MORE THAN MEETS THE EYE

(re)Discovering Ancient Portable Rock Art

MORE THAN MEETS THE EYE

(re)Discovering Ancient Portable Rock Art

Carl Lehrburger

2023

NewHistoryofAmerica.com

More Than Meets the Eye
(re)Discovering Ancient Portable Rock Art

Contact the author at:
author@newhistoryofamerica.com

Or through the website at:
www.newhistoryofamerica.com

ISBN: 979-8-218-26906-7

Editing and Book Design:
Vivian Freeman Chaffin
vivian.freeman@yellowrosetype.com

Printed in the United States of America

. . . And as I walked alone, I heard the sun singing
as it arose, and it sang like this:

With visible face I am appearing.
In a sacred manner I appear.
For the greening earth a pleasantness I make.
The center of the nation's hoop
    I have made pleasant.
With visible face, behold me!
The four-leggeds and two-leggeds,
    I have made them to walk.
With wings of the air, I have made them to fly.
With visible face I appear.
My day, I have made it holy.

—*Black Elk Speaks*
John G. Neihardt

CONTENTS

KEY ARTIFACTS

Among the many examples of paleo art on stones presented in this book, the following are among the author's best representations of the ancient art platform referred to as Portable Rock Art.

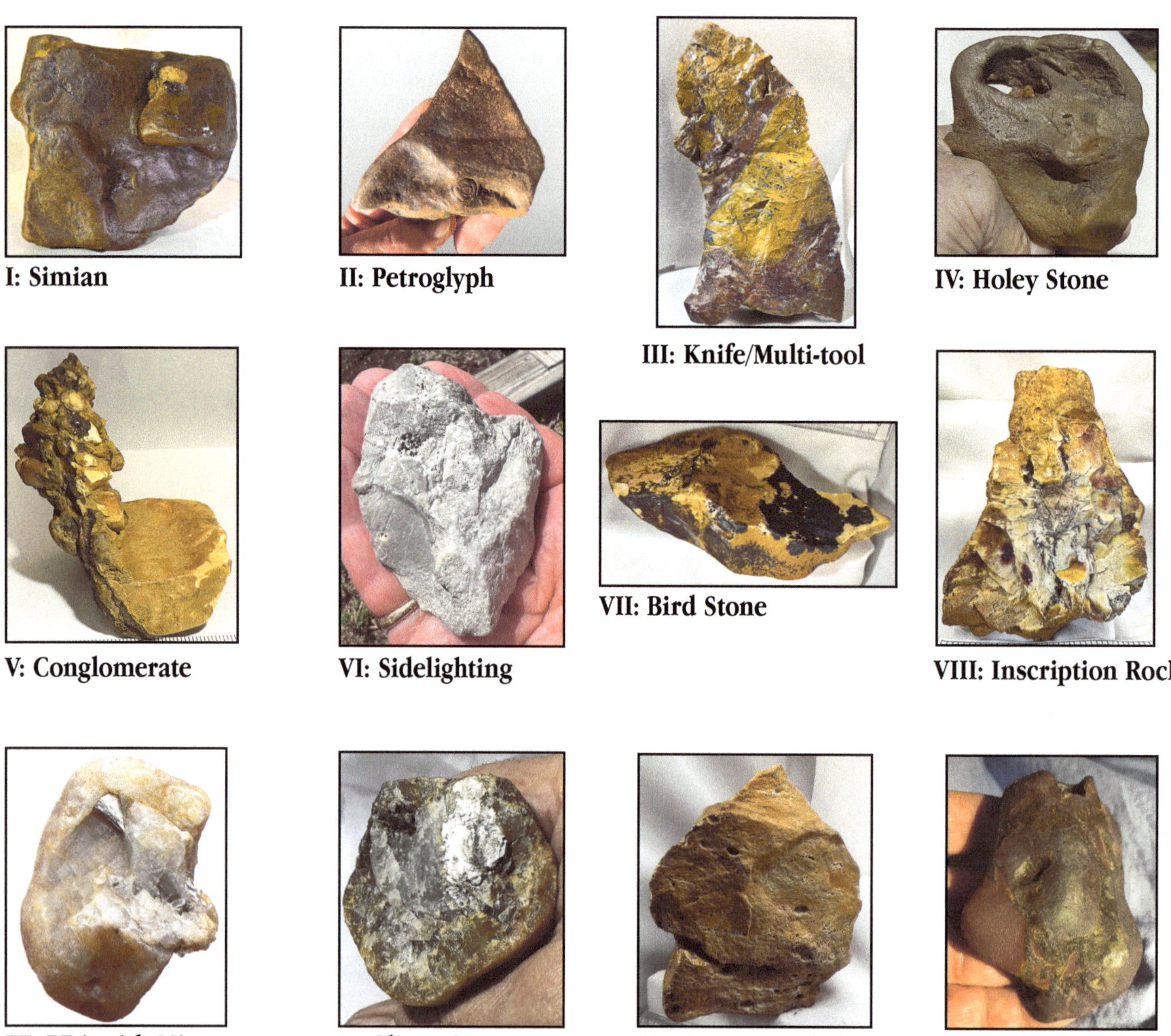

I: Simian

II: Petroglyph

III: Knife/Multi-tool

IV: Holey Stone

V: Conglomerate

VI: Sidelighting

VII: Bird Stone

VIII: Inscription Rock

IX: PRA with Mica

X: Glitter Serpent

XI: Pointy Head Guy

XII: Whistle

LIST OF FIGURES

ACKNOWLEDGEMENTS

The author acknowledges primary source material and significant contributors below.

Primary Source Material

Secrets of Ancient America: Archaeoastronomy and the Legacy of the Phoenicians, Celts, and other Forgotten Explorers, Carl Lehrburger, (Bear & Company, 2015).

Ancient American Inscriptions: Plow Marks or History? William R. McGlone, Phillip M. Leonard, James Guthrie, Rollin Gillespie and James Whittall Jr. (1993).

The Hidden Maya (1998) and the *Stones of Time* (1994), Martin Brennan.

"Palaeoart at Two Million Years Ago? A Review of the Evidence," along with many other articles by Dr. James B. Harrod.

(Refer to the endnotes for full citations.)

Significant Portable Rock Art Contributors

Tim Banninger from Kansas introduced me to the world of PRA, shared his many years of experience and provided a multitude of the examples presented here. Clay Mathis from Kentucky shared his extensive collection, techniques and knowledge, along with the many exquisite artifacts featured in this book. Chris Penney from Michigan, fellow researcher, videographer and producer of *The Ancient Artifact Hunters,* has documented many aspects of PRA and shared his deep experiences and stories.

Photo Contributors

All photos and drawings by author except where noted. Photo contributors include George L. Davis, Tim Banninger, Carey Bell, Alan O'Hara, Chris Penney, Alan Day, Kimra Manion, Ursel Benekendorff, Keli Brooke Bradley, Andy Mabbett, Leonardo L. Lujan, Jamie Collier, L. Benson, J. A. J. Gowlet, Bill Waters, Peter A. Bostrom, Jan Van Es, Jul Jones, Robert G. Bednarik, Greg Darby.

Colleagues

Over decades, I have worked with many collaborators in the rock art realms, some listed above, who I gratefully acknowledge and thank for their contributions to my work: William R. McGlone, Phillip M. Leonard, Ted Barker, Martin Brennan, Hugh Gardner, Kean Scott Monahan, Roderick Schmidt, Dorian Taddei, Arlo Acton, the guy with eye from Pueblo, along with the many who are not mentioned, thank you.

PREFACE

Finding an arrowhead as I ran down a mountain trail in Colorado was one of the most ecstatic childhood experiences I can remember. Its neatly fashioned shape, pointy tip and sharp edges felt natural in my hand (*Fig. 1*) as if there was a magnetic attraction.

I could not imagine what an impact this find would make on my life going forward. But perhaps more important than the find was the lesson I learned losing the arrowhead several months later.

Something important was left behind when I misplaced that prize. From that day, I have looked down not up, searching the ground for stone tools, workings or anything touched by the Ancients. Unraveling and seeking to understand the mysteries they left behind became a passion. Since finding and losing that arrowhead, I continued to pick up rocks and for some unexplained reason kept them. No matter where I moved around the country, my rock collection traveled with me. Only in recent years did I take a closer look with a new set of eyes. It turned out some of those not-so-random collectables were human-crafted Portable Rock Art objects.

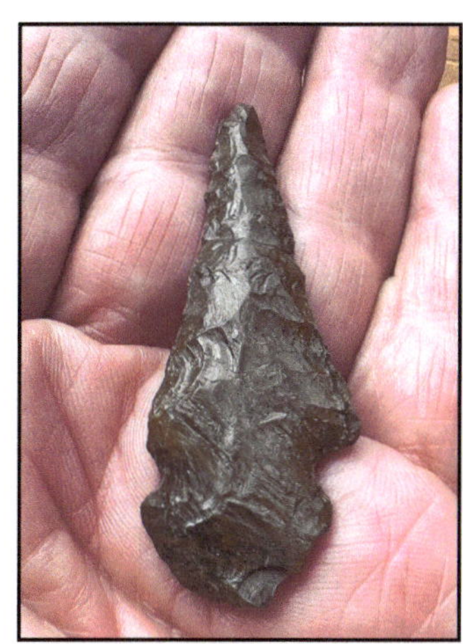

Figure 1: Arrowhead: A spear point from Colorado.

Not long after losing the arrowhead, a second experience proved to be fortuitous and educational regarding my future interest in rock art. An elderly neighbor, who happened to be a retired geologist with a significant rock collection, gave a show-and-tell demonstration to the neighborhood kids of his many stones. Among these was a geode, the size of a fist, that he had cut into sections using a lapidary saw. In sequence, he revealed each section to the captivated onlookers, as if turning pages of a picture book. He first removed the end piece section of the chunk of agate, revealing a smooth inner first layer that had the likeness of a face. As he unveiled the next section, the shiny agate piece became a likeness specific to the profile of a Native American (*Fig. 2*), which became even more apparent as the next section was revealed. Finally, exposing the most inner section of the polished stone brought forth an almost exact image of the face from a U.S. Indian Head penny, feathers and all. My friends and I

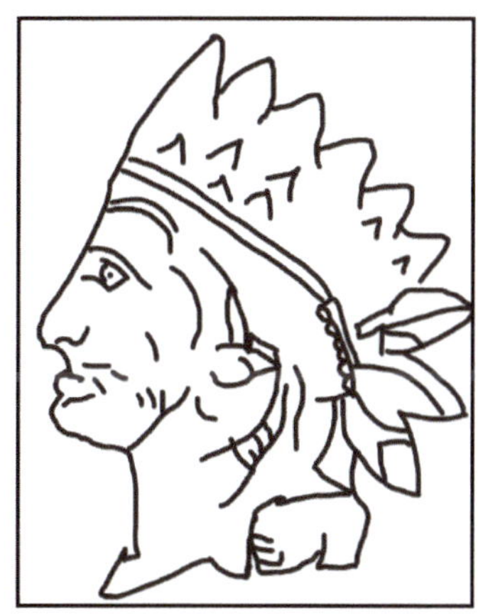

Figure 2: Drawing of Indian Head: The center of a stone cut into layers resembled the image of a U.S. Indian Head penny.

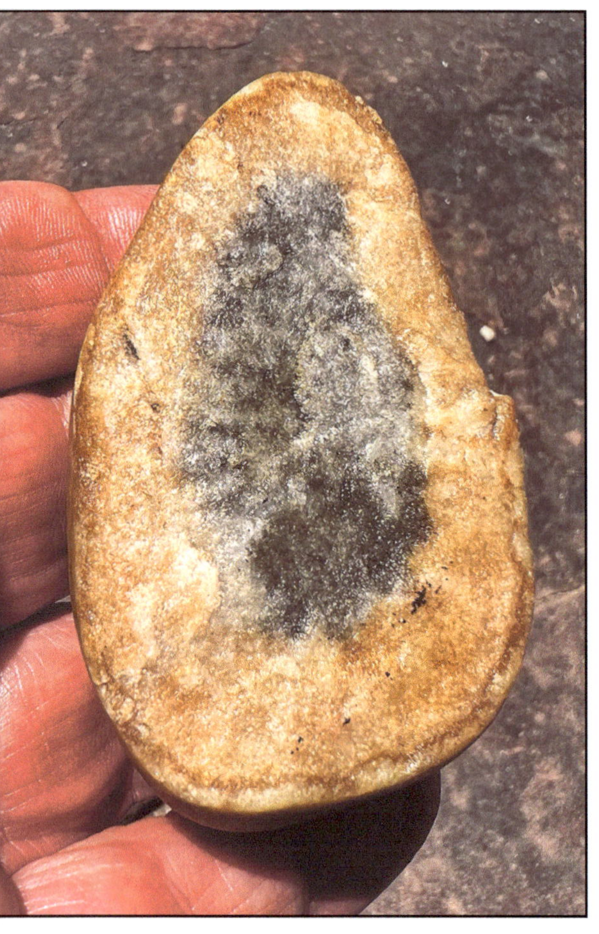

Figure 3: Natural image in center of stone from Colorado.

were captivated and perplexed. How was it possible? I later came to learn that this was pareidolia, where natural phenomena, including stones, appear to have recognizable images, notably faces (*Fig. 4*).

Although my journey began in childhood, I learned early on that natural rocks can and do resemble recognizable images to the point they appear to be nearly indistinguishable from the real thing. This encounter involving pareidolia, demonstrates one of the central controversies involving Portable Rock Art: *Is it human crafted or natural with familiar appearances?*

In evaluating rock art, I harken back to my experience seeing the naturally created Indian likeness in the center of a rock, recognizing that many likenesses considered to be art on rocks are natural.

These life events before I was ten years old influenced my (re)discovery of paleo (stone) art, interweaving the past into a future passion for exploring the world of rocks and archaeology. Years later, my travels and experiences at sacred sites and my investigations of ancient petroglyphs and rock art helped me to appreciate better what it means to be human.

Connecting the past and the future is the present. In the present, we can still appreciate and learn from the Ancestors, for they have left us many opportunities to experience our human heritage. I hope in your journey between the book's covers and beyond you also come to learn more about what it means to be human.

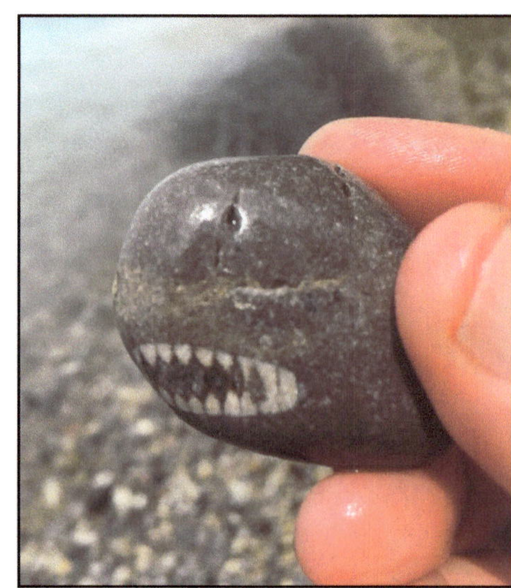

Figure 4: Pareidolia sample of natural stone with shark-like appearance (Greg Darby).[1]

MORE THAN MEETS THE EYE

(re)Discovering Ancient Portable Rock Art

INTRODUCTION

My first book, completed in 2015, addressed many mysteries uncovered in a quest to understand the prehistory of the Americas. *Secrets of Ancient America: Archaeoastronomy and the Legacy of the Phoenicians, Celts, and Other Lost Explorers* is very much a history book with a focus on the expeditions of pre-Columbus explorers from around the world to the Americas. *Secrets of Ancient America* documented the stone workings of the Ancients with an intention of reconstructing a lost history while discovering, preserving and presenting paleo artistry previously unknown. In offering a contrarian historical narrative to the "Columbus discovered America" story, I focused on the travels of Celtic people from Europe but also included evidence of pre-Columbus Roman, Egyptian, Chinese, and other explorers.

In *Secrets of Ancient America* as well as describing portable paleo rock art in this present work, I rely on three foundational pillars as guides in my quest to identity and decipher rock art. These core constituents to my endeavors are **petroglyphs**, **archaeoastronomy**, and the expertise and experience of **collaborators and earlier researchers**.

Detailed examinations of petroglyphic rock art are a significant part of both books. They are found predominately on fixed boulders, large rocks, rock outcroppings, and cave walls and were created principally as two-dimensional pictures. The word **petroglyph** comes from the Greek words ***petros*** meaning "stone" and ***glyphein*** "to carve." Petroglyphs are found throughout the world, with significant concentrations in the American southwest.

In addition to my pursuit of observing and recording petroglyphs, *Secrets of Ancient America* relied heavily on **archaeoastronomy**. Archaeoastronomy is an integrated field of study relying on astronomy, archaeology, anthropology, philosophy and epigraphy to identify and interpret the meaning of astronomical alignments at large structures and on petroglyphs. Stonehenge in southern England is the

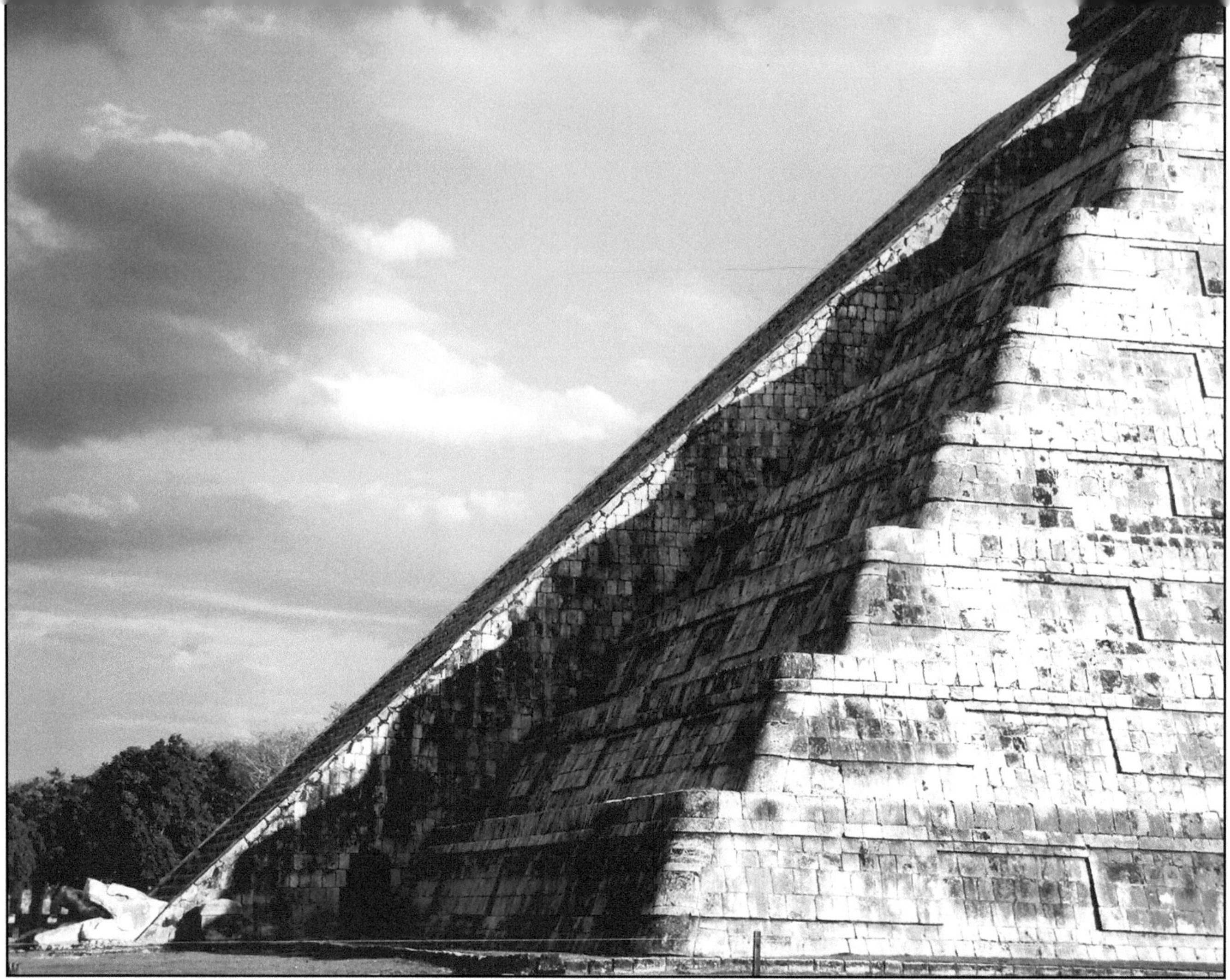

Figure 5: Temple of Kukulkan Equinox Alignment at Chichén Itzá, Mexico.

most famous archaeoastronomy structure in the world, but there are many others including Chichén Itzá in Mexico (*Fig. 5*).

Located in southern Mexico, the Temple of Kukulkan at Chichén Itzá is known for its Equinox alignment with light and shadow interplay mimicking a descending giant serpent on the pyramid. The **Equinoxes**, when day and night are equally divided, occur twice each year around March 21 and September 21. Archaeoastronomy reveals the ancient Maya, in addition to many ancient cultures worldwide, designed their architecture so precisely that only on the Equinoxes would this heliolithic animation (light show) be revealed at sunrise.

As a result of studying with mentors and researchers William R. McGlone and Phillip M. Leonard, I came to learn the intimate relationship between the rock art (petroglyphs) and the position of the sun to create intentional alignments at designated days of the year. Just looking at a petroglyph is often not enough to understand its meaning. The precise movement of light and shadow on fixed petroglyphs can create alignments, akin to moving pictures that convey a story, but one must be looking at the petroglyphs on a specific day and time of day to see intentional conjunction of the light and shadow interplay on the petroglyphs. These insights proved to be extremely relevant to Portable Rock Art. Instead of the sun's movement on fixed petroglyphs, it's moving the handheld artifact that can amplify 3-D views.

The first sacred site Bill shared with me was the Pathfinder, located above the Purgatory River Valley in southeastern Colorado. This thousand-year-old Native American rock art panel was determined by McGlone to be a sunrise Equinox marker. It was propitious enough to be working with the aging McGlone, but to be among the first Moderns to see and study this remarkable creation propelled my interest and motivated me to draw the complete sequence of Native American petroglyphs at the Pathfinder. My participation in McGlone's research lasted through multiple investigations, documenting the Pathfinder's morning Equinox alignment.

Through my own research I observed and documented a second Equinox alignment, a remarkable noontime heliolithic animation, described in detail in several articles[2] and in *Secrets of Ancient America,* involving the appearance and movement of a sun dagger through a series of petroglyphs. Phil Leonard also observed the petroglyphic images and proposed one figure in particular represented the main protagonist in the story of "Changing Women," also known as *Widapokwi,* considered to be the First Mother and the Mother of Mankind in Native American mythologies, including a Yavapai-Apache tradition.

Pathfinder's sun dagger (*Fig. 6*) descends from a hole above and at noontime on the Equinox strikes petroglyphs in a sequence that tells the story of Changing Woman. In the first photo the sun dagger approaches a glyph in the shape of a phallus. In the second photo the tip of the sun dagger strikes the petroglyph image, but only on the Equinox.

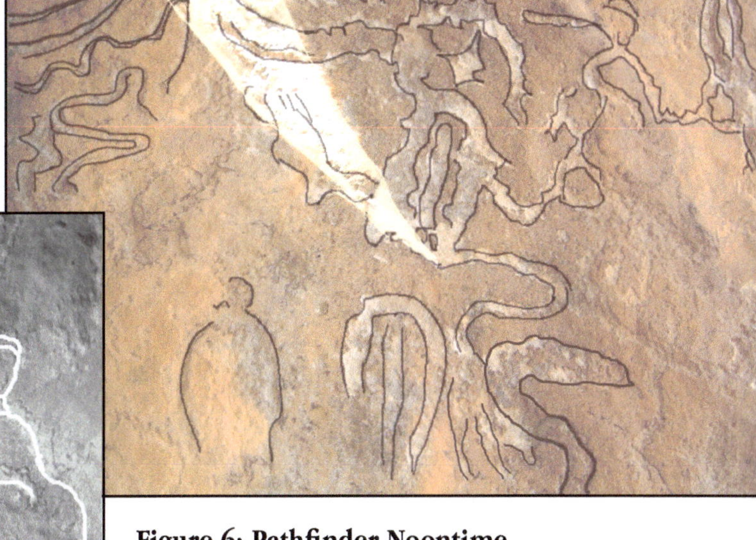

Figure 6: Pathfinder Noontime Equinox Sun Dagger Details.

The more I dissected the imagery as suggested by Phil, the clearer it became the Pathfinder's seventeen-foot-long Equinox sun dagger illuminated a series of petroglyphs in sequence as the light dagger moved across the rock art panel that told the story of Changing Women consistent with the Native American tales.

The Pathfinder site has been closed to researchers for over a decade, but McGlone and Leonard's book on the archaeoastronomy of the region[3] and my published articles on the Pathfinder[4] document this impressive Native American rock art creation.

As a result of the *Ancient American Magazine* articles, I published on the Pathfinder and Celtic archaeoastronomy sites in the American Southwest, I was encouraged to visit an eastern California petroglyph site referred to as Mojave North by resident expert Roderick Schmidt. Rod had been studying Mojave North for over a decade, working toward an archaeology degree at the time. He shared his knowledge of the many archaeoastronomical alignments he had observed on the small, approximate one-acre site, including a petroglyph panel where a wedge of light with likeness of a serpent with open jaws approaches and ultimately engulfs or "eats" the center of a series of concentric circles, the target for this Equinox alignment. The precise conjunction of the moving light/shadow serpent image (*Fig. 7*) with the fixed petroglyphs only occurs on Equinox morning in a particular sequence that conveys a story, just like the Pathfinder's light serpent created thousands of years later.

Rod and others had documented alignments at Mojave North on the Equinoxes, **Solstices** (the longest and shortest days of the year around June 21 and December 21 respectfully) and **cross-quarter**

Figure 7: Mojave North Equinox Light Serpent Morning Alignment. Like many other Equinox alignments, the light and shadow lines create the shape of a dagger that traverses the petroglyphs with the movement of the sun. Only on the Equinox is there an exact alignment with the petroglyph.

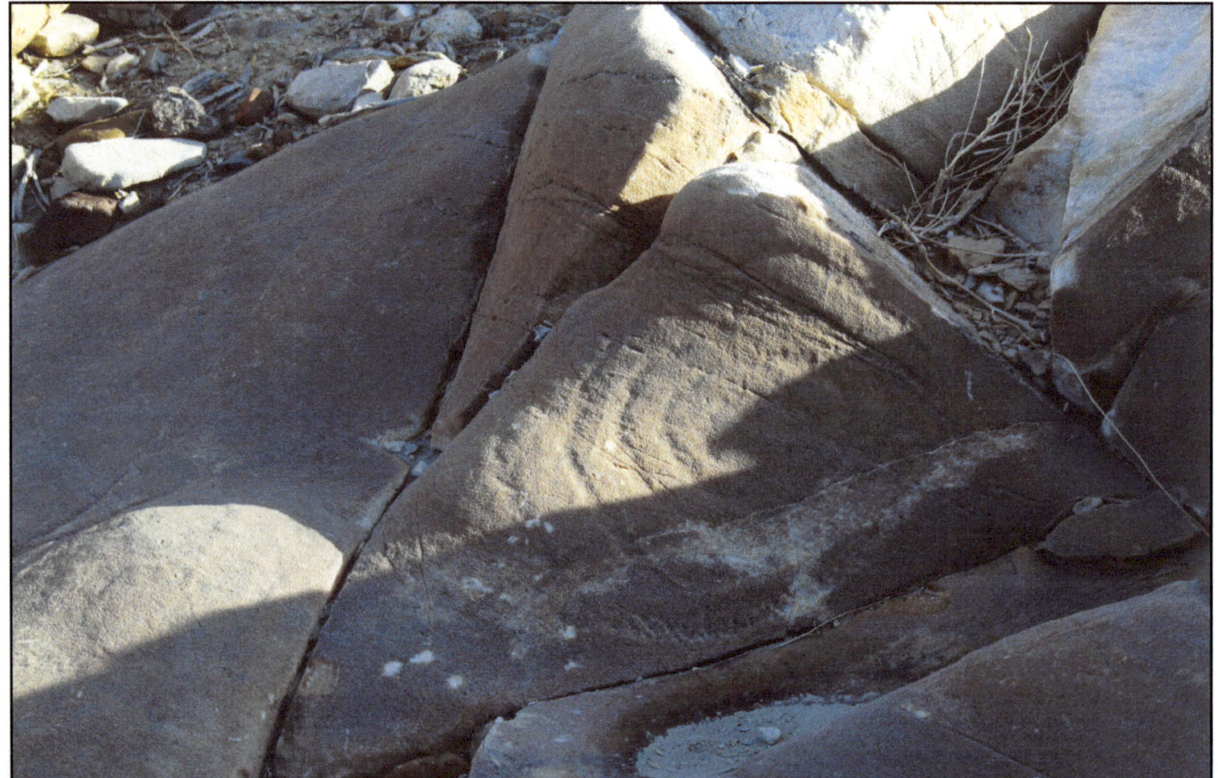

days (the 4 days that occur between Equinox and Solstices in early February, May, August and November).

Among the 12 celestial alignments at Mojave North, I observed the Sunset Equinox Animation (SEA) rock (*Fig. 8*), which was my first glimpse into the ancient artistic platform employed in Portable Rock Art, the subject of *More Than Meets The Eye.* The SEA petroglyphic image of a pointy-hat man changed shape as the sun moved lower in the sky toward sunset, revealing a second "hidden" petroglyph image not previously visible in direct sunlight, which can be described as a "face-in-face" image, also found abundantly in PRA. I described the SEA rock alignment[5] in a 2010 article

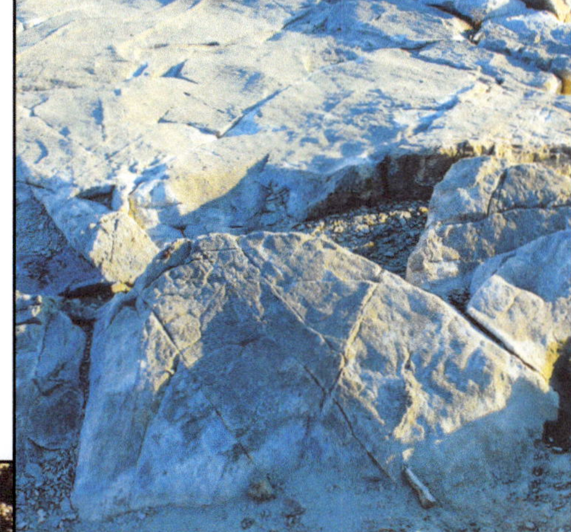

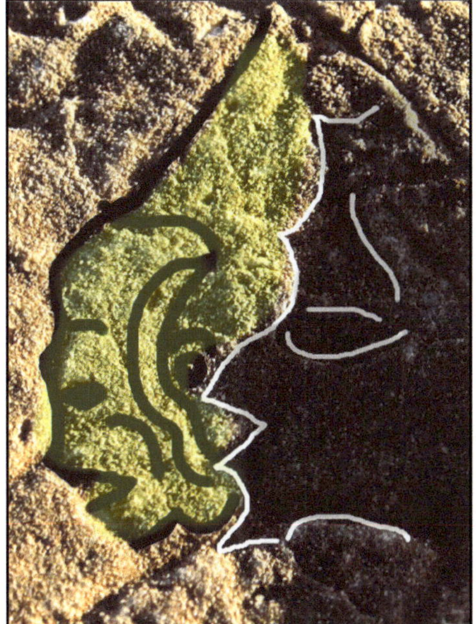

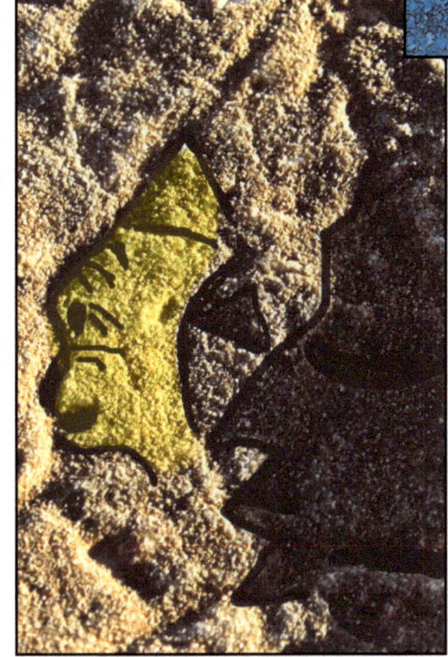

Figure 8: Mojave North Sunset Equinox Alignment.

(above) Mojave North boulder with SEA petroglyphs.

(left) This ancient petroglyph was intentionally aligned to the Equinox. As the sun moves toward the horizon, the lower half of the etched profile is enveloped in shadow and a hidden upper face is illuminated.

(below) The action of the Equinox animation unfolds during sunset as the shadowed profile moves toward the etched profile until the two profiles are precisely aligned, as the last rays of light reveals the shape of a monkey.

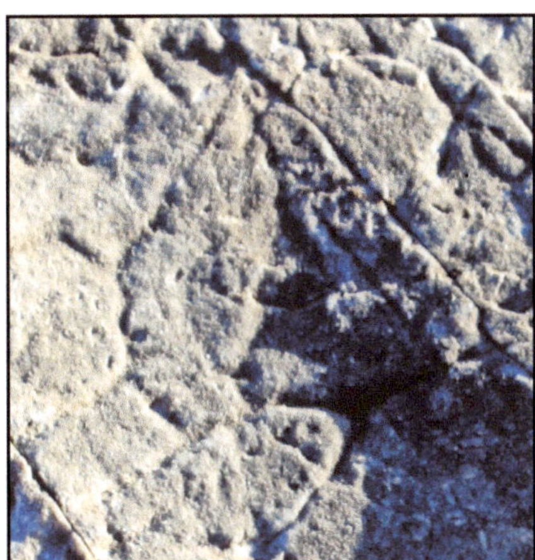

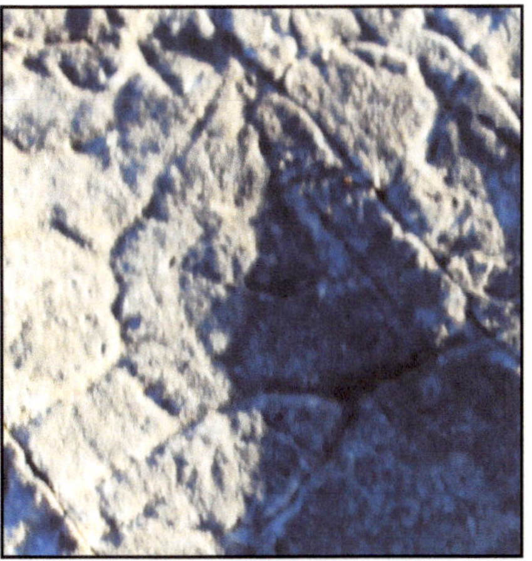

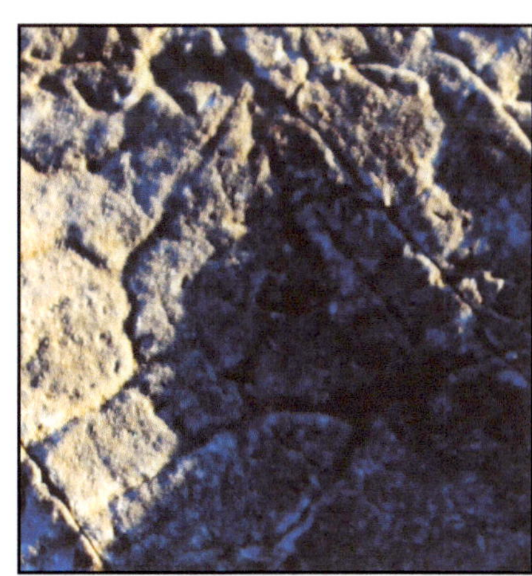

for *Ancient American Magazine*[6] and also in a video. Unlike PRA that relies on moving the stone in one's hand, the interaction of the moving shadow on fixed petroglyphs enables one to see an example of face-in-face imagery common to Portable Rock Art.

At the time of the SEA animation discovery, I didn't realize the artistic mastery that created the Equinox alignment would extend to rock art on smaller, portable Figure Stones, as they are commonly known. These and other archaeo astronomical alignments are directly relevant to PRA, as they document intentionality, provide key details to the petroglyph meanings, and they demonstrate the necessity of knowing what to look for at the right place and right time.

It was only after being contacted by Tim Banninger from Kansas that I became aware that the artistic platform that I had observed at the Mojave North SEA alignment was but a small representation of how the Ancients applied artistic features to rocks. Banninger showed me stones that appeared to be carved animal likenesses (*Fig. 9*). However, unlike fixed petroglyphs, these hand-held objects allow one to move and see three-dimensional art involving different facets and sides. Because of my previous work with the SEA animation at Mojave North, I immediately grasped what Tim was trying to show me. The same artistic paleo art platform I glimpsed at Mojave North was imbued in smaller portable rocks by the Ancients.

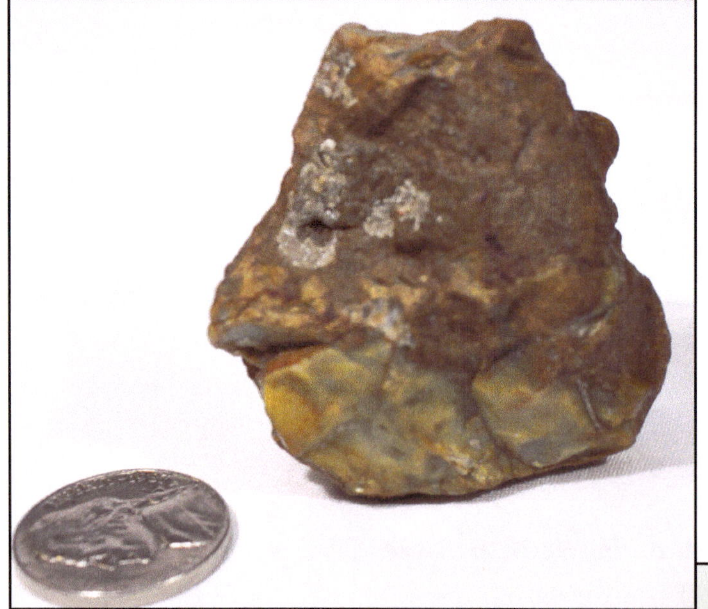

Figure 9: PRA examples from Kansas (Tim Banninger).

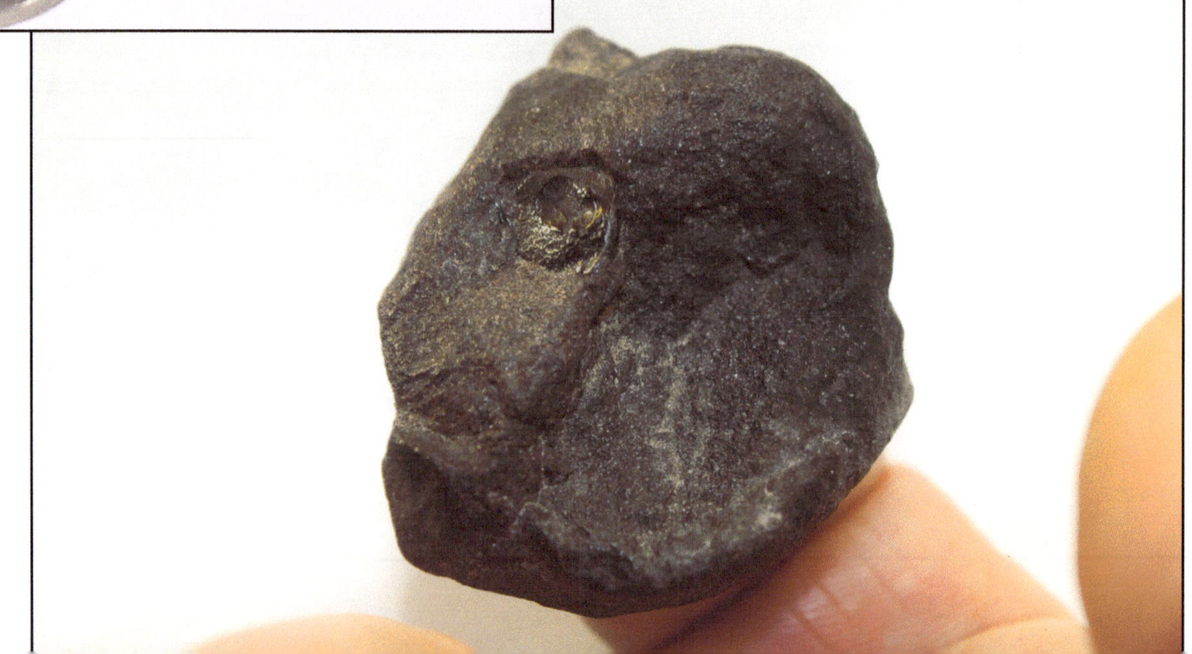

With Tim's guidance, I began noticing and finding portable rock artifacts, only to learn these stone artistic creations are quite abundant and available to those able to identify them. What I discovered is that the Ancients employed a three-dimensional artistic platform to create rock sculptures, which heretofore have gone unnoticed by Moderns.

Over several visits to Kansas, I learned how to identify Portable Rock Art and acquired a collection of fine pieces thanks to Tim, resulting in my first PRA article in *Ancient American Magazine.*[7]

The article attracted the attention of Clay Mathis who encouraged me to visit him in Kentucky to see his extensive PRA collection. On two visits during 2020, I experienced even more paleo sculptures than I thought possible (*Fig. 10*).

Clay had discovered a significant cache of PRA objects at the base of an operating gravel mine, well over twelve feet below the surface. Through his guidance I learned more about how to find, identify and clean these ancient artifacts. Many of the artifacts pictured in *More Than Meets The Eye* originate from my Kentucky excursions.

Upon returning from Kentucky, I wrote my second article on PRA, published in *Ancient Origin Magazine.*[8] As was the case with previous articles, fellow researchers, PRA enthusiasts and collectors contacted me. These included videographer Chris Penney, who joined me on a second trip to Kentucky where he documented Clay's excursions collecting PRA at the gravel pit site. Other collectors also contacted me, some of whose PRA photos are included in *More than Meets the Eye.*

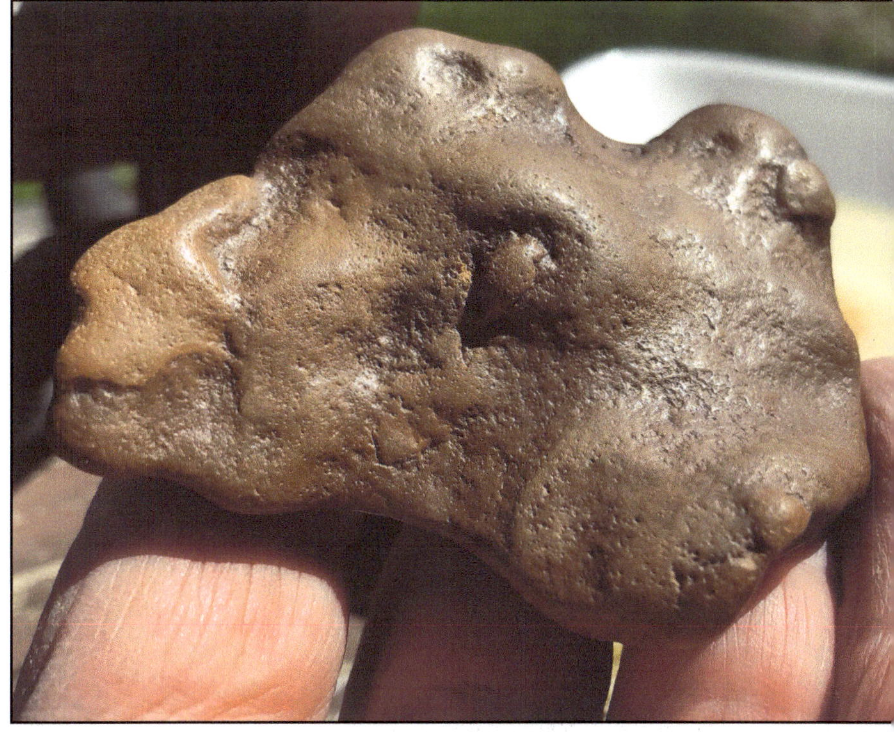

Figure 10: PRA from Kentucky gravel pit.

I am not new to being associated with archaeological research deemed "fake" by many archaeologists, including my publications on evidence of Celtic travelers in North America before Columbus, based on Bill McGlone and Phil Leonard's decades of documentation.[9]

Although McGlone and Leonard's initial findings were based on archaeoastronomical and petroglyphic evidence and published thirty years ago,10 the pre-Columbian exploration of America remains virtually unknown. Quite often those of us who research and document contrarian perspectives to the archaeological community are ignored or denigrated. The same is true with Portable Rock Art. In spite of

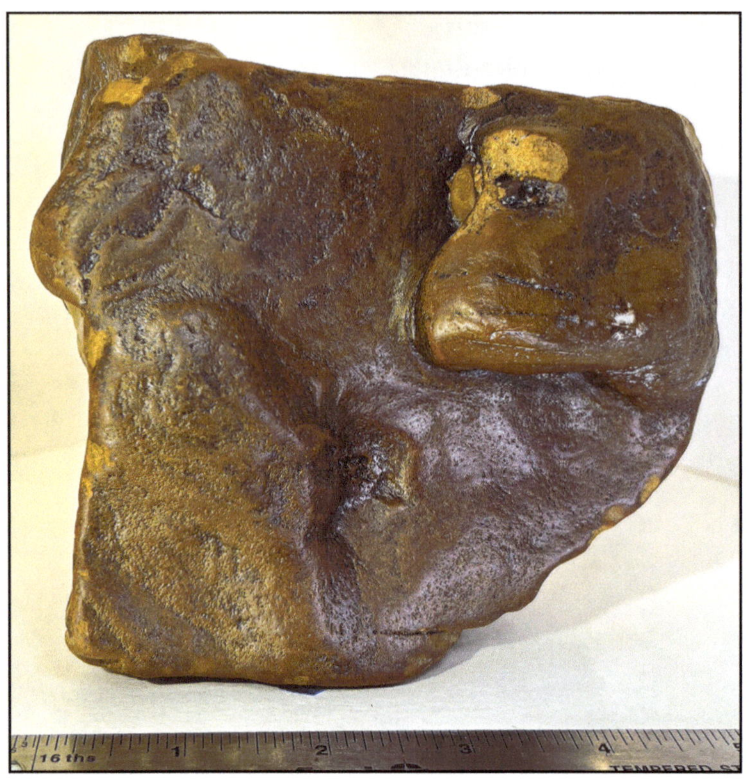

Figure 11: Artifact I, Simian (monkey), Kentucky (Clay Mathis).

meticulous research and discoveries by many, inclusive of those detailed in More than Meets the Eye, the subject matter has remained taboo.

How is it that there appear to be so many of these paleo artifacts both in an archeological context and also available to collectors, but so few Moderns know about them? Why are these ancient artistic creations not recognized by the established archaeological order? Is there a lost "language" associated with what most consider to be ordinary stones? These are among the questions that *More Than Meets the Eye* address.

Throughout this book, the terms ***Ancients*** and ***Moderns*** are capitalized to differentiate human ages, with the authors dividing line between them being the Conquest of the Americas by the Spanish, Portuguese and others. Prior to the 1500s, indigenous cultures relied on stone tools, which were mostly abandoned after the Conquest. The millennium-old traditions and skill sets employed to exquisitely craft paleo art, going back to the earliest humans, disappeared within several hundred years along with the ability to recognize it. While some suggest that PRA died out earlier, in the author's view PRA was in use as late as 250 years ago in North America.

In spite of the conquest and destruction of Native cultures worldwide, the artistic achievements of the Ancients survive. Wherever the Ancients lived, particularly those dependent on stone tools and implements, Portable Rock Art can be found. In the Americas, this means practically everywhere.

More Than Meets The Eye aspires to tell a story, reveal a lost history, and present opportunities to honor and preserve shared human traditions preserved in PRA. As we stand on the precipice of the future, it's not too late to recognize and celebrate our human roots, shared heritage, and connections to Nature.

PART I

INTRODUCING PORTABLE ROCK ART

Deconstructing the Past

A friend, steeped in conventional archaeology once asked, "Even if these rocks you're finding do have some human artistic quality, so what?"

Is it possible that what appears to be plain old rocks can actually be messages from ancient ancestors? The abundance of ancient stone

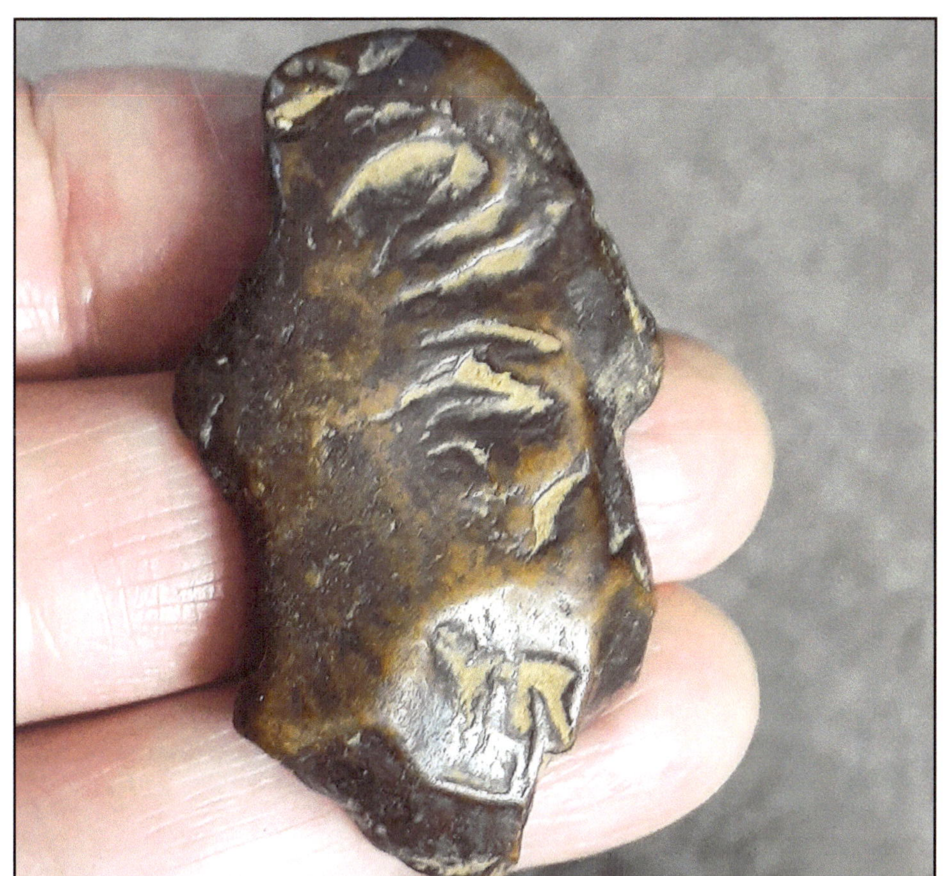

Figure 12: PRA head variant, Alabama (George L. Davis).

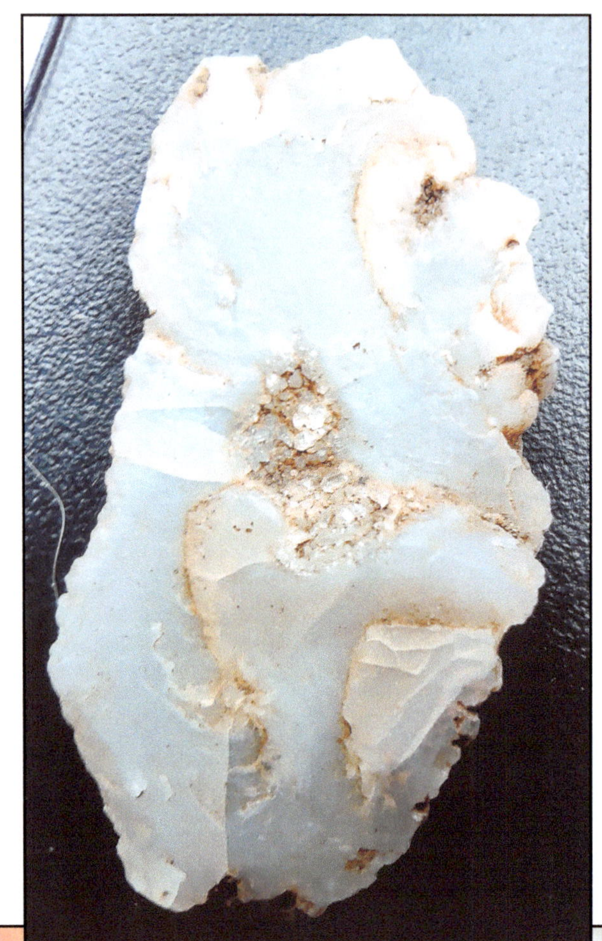

artwork, heretofore unrecognized, demonstrates that millennia-old artistic techniques and creations have escaped modern view, as a new chapter of humanity is being revealed.

Portable Rock Art, also referred to as Figure Stones, handheld paleo sculptures, microlithic sculpture[1] as well as "anthropomorphic paleolithic sculptures," is a classification of stone creations consisting of lithic assemblages or technological characteristics.

These include representations of faces and animals worked onto stones and stone tools by ancient humans (*Fig. 13*). These handheld paleo artifacts have mostly been ignored in spite of the evidence they embody a long practiced ancient art implemented continuously over millions of years. PRA has a wide variety of groupings, ranging from slight artistic additions to extensively art-laden embellishments that seem to have little functionality whatsoever.

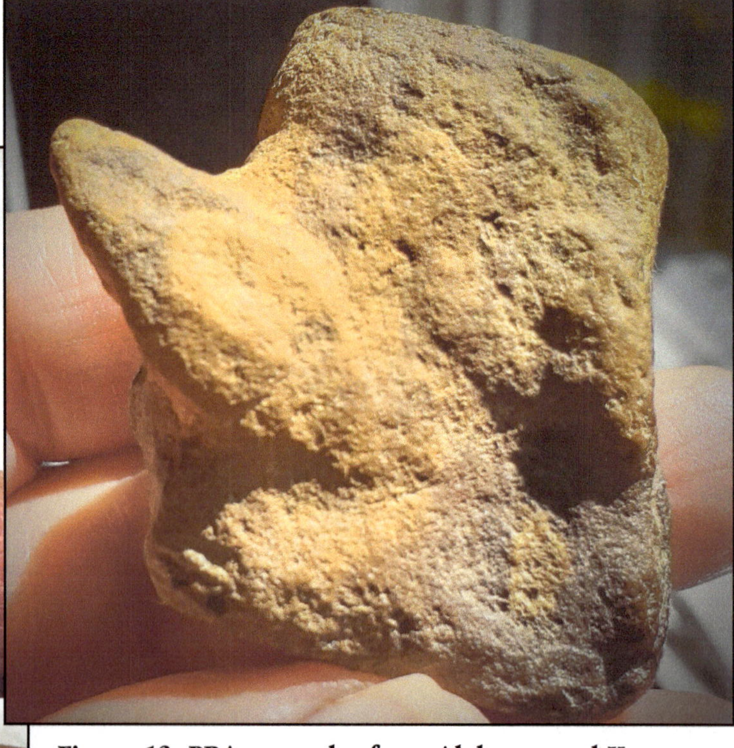

Figure 13: PRA examples from Alabama and Kansas: (top) Paleolithic tool with carvings, blue chalcedony, Alabama (George L. Davis); (left) PRA animal-shaped multi-tool found in Kansas (Tim Banninger); (above) A "Big Nose Guy" with an awl as a nose (George L. Davis).

Broadly speaking, the archaeological community remains skeptical of PRA because it tends to be subjective, meaning two observers viewing the same piece may see something completely different. Admittedly, many PRA pieces are mistaken for natural or pareidolia look-alikes. However, as described herein, pareidolia was integrated into the art platform itself. For example, a beginning point for identifying PRA is the natural shape of the stone with human- and animal-like features (*Fig. 14*). As this book seeks to explain, there is often a fine line between human crafted ("worked") stone with artistic enhancements and natural stones with apparent imagery. Even so, as this book describes, there are ways to distinguish and validate PRA.

With a world fixated on money, or in some cases focused on survival, spending hours seeking, cleaning, brushing, washing and admiring newly found ancient artifacts sounds trivial and fanciful. Yet, these traditions connect us to our deepest human stories, mythologies and memories through perplexing and abundant ancient paleo creations.

PRA consists not merely of ***effigy*** stones (a singular sculpture, image or representation, especially of a person), conventional portable artifacts, or purely subjective pareidolia (natural) phenomena.

The examples provided in this book and thousands of others found in hundreds of collections, demonstrate what few in the academic and

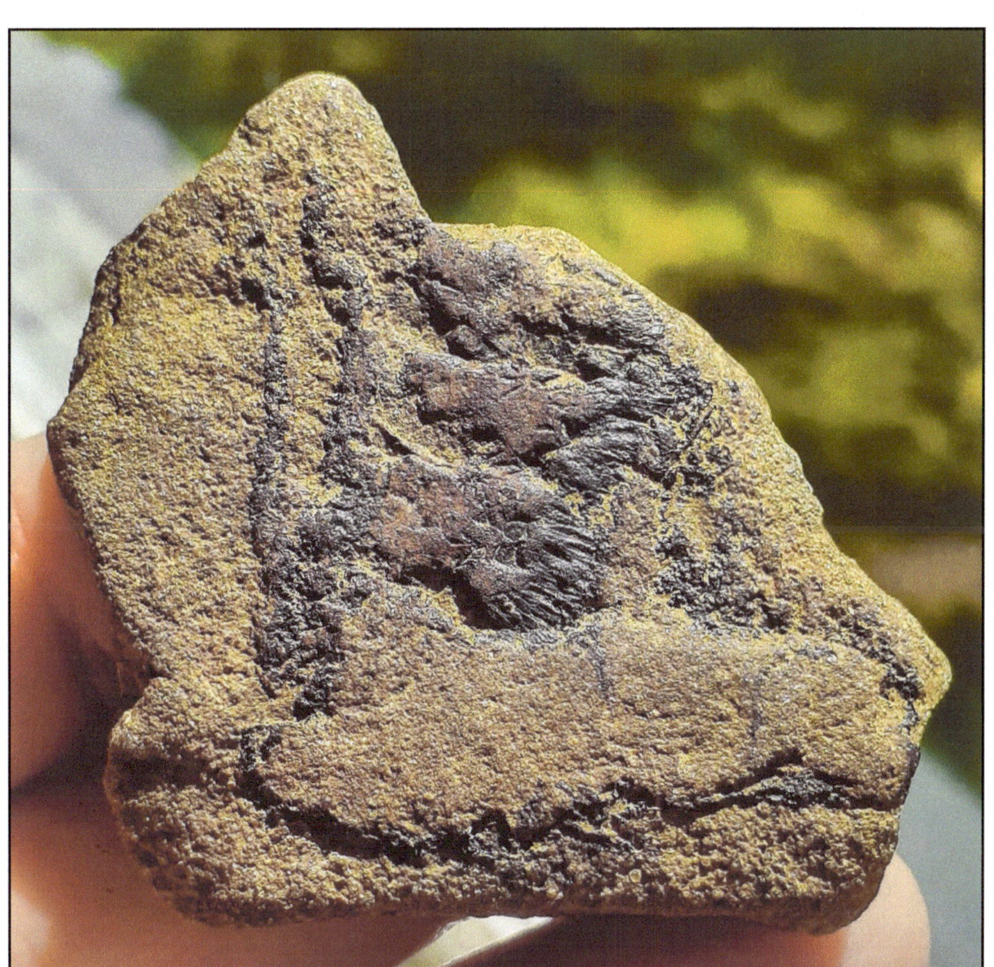

Figure 14: Animal-shaped PRA, Alabama (George L. Davis).

mainstream archaeological communities have been willing to explore or acknowledge—the sheer abundance of PRA is astounding. PRA hounds, along with amateur and professional researchers worldwide, have assembled collections, including a host of online PRA photo galleries displaying thousands of diverse PRA artifacts.

Even more surprising, significant repositories can be found in numerous urban areas across a broad geographical spectrum. Exquisite PRA with human-crafted artistry can be discovered while walking through a neighborhood, on a dirt road, along a country path or near a stream.

Figure 15: Handheld tool with PRA features, Kentucky (Kimra Manion). The 5.25-inch long artifact has sharpened edges and worked tool extension on top.

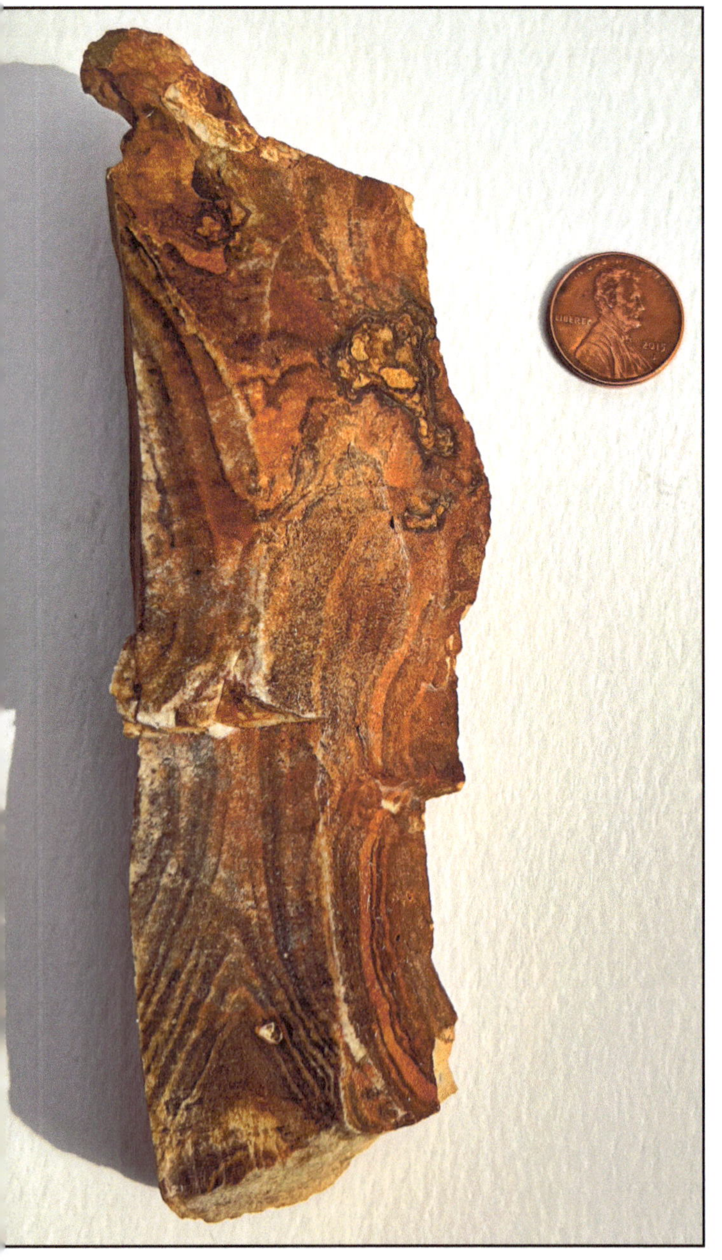

In the recent past, finding an arrowhead was pretty common, but after scouring surfaces for centuries, this is no longer true. More common and accessible, however, is the chance of coming across PRA. Those with a trained eye and knowledge of where to look have amassed significant PRA collections in Arkansas, Kentucky, Virginia, Oregon, Kansas, Arizona, Colorado, throughout the southeast USA, throughout Europe and many other locations.

I like to consider PRA as being "not this or not

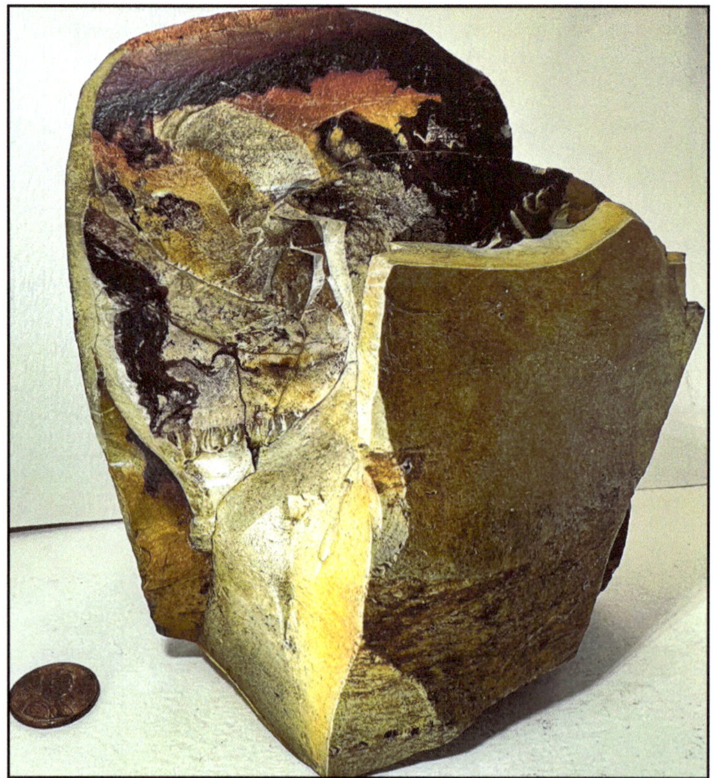

Figure 16: PRA with head variants, Kentucky (Kimra Manion). PRA with apparent head variants among natural features without utilitarian aspects.

that" when trying to explain it. By defining, interpreting, and naming artifacts we can limit our understanding of what they actually are. Rather than a singular image, PRA artifacts often have many dimensions and are often multi-purpose creations for our imaginations to behold.

Examples from a variety of locations demonstrate that an abundance of unrecognized artifacts remain from a widely practiced, millennia-old tradition of enhancing stones, including tools, and presents a new and exciting chapter of understanding ancient cultures. These artistic creations are a phenomenon to experience, explore and something profoundly important for humanity. Understanding and appreciating the many different dimensions of PRA is only limited by our lack of imagination and resistant to new ways of seeing the world.

Welcome to a whole new universe.

Why Is Portable Rock Art Important?

Something important is revealed in PRA. At first, it takes effort to see what had been created on what appears to be unremarkable rocks. Whether it is a lack of interest, imagination and/or effort, modern archaeology has ignored the PRA phenomena. Thus, PRA is waiting to be (re)discovered, experienced and appreciated.

So, why is PRA important for Moderns? Figure Stones can reveal an ingenious ancient art form widely practiced over millions of years. This 3-D artistic platform is an ancient language that comes alive by moving a PRA artifact to see the changing imagery. Understanding the lithic techniques and being able to grasp the PRA three-dimensional petroglyphic sculptures requires a growing awareness, artistic appreciation and imagination.

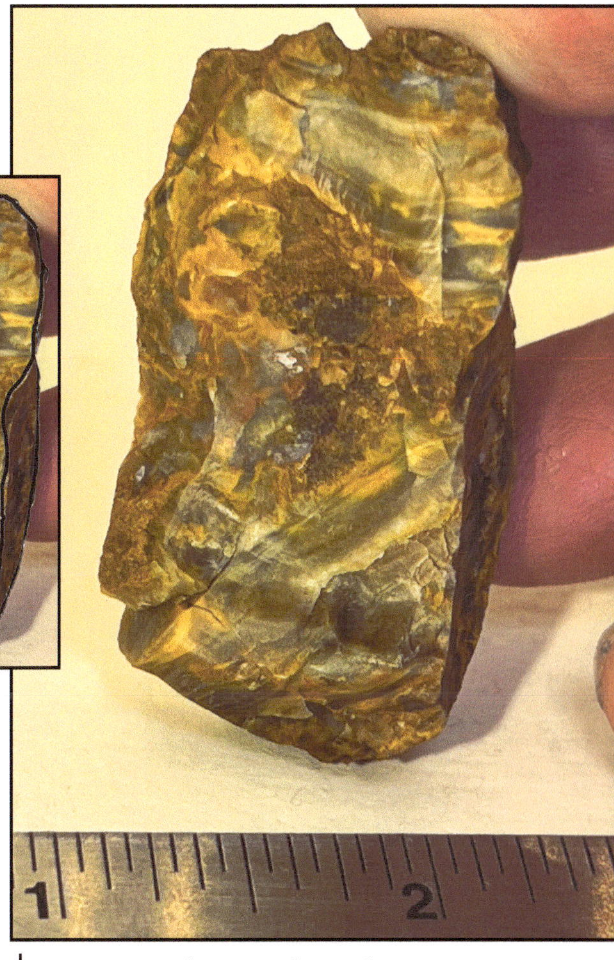

Figure 17: Chert, multi-tool/scrapper from Colorado with PRA imagery.

Professional researchers have recovered PRA from sites within a cultural stratum; but most PRA examples presented in this book and in other PRA collections have no cultural context or provenance because they were found in disturbed venues, making accurate dating and determining cultural origins difficult, if not impossible. From a scientific perspective, these commonly found ***artfacts*** may have little "scientific" value. Even so, the importance of PRA extends beyond any archaeological meaning. PRA often involves complex, multi-dimensional lithic enhancements, apparently difficult for Moderns to recognize. Can we learn to open our eyes to differentiate and see it? Can we expand our neural (brain) network to better comprehend and appreciate ancient paleo art?

Due to the sheer number of examples identified by independent researchers, PRA offers another dimension to understanding ancient cultures by contributing to education, art appreciation, art history, archaeology, anthropology, Native American studies, historical preservation and human enjoyment. Isn't it time to begin appreciating this newly (re)discovered artistic tradition from age-old cultures, perhaps leading to a more mindful and creative future? I suggest the answer is a resounding "Yes!"

Figure 18: PRA from Kentucky (Clay Mathis). Example of a large handheld paleo sculpture. Most PRA examples are much smaller creations. Notice the white ear on the left is a left-facing image—a face within a face.

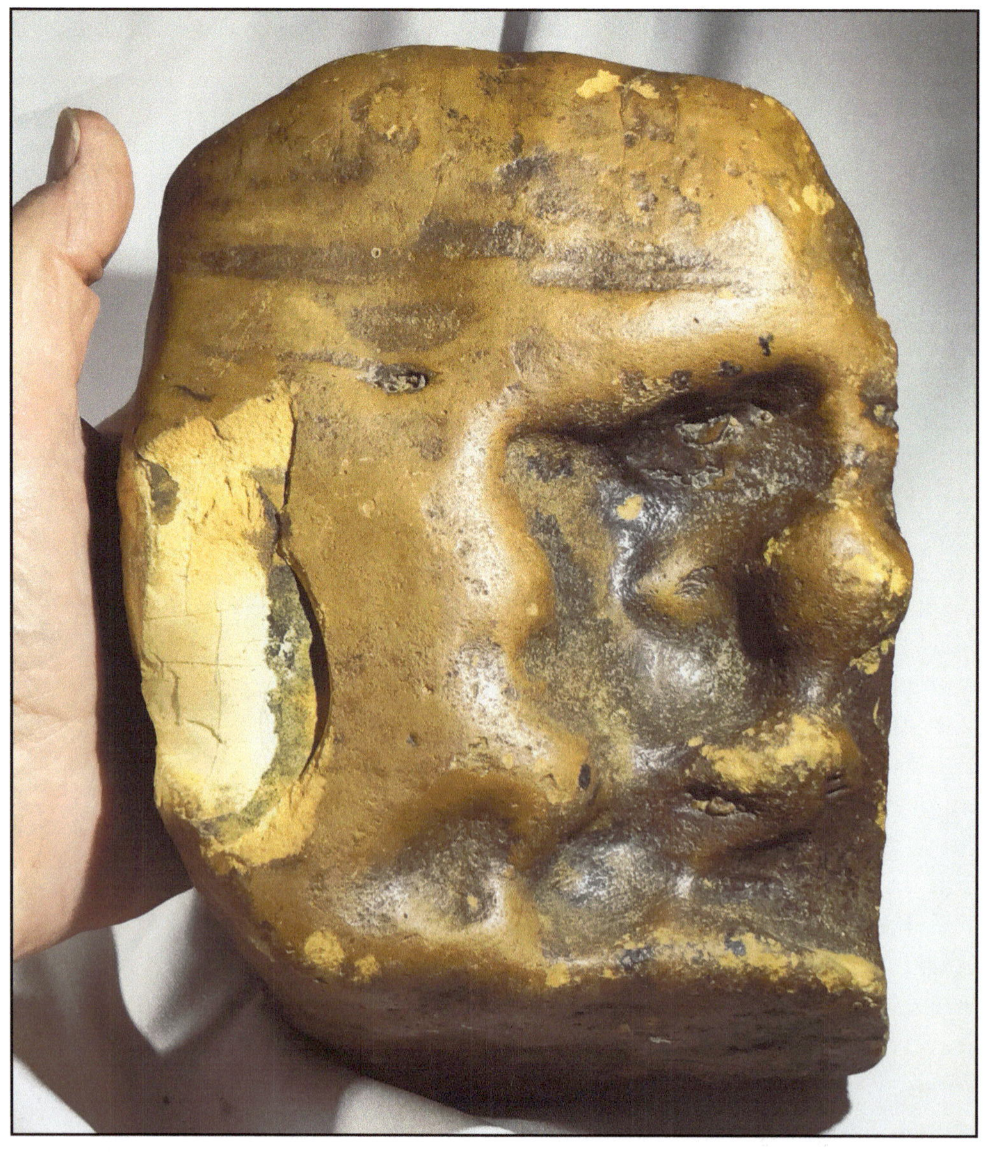

PART II

PRA TRAILBLAZERS

Paleo Rock Art Pioneers

In America, it is quite common for beginners who become interested in PRA to believe their "discoveries" are unique and unparalleled. In the excitement of discovery, few realize PRA and related 3-D imagery have been studied for centuries. Researchers previously have and continue to pioneer a greater understanding and appreciation of the many different types of paleo art, including PRA.

Reconstructing the past can be an arduous and uphill battle when new ideas and ways of thinking challenge conventional thought. Even though most academics and archaeologists have yet to recognize these ingenious ancient creations, notable researchers have blazed the trail with insights and discoveries. Beginning with European-based researchers, the following are notable Portable Rock Art leading researchers.

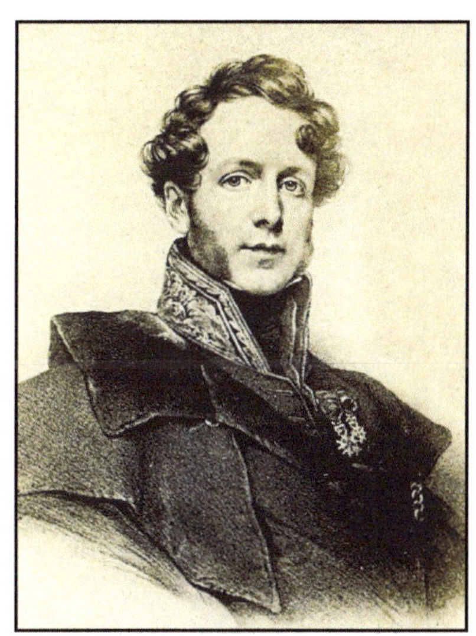

Figure 19: Jacques Boucher de Crèvecœur de Perthes (1788–1868)

Jacques Boucher de Crèvecœur de Perthes

Perhaps the earliest of these pathfinders was Jacques Boucher de Crèvecœur de Perthes (1788–1868), considered in France to be the "Father of Prehistory." In spite of his advanced insights, his discovery and descriptions of lithic sculptures was universally rejected by archaeology for decades. In more recent years, researchers including Pietro Gaietto and James Sackett have revived interest in de Perthes discoveries.[11]

Boucher de Perthes published the first in a series of volumes

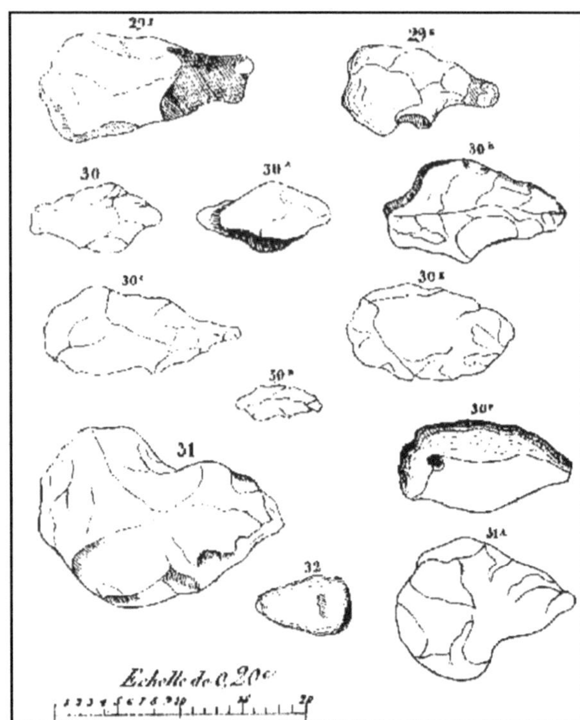

Figure 20: Boucher de Perthes' drawings of tools (Pietro Gaietto).[12]

entitled *Antiquites celtiques et antediluvienne* between 1846 and 1864, where he categorized worked lithics by tools, sculptures and symbols. Even though European archeologists eventually accepted the stone tools documented by Boucher de Perthes as worthy, the sculptures and symbols he identified were never widely recognized.

Boucher de Perthes identified and documented lithic figures, which were predominately faces and birds (*Antiquités Celtiques et Antédiluviennes*). His drawings demonstrate his eye for seeing what professional archaeologists and academics could not.

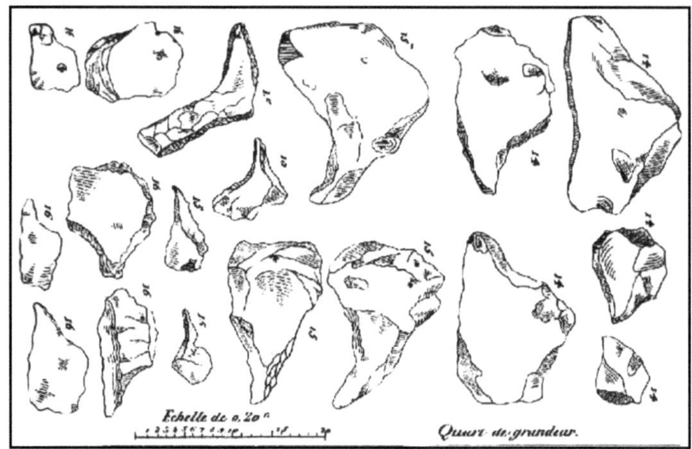

Figure 21: Boucher de Perthes' drawings of bird images (Sackett 2014).[13]

Mary Leakey

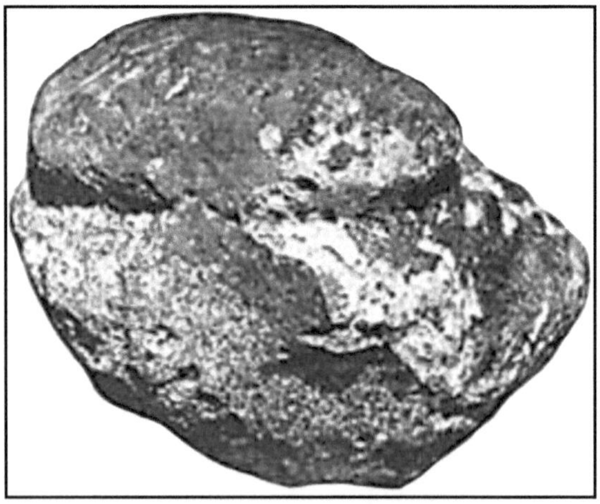

Figure 22: Grooved and pecked cobble, Olduvai Gorge.[15]

Mary Leakey (1913-1996) was a British paleoanthropologist who discovered an extinct ape skull believed to be an ancestor to humans along with other skulls at Olduvai Gorge or Oldupai Gorge in Tanzania, Northeast Africa.

In addition to being known as an archeologist from the famous Leakey family of archaeologists, she was also an accomplished archeological illustrator who documented an unquestionably artificially shaped "pebble of many faces" in the 1970s. She observed, with oblique lighting, pecked grooved facial elements could be identified on the artifact from the Olduvai Gorge, where anthropologists have found some of the earliest human remains going back two million years ago.[14]

The pebble is a fine-grained igneous rock (phonolite) referred to as a cobblestone (79 x 54 x 49 mm) with almost the entire original cortex removed by pecking and battering. Emphasizing the importance of the cobblestone, Leakey said, "This stone has unquestionably been artificially shaped, but it seems unlikely that it could have served as a tool or for any practical purpose."

Ursel Benekendorff

A highly recognized researcher and avocational archaeologist, Ursel Benekendorff has been documenting PRA since 1984. She has devoted much of her life to the recovery, preservation, and analysis of paleo art creations, many of which were recovered from a gravel quarry near Hamburg, Germany. Initially looking for fossils, she soon discovered an assortment of flint tools along with artistically embellished objects.

Born in 1941, she made contact with fossil-collectors from the Netherlands and published in their magazine *Archaeolgishe Berichten,* under the title "Picture Book of the Stone Age." She organized meetings and personally founded an International Study Center of Schleswig-Holstein, for the "protection and rehabilitation of paleolithic sculptures and symbolism."

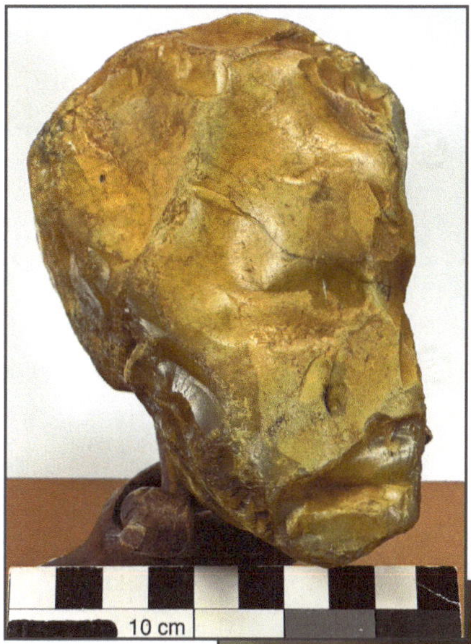

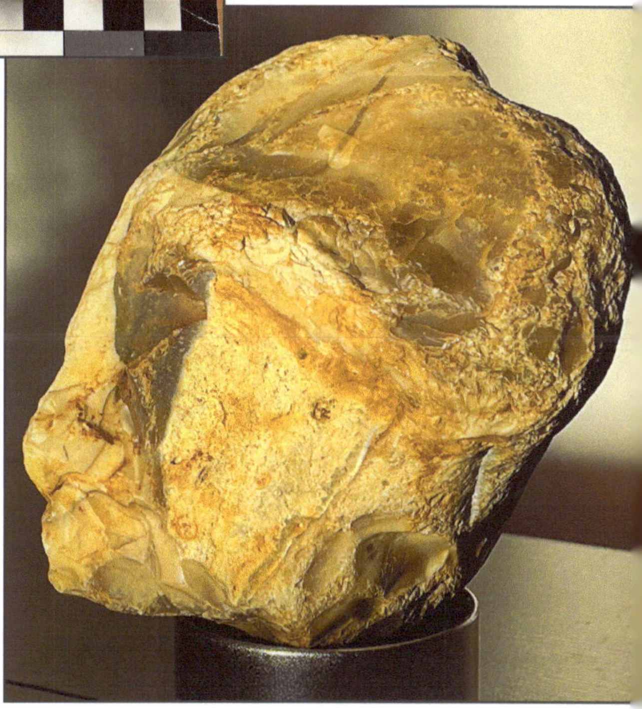

Figure 23: Lower Paleolithic Figure Stones recovered by Ursel Benekendorff from the Ohle gravel pit, Gross-Pampau, Germany. (Ursel Benekendorff; published with permission; all rights reserved.)

Ms. Benekendorff has rescued thousands of these millennia-old relics as she picked them off the conveyor moving the stones to a rock crusher. More recently, some of her Figure Stones and Acheulean handaxes (stone tools characterized by the distinctive oval and pear shapes linked to early humans) have been conclusively confirmed as artifacts by professional archaeologists.

Ms. Benekendorff writes:

> *After finding such tools (Acheulean handaxes) I began to notice that the dredge was also bringing up stones with worked traces that seemed to show zoomorphic and anthropomorphic figurations. The examination and study of Ohle [gravel pit] figure stones has been the focus of my research ever since.... When I presented my materials to*

museum officials as artifacts, they were rejected. They had never seen anything like them before. A lot of learning lay ahead of me and lots of material to sample. All in all, several thousand objects from the quarry pit have passed through my hands, not all artifacts by any **means.**"[16]

Ursel Benekendorff''s website has many photographs documenting Portable Rock Art.[17]

Jan van Es

Beginning in the 1970s, Jan van Es documented a microlithic industry in the Netherlands including tools and microlithic sculptures. Referred to as the Boukoulian find from Boukoul, Netherlands, artifacts identified by van Es were dated 400,000-450,000 years before the present era.

Jan van Es writes:

Using these techniques of "looking," one discovers a shadow language. By turning and overturning the sculptures with this technique... one can "read" a story.[18] (Trans. J. Huber).

Paleo art images documented by Van Es include female figures, zoomorphs and heads/profiles/masks.[19]

Remarkably, while the artifacts he studied that ranged in size from about 1/8th to 1-1/2 inches (0.5-4 cm), 95% are less than an inch (2 cm).

Van Es has collected many different types of PRA and is referenced by other rock art researchers.[20]

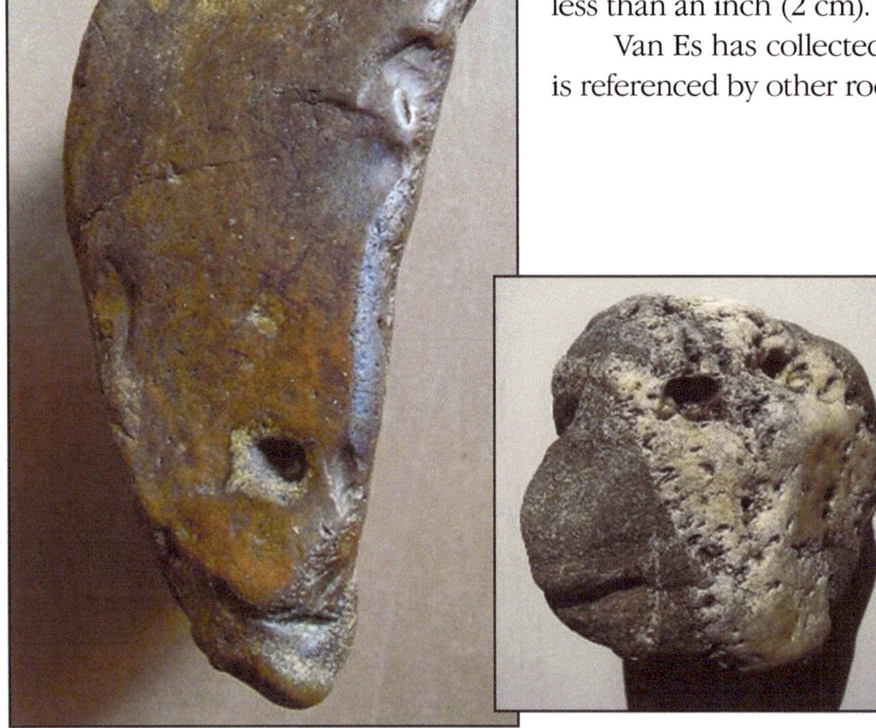

Figure 24: Figure stones from Jan van Es collection, Limberg site, Beegden, Netherlands. [21]

Brett Martin

Mr. Brett Martin from England describes Figure Stones as having multiple images that are best-seen while holding and rotating the stones for different viewing perspectives, noting the importance of the eye depictions in recognizing the often-subtle imagery.[22]

Mr. Martin references Figure Stones and writes:

> *What are Figure Stones? (French:* Pierre's figures*) are a type of Portable Rock Art. A figure stone may depict one or more glyphs or symbols (Ecoglyphs, q.v.), possibly used as a mode of voiceless communication or primitive writing. Symbols portrayed are thought to stem from the palaeolithic era but can also be recognized in more modern finds. Many authenticated palaeolithic flint tools and hand axes are decorated with similar glyphs so can be considered also to be Figure Stones carrying much of the known eoglyph symbology.*[23]

Alan Day

Since 1987, Mr. Alan Day has been researching an early habitation site in southeastern Ohio known as Day's Knob, and in the process recovered and identified examples of PRA. His research has been aided by professional archaeologists and scientists and is among the most credible studies of a North American archaeology site yielding PRA.

Mr. Day writes:

> *The lithic artifacts found so far at Day's Knob are carved, chipped, flaked, split, and abraded mainly from the local limestone, sandstone, hematite, and limonite. Heavy V-profile incision marks (seemingly decorative or symbolic in most cases) are a distinctive characteristic of this*

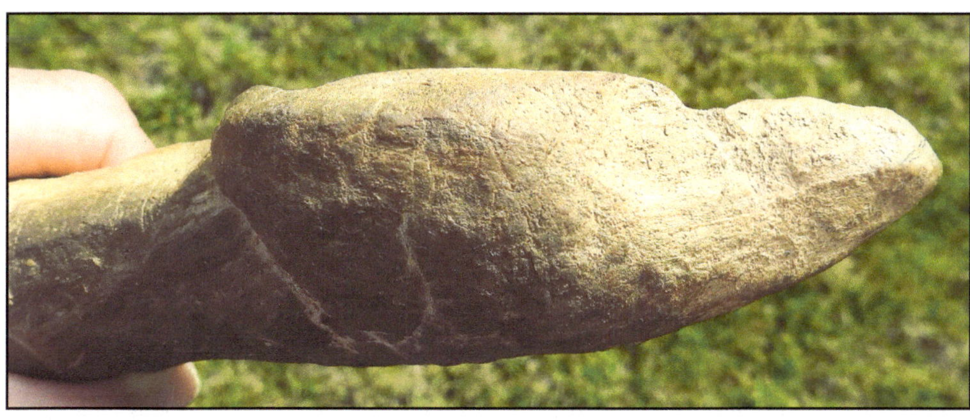

Figure 25: PRA example from Day's Knob (Alan Day).

assemblage. A few of the simple tools are made from non-local igneous or metamorphic rock.[24]

Mr. Day notes that artifacts have been discovered in significant quantities near the surface to over a meter below the surface.

Among his many contributions to the study of PRA (which he commonly refers to as Figure Stones) is his identification of a shaman-like bird-human figure from Day's Knob, also found in other locations around the world.

He writes:

Whatever the age of this material might prove to be, it seems to point to an important if unrecognized anthropological and cultural phenomenon—the almost ubiquitous shaman-like bird-human figure characterizing the rock art at this site, remarkably consistent in its arrangement of readily identifiable sub-components. Strangely, this figure incorporates iconography quite evident in modern but traditional Inuit/Yupik art, and also present in European Paleolithic artifacts, as well as in Australian material of unknown age, apparently a Primal Image. (The presence of portable rock art or mobile rock art has long been recognized in European artifact material, and is starting to be seen for what it is at sites in North America. At this site and others, it is often incorporated into simple lithic tools.)[25]

Since 2003 to the present, Mr. Day has been pursuing serious, credible investigations including dating studies of artifacts from the southeastern Ohio site. His website provides viewers many examples of PRA, as well as championing professional investigation "to ensure the credibility of research into this subject so fraught with controversy and official disapproval."[26]

James Harrod, Ph.D.

James Harrod, Ph.D., Director of the Center for Research on Origins of Art and Religion, has provided among the best scholarly documentation for the origins of paleo stone art. He has authored articles on the decipherment of Upper Paleolithic European protolanguages and has also published on the origins of symbols as evidenced in the paleo art of Oldowan artifacts from Africa, resulting from a widespread prehistorical stone tool industry. Dr. Harrod has suggested some specimens were non-utilitarian art representing symbolic behavior.[27] In his research into symbolic language and meaning, the rock art galleries on his website provide ample evidence that PRA is among the earliest human art.

Addressing one of the most fundamental issues and controversies, determining the intentionality of paleo art, Dr. Harrod writes:

> *With respect to any proposed object and for each category, to establish symbolic intent requires first determining whether, or to what degree, the object is an artifact or geofact (nature-fact) and if it has artificial working traces whether they are intentional or accidental. Determination must be made whether the object is utilitarian (usually considered to mean "tool") or non-utilitarian ("not a tool" and not simply toolmaking "waste" or tool use "damage" or "battering"). Of course, an artifact may be classed as a decorated tool with utilitarian and non-utilitarian aspects. If there appear to be markings or marker placements it must be verified microscopically or otherwise that to what degree they are totally natural, natural and artificially enhanced, or fully artificial. Both symbolic and non-symbolic alternative explanations must be hypothesized, and the non-symbolic explanations ruled out to rule in possible symbolic behavior."*[28]

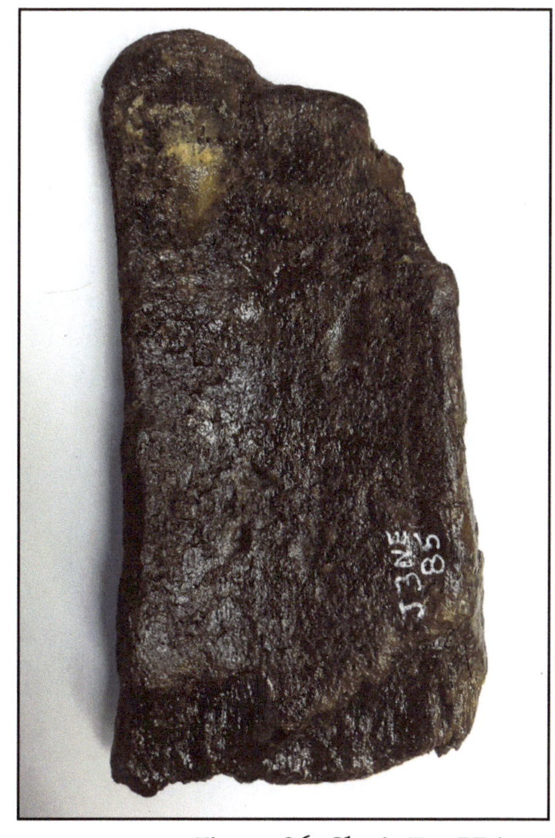

Figure 26: Clovis Era PRA. Hiscock site in Western New York, a mammoth sculpture on tusk ivory (James Harrod).[30]

Dr. Harrod's work is also referenced in Section 4, including a table entitled "Symbolic Behavior—Taxonomy,"[29] in which he lists criteria for determining intentionality found in paleo art.

Kenneth B. Johnston

An American-based PRA pioneer is Kenneth B. Johnston (1963-2020). Ken was an amateur collector of PRA and ancient hand tools he found in Licking County, Ohio. His work as a collector and developer of hypotheses about Portable Rock Art was his passion. Through his PRA website, he became a pioneer and focal point in recognizing the archaeological value of crude stone tools with rock art.

Jul (Rocky) Jones

Mr. Jones is curator of the Portable Rock Art Museum in Grand Falls, New Brunswick, and manages an extensive online resource with commentary articles on PRA and thousands of examples of PRA in well-organized photo galleries. He has created an online platform where members upload and share their PRA finds. Mr. Jones has posted thousands of links to articles and PRA research. The Portable Rock Art Museum website also has an on-line PRA marketplace with thousands of PRA stones on display and for sale.[31]

According to Mr. Jones:

> *. . . Prehistoric man routinely enhanced the attributes of naturally formed rock. To create such artwork, not only artistic ability but 3D spatial aptitude and cognitive abilities were needed, especially using* stone age tools.*”*[32]

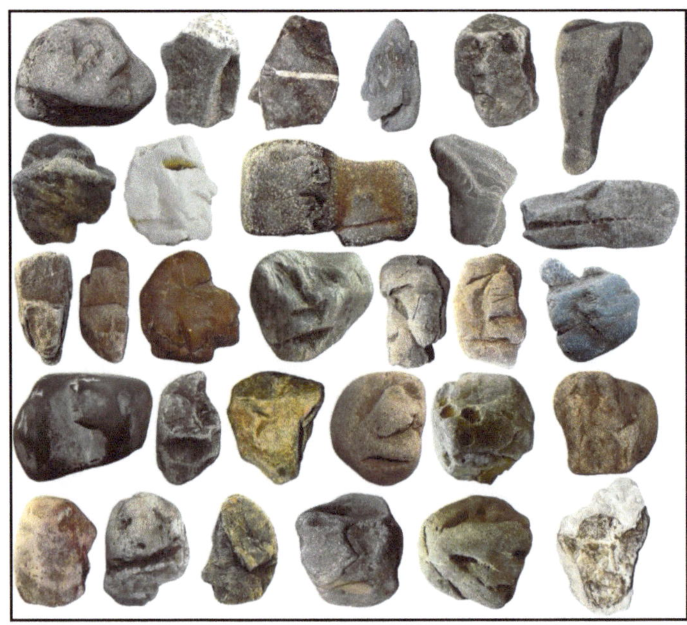

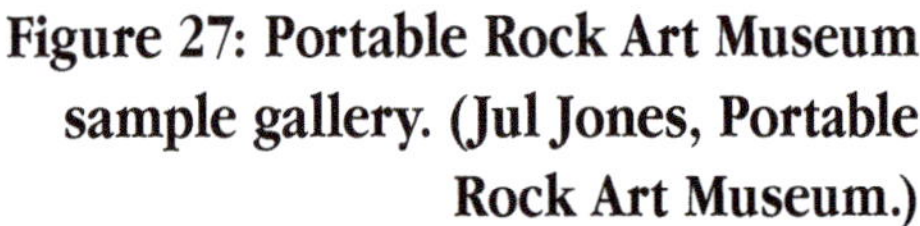

Figure 27: Portable Rock Art Museum sample gallery. (Jul Jones, Portable Rock Art Museum.)

Robert G. Bednarik

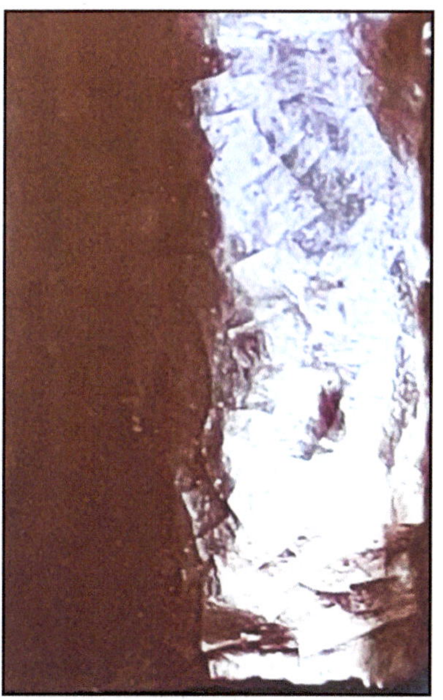

Figure 28: Example of face-like pareidolia imagery resulting from reflection of a white candle on bathroom tile.

One of the most published researchers in the field of rock art and pareidolia phenomena is Robert G. Bednarik. He is included here not as a PRA enthusiast. Quite the contrary, Professor Bednarik is one of the leading critics of PRA and Figure Stones.

Professor Bednarik is an expert in the fields of rock art and paleolithic portable art with over seven hundred publications addressing paleoart, human evolution, psychology and replicative archaeology among other areas. Professor Bednarik is also an expert in dating rock art and is responsible for developing non-invasive rock art dating methods.

Mr. Bednarik has written extensively on pareidolia being the primary explanation for PRA and Figure Stones. His descriptions of how the human brain overlays pareidolia imagery onto random and natural stones to appear as human-made rock art is fundamental reading for anyone wanting to understand pareidolia and how it can impact perception of rock art.

Mr. Bednarik also concludes that Moderns lack the abilities to interpret ancient petroglyphs:

> *Unless there is sound ethnographic information available, the determination of the meaning of petroglyphs or other rock art lies outside the proper science. Nevertheless, it is the approach favored by most archaeologists and therefore requires attention. All iconographic interpretations of rock art involve pareidolia, the experiencing of meaningful patterns in random stimuli. Since modern beholders of such imagery lack the brain structure and composition, and therefore the perception, of its producers, the modern observers cannot determine the emic meaning of supposedly figurative motifs. We can only function as human beings in the context of our societies here and now; we have no way of understanding the conceptual world of people thousands of years ago.*[33]

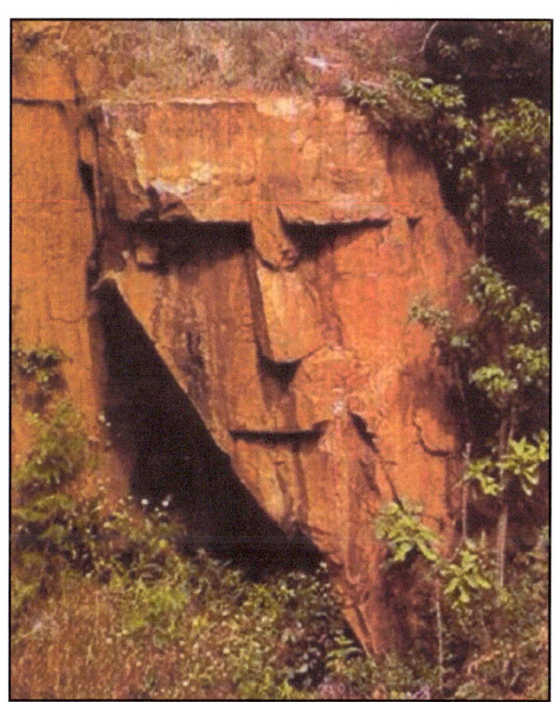

Figure 29: Pareidolia image of a rock outcropping. Owl Mountain (also known as the Sleeping Indian), Colorado Rockies.

While Bednarik's critique of PRA is essential, validation methodologies can verify human workmanship, and head variants can be identified as reoccurring imagery in PRA. His website offers references to his numerous articles.[34]

Additional references to Professor Bednarik's research and publications are presented in "Part Four, Grand Artistry or Pareidolia."

A Growing Community

More recently, I have become acquainted with collectors and researchers across a wide geographical area. Chris Penney, a videographer from Michigan, is another active PRA researcher.

Chris has interviewed dozens of PRA collectors and detractors in pursuit of documenting and bringing to the light the PRA phenomena. His 2023 documentary on PRA, "Ancient Artifact Hunters", explores the various aspects of PRA, including interviews with collectors.[35]

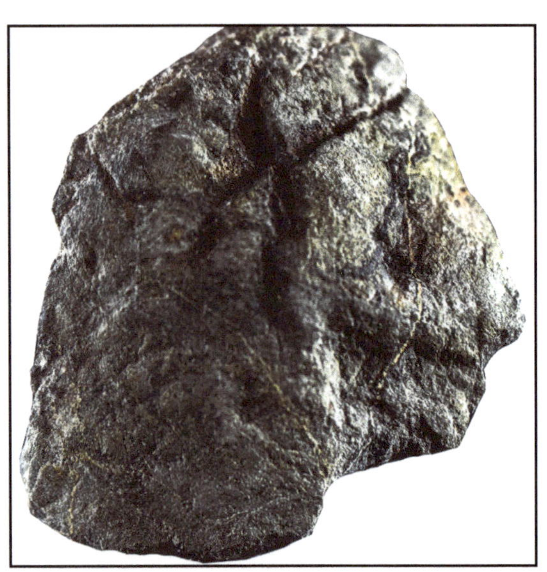

Figure 30: PRA found two feet beneath the surface at an early archaic site in Kent County, Michigan (Chris Penney).

In addition to these modern pioneers, I have been in contact with dozens of collectors throughout the U.S. where PRA has been found. These mostly non-professional enthusiasts possess excellent PRA collections from significant caches, found both below and on the surface.

Each collection consists of common PRA artifacts featuring human and animal head variant shapes, along with noteworthy PRA examples. While most PRA finds are on or near the surface, some like those from Kentucky featured in this book were retrieved from below the surface which may in the future provide a context for dating and better understanding.

There are differences and schisms among PRA experts and enthusiasts (professional vs. nonprofessionals, seasoned researchers vs. newcomers, artistic vs. scientistic outlooks, etc.); nevertheless, we all have seen/experienced something extraordinary and want to share and learn more about these amazing artifacts.

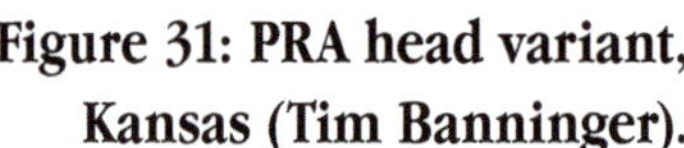

Figure 31: PRA head variant, Kansas (Tim Banninger).

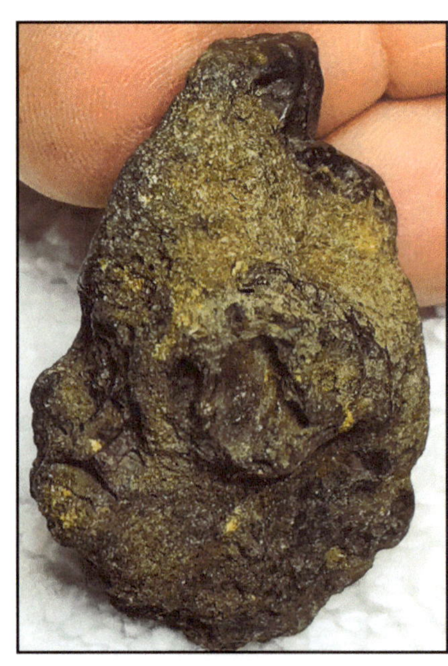

PART III

HAND HELD, MULTIFACETED PALEO ART

Petroglyphs, Rock Art, and Portable Rock Art

Paleo, stone-age art from around the world ranges in style, method, and age, and includes cave paintings, petroglyphs, pictographs, and polished and engraved stones as exemplified by portable stone ceremonial objects.

The word ***petroglyph*** means to shape, fashion and sculpt. By this definition, a 3-D sculpted image on PRA is literally a petroglyph, although the term itself is not associated with 3-D images.

Petroglyphic images are inscribed in stone and found predominately on fixed boulders, large rocks, rock outcroppings, and cave walls. Petroglyphs were created by removing part of a rock's surface through a process of pecking, abrading, incising, and/or etching, and are generally associated with large rock surfaces. ***Pictographs*** are images painted onto rock surfaces.

Petroglyphs are most often assumed to be two-dimensional creations (width and height) as found on fixed rock surfaces. In contrast PRA is a three-dimensional (3-D) artistic platform often replete with sculptures and micro-sculptures, not generally recognized to be petroglyphs or even human creations. The commonly held and limited view of petroglyphs (literally carved, sculpted and shaped stone works) has restricted the ability of Moderns to recognize the human-created art found on PRA.

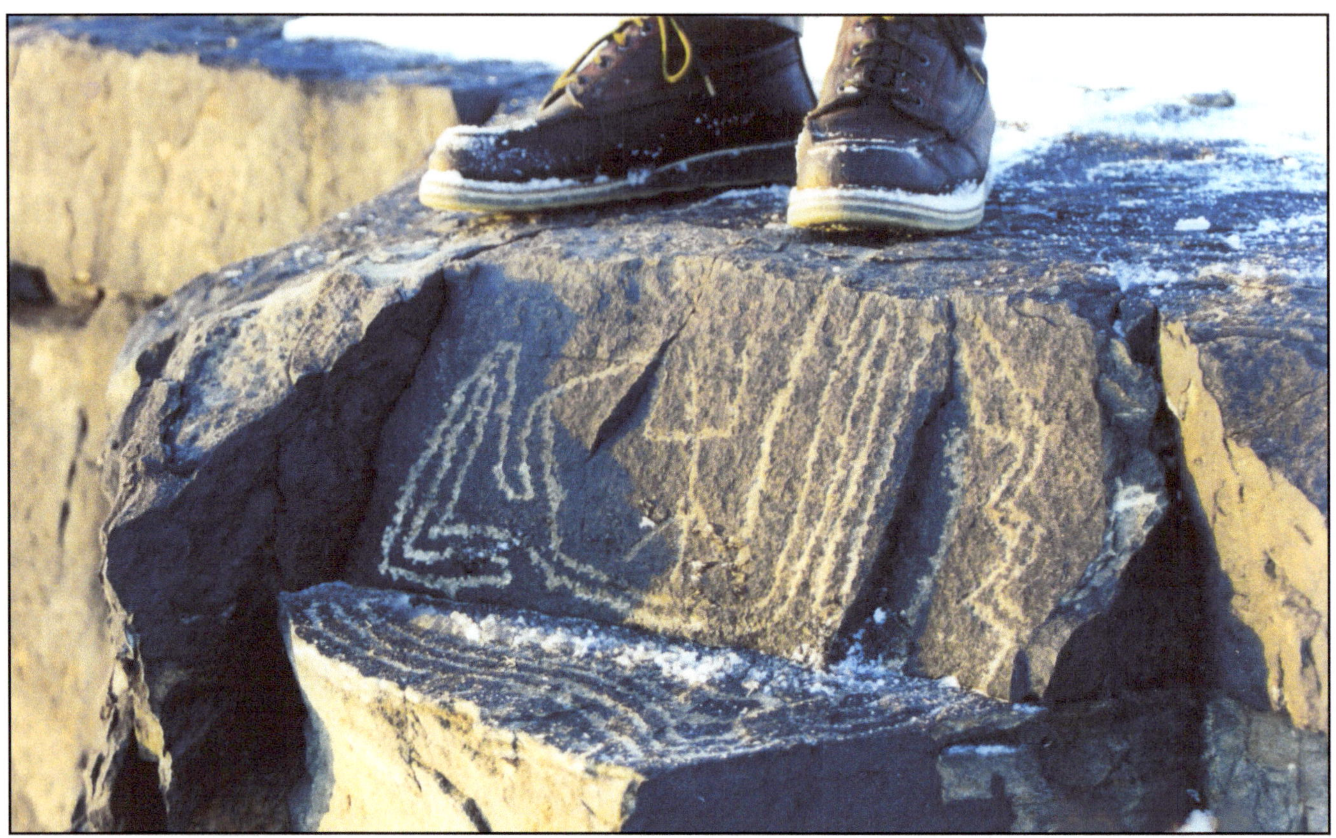

Figure 32: Petroglyph marking winter Solstice, Southeast Colorado.

Unlike most petroglyphs carved on a single plane, Figure 32 shows an unusual configuration using three different planes (top horizontal, vertical and bottom horizontal with snow). When looked at standing above or from below, a three-dimensional (3-D) image is portrayed. The meaning of the series of petroglyphs from the Purgatory River Valley of southeastern Colorado is revealed only at sunrise around the Winter Solstice (December 21), when a triangular point of the shadow strikes the extended phallus of the central figure on the vertical surface. This Winter Solstice archaeoastronomical alignment validates intentionality and provides a context for interpretation. As it relates to PRA, instead of the sun's movement creating light/shadow imagery at a specific time of year on a petroglyph, it's the movement of an artifact aligned to one's viewing position that reveals intentionally created art.

Rock art sculptures appear where you may not expect them. While most petroglyphs on fixed surfaces are two-dimensional images, the cemetery "bench" (*Fig. 33*) has 3-D imagery on its side. The extended triangular shaped pointy-head petroglyph demonstrates several important aspects of rock art, including a 3-D configuration and use of natural layers and strata to create faces and art typically found on smaller portable artifacts.

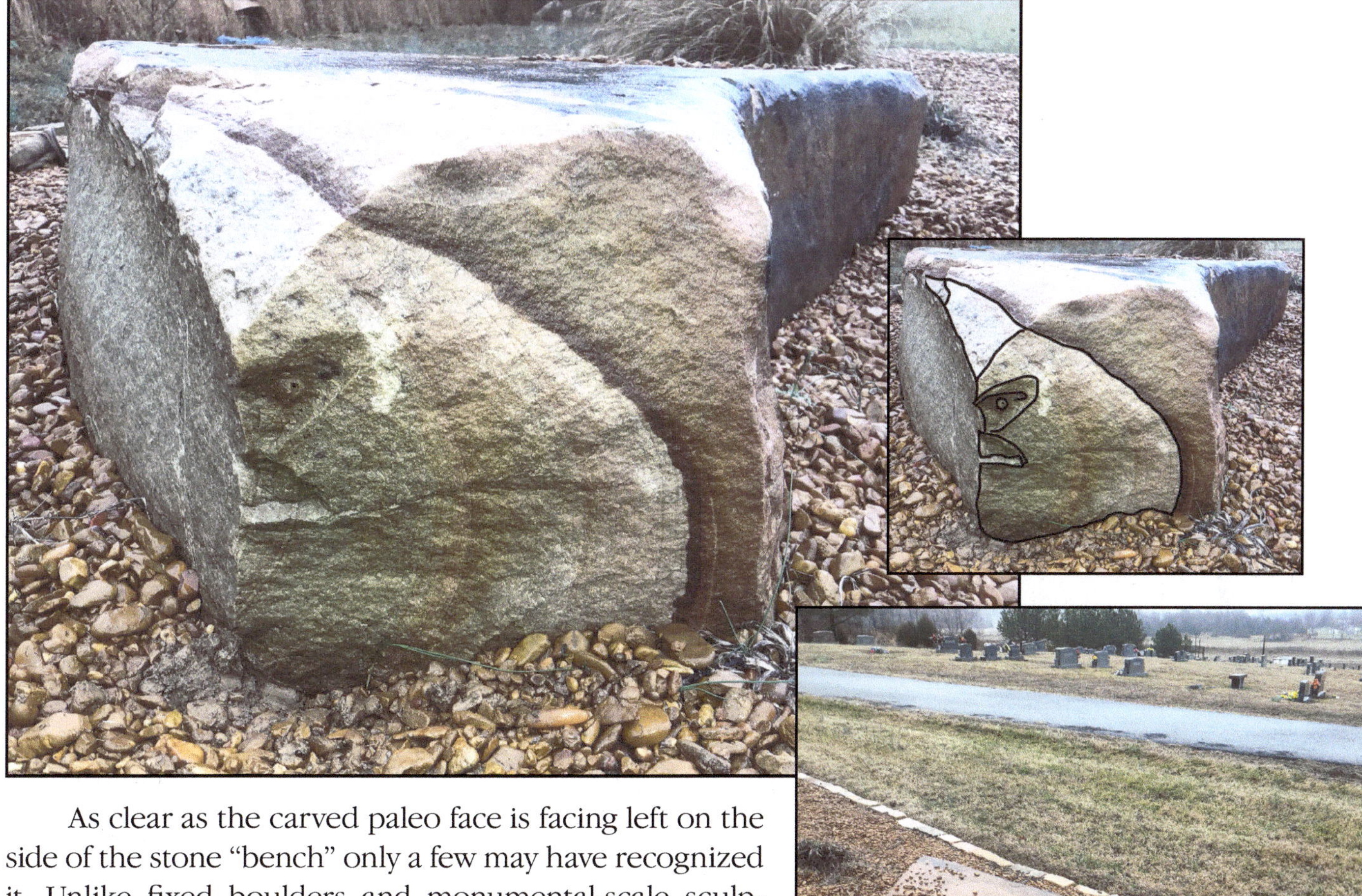

Figures 33: Cemetery bench featuring pointy-head petroglyph.

As clear as the carved paleo face is facing left on the side of the stone "bench" only a few may have recognized it. Unlike fixed boulders and monumental-scale sculptures, PRA objects are portable, ranging in sizes from less than one-inch pebbles to handheld stones.

A growing body of evidence gathered from locations throughout North America, Europe and Africa confirms that, in addition to traditionally understood petroglyphs on fixed rocks, there is an abundance of unrecognized Portable Rock Art remaining from a widely practiced, age-old tradition of enhancing stones with art, as documented by Mary Leakey, James Harrod and other archaeological researchers.

PRA relies on shapes/profiles using the whole stone most often resembling a human and/or animal shape or head variant along with sculpted shapes/images on facets/planes/appendages. Etched, pecked and carved petroglyphs with symbols are less common and most often are hidden by built up residue referred to as **patina.**

The best examples of PRA often have more than just shapes appearing as human and animal head variants, but encompass other petroglyphic aspects including detailed sculptures. Learning how to identify and distinguish them from natural looking phenomena is the task at hand for rock art readers.

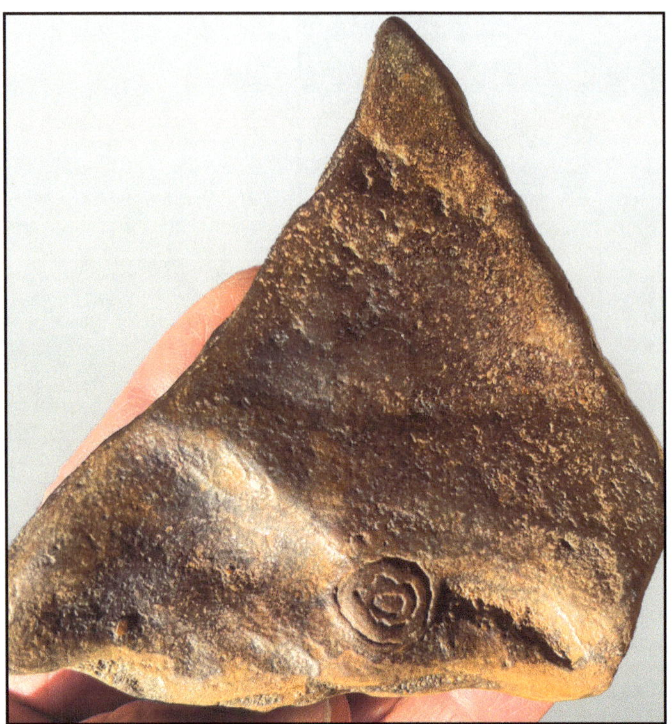

Figure 34: Artifact II (above), Triangular PRA petroglyph with detailed face-in-face motif (below), Kentucky (Clay Mathis).

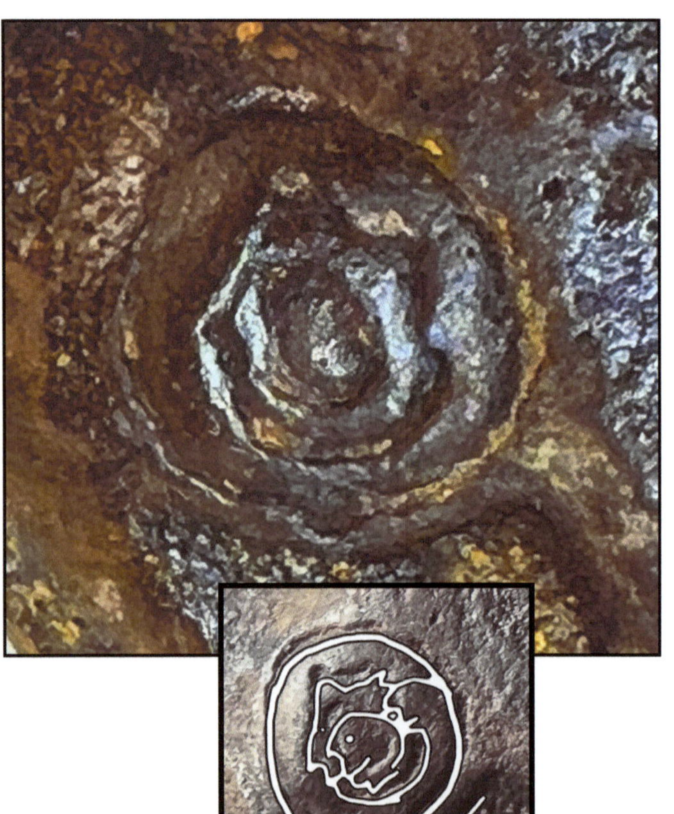

ARTIFACT II:
Triangular Shaped PRA with Petroglyph and Sculptures

While most PRA specimens do not appear to have "petroglyphs" in the traditional sense, Artifact II is inscribed with three concentric circles, which fits the stereotype of conventional petroglyphs. This example of a clearly inscribed glyph may be an exception to most PRA, which rarely have such clear symbols.

On close examination, the "circles" on Artifact II are a more complex set of images.

The front of Artifact II hosts the etched glyphs (*Fig. 34*). What appear to be three concentric circles are a detailed design consisting of a face-in-face motif. While a persistent layer of black remains, the cleanings thus far reveal underlying shallow workings that are integral to sculpted shapes.

The backside of Artifact II on the opposite page (*Fig. 35*) appears to include a side view of a female motif. This is noteworthy as most PRA human head variants appear as male characters. The lighter color of the backside compared to the front demonstrate the natural color of this 4.5x4.5x3.5-inch paleo sculpture.

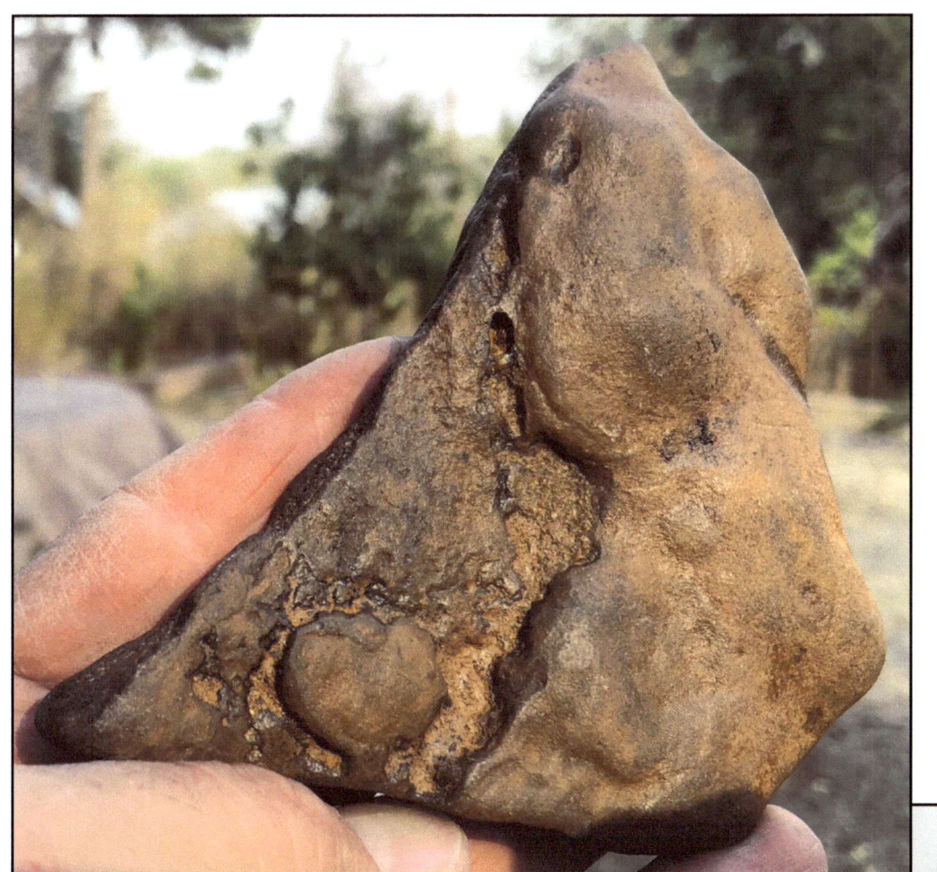

Figure 35: The backside of Artifact II (left), with one of the sculptures highlighted (below).

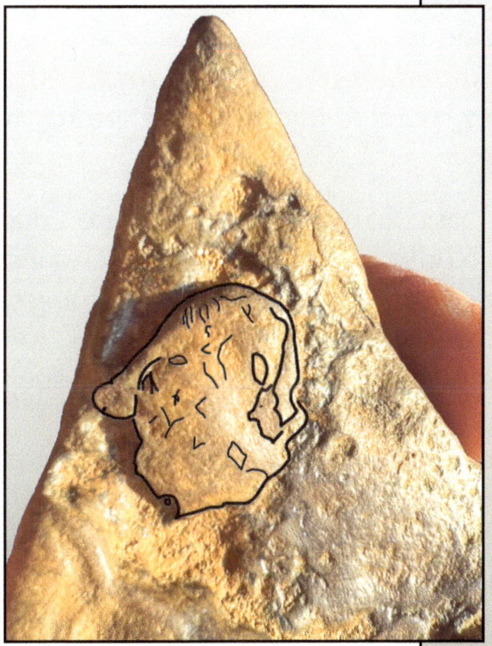

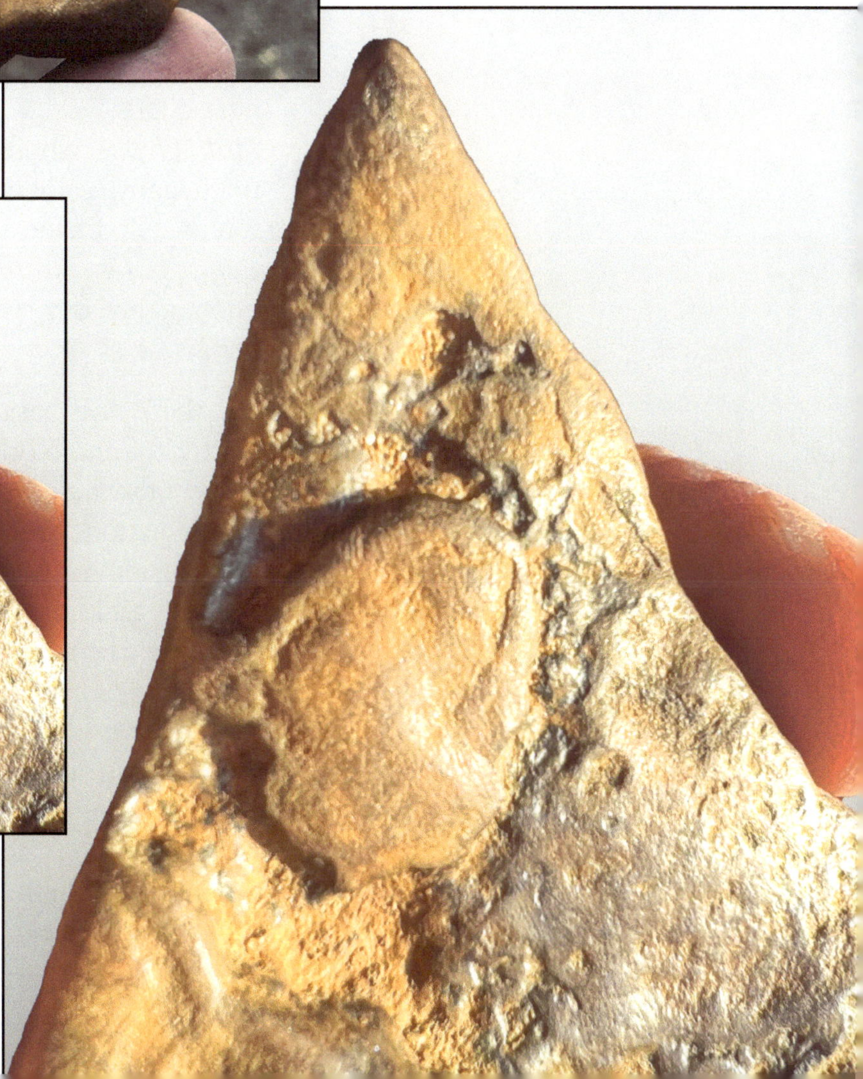

Portable Rock Art Basic Elements

Proper positioning is critical to perceiving intentional rock art. When inspecting petroglyphs on fixed surfaces (panels, boulders, etc.) the observer has a coherent orientation to see the plane onto which petroglyphs were created and the intended viewing angle. In contrast, PRA presents multiple ways of viewing an artifact, including rotating it in one's hand. This adds to the dimensionality and complexity of the piece and contributes to the challenge of recognizing intentionally created rock art enhancements among natural features.

PRA incorporates many artistic techniques of which five basic types of enhancements are noted here and detailed further in Part VII, Recognizing Petroglyphic Features.

- *Profiles/sculptures* of whole stones resembling a human and/ or animal. This is the most important aspect of recognizing most artifacts. Often there are different intended profiles on different sides and planes.
- *Sculpted shapes/images on facets/planes/appendages.* These enhancements are chipped/scratched/carved to create images within the greater shape of the object.
- *Etched glyphs* on rock surfaces, often on a single plane, sometimes appearing in a series of glyphs and extending around or near edges.
- *Multi-glyphs,* where a single petroglyph or sculpture incorporates many connected images, including "faces-in-faces" and totem-style imagery.
- *Edges, holes and indented/depressed surfaces* that incorporate and are incorporated into micro-sculptures and petroglyphs.

While these five basic artistic perspectives are critical to understanding PRA, there are other techniques and dimensions of paleo-enhancements not included above. These include adorning tools with art; heliolithic animations employing light/shadow effects; rotating objects to achieve "moving picture" imagery; artifacts making sounds including whistles; games and other utilitarian qualities; along with more esoteric features relating to energetics, rituals, and other Ancient practices. *(See Figs. 55, 56 and 57 for more details.)*

Examples of exceptional PRA found on the following pages *(Figs. 36-39)*, demonstrate these five basic artistic techniques employed in utilitarian and non-utilitarian PRA. In addition to their detailed micro sculptures, multi-glyphs and etchings, what sets these two specimens apart from more common Figure Stones is the occurrence of holes that penetrate the entire stone.

ARTIFACT III: *Tool from Arizona*

1. Evidence of workmanship (knife edges)
2. Profiles using whole rock
3. Sculpted images on appendages
4. Multi-glyphs
5. Divots, holes for mouth
6. Other PRA attributes

---

1. **Tool**. Worked double edges for cutting, fits well in one's hand, functions as a knife.

2. **Profile using whole stone**. Right facing image with mouth in yellow, head in brown, and eye in red strata.

3. **Images on appendages**. Left facing head variant.

4. **Multi-glyph** includes forehead of left facing head variant with large nose.

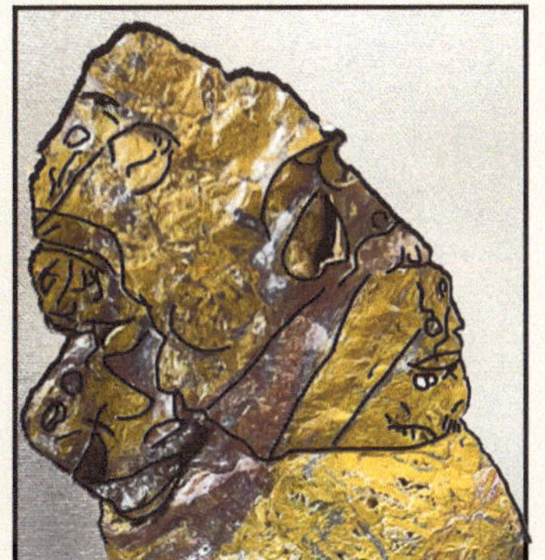

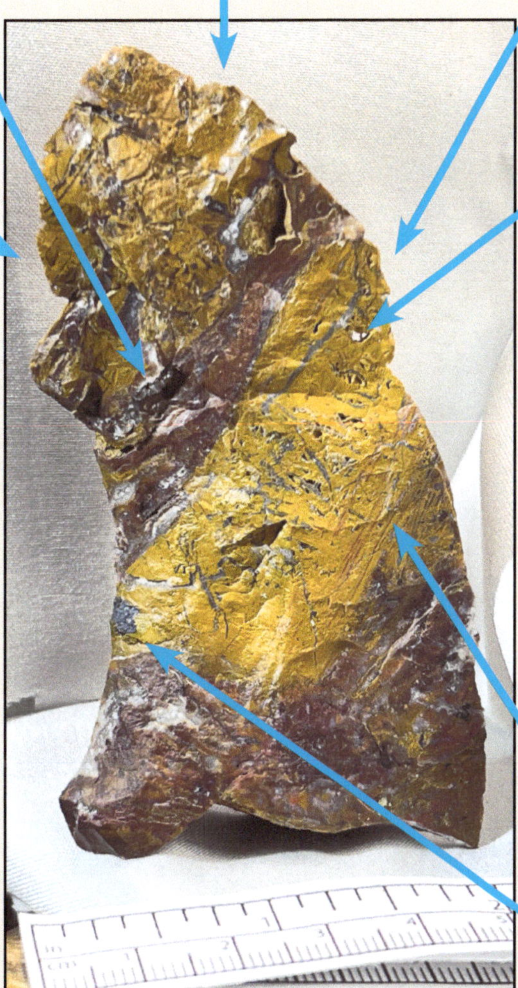

5. **Several Tiny Holes** that penetrate both sides are positioned where the mouth of the head variant is located.

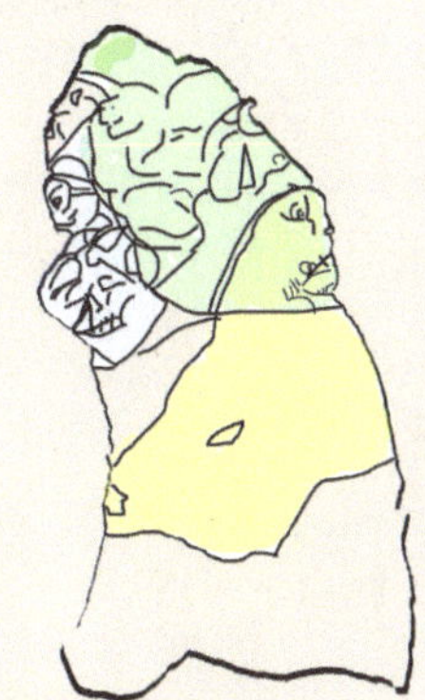

6. **Other artifact attributes** include use of natural strata colors in artifact left- and right-facing. imagery. Holes on right side are an imaginative creation.

3. **Images on appendages**. Left facing head variant.

4. **Multi-glyph** includes forehead of left facing head variant with large nose.

Figure 36: Tool with PRA elements found in Arizona.

ARTIFACT IV: *Holey Stone from Kentucky*

1. Shapes, etchings, sculptures show workmanship
2. Profile using whole rock
3. Sculpted, etched images on appendages
4. Multi-glyphs
5. Edges and holes
6. Other PRA attributes

1. **No apparent utilitarian use.** Detailed carvings and shapes are indicative of workmanship, especially about and within "eye" holes.

5. **Hole penetrates** both sides, is adorned with sculptures and etchings. Shallow area forms right eye.

2. **Profile using whole stone.** From this perspective, large, oval eyes, pronounced nose and a smile. (See next page for other head variant shapes from different positions.)

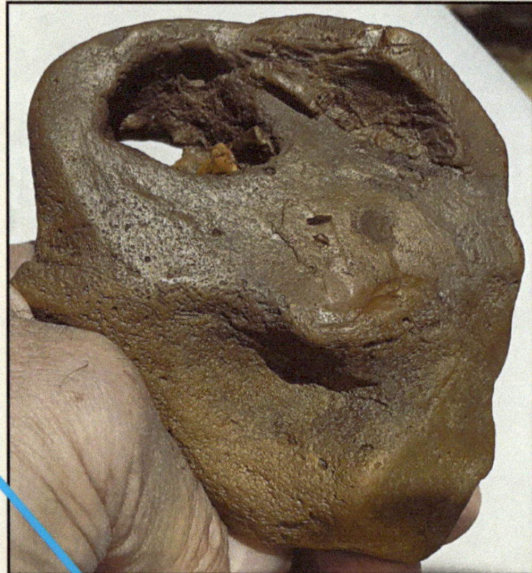

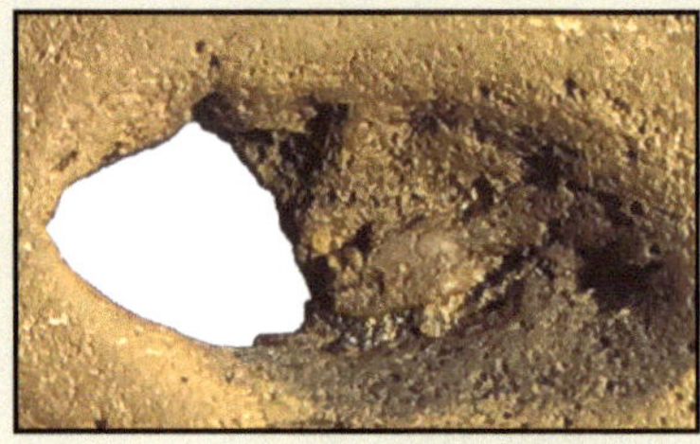

3. **Images on appendages.** Left facing head variant with micro sculptures

4. **Multi-glyph** above left facing head variant includes a serpent with an etched Pointy Head Guy above.

6. **Other attributes** include the detail etchings in the interior of the hole, etched decorations on the eye pebbles and the diverse profiles employing the artifact's many sides.

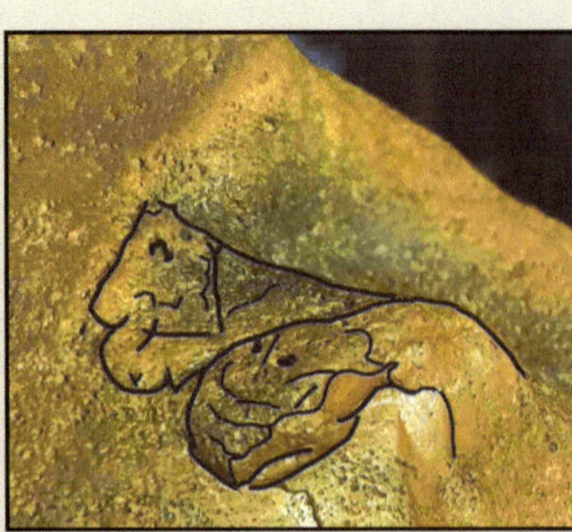

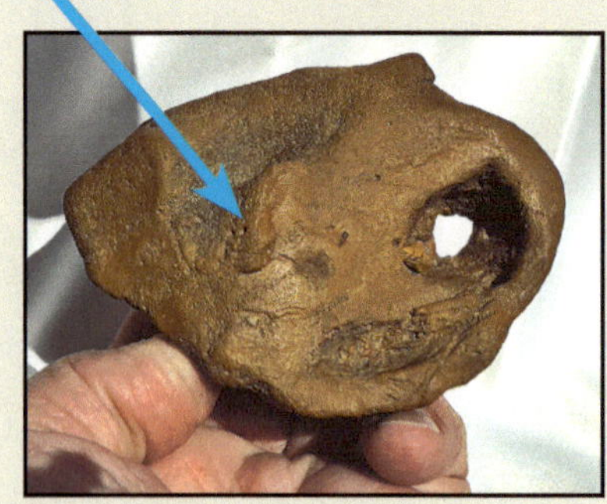

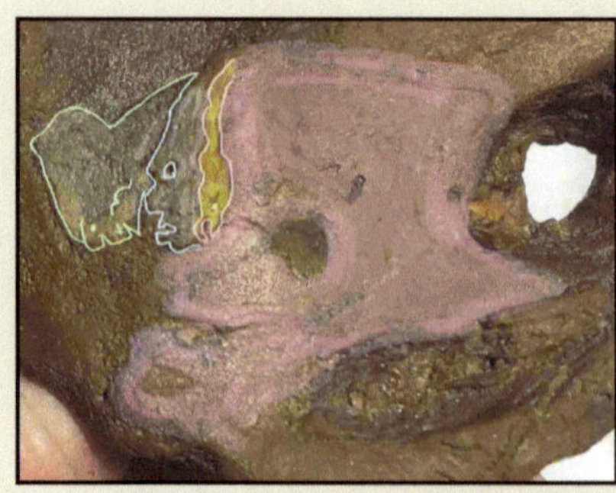

Figure 37: Example of apparent non-utilitarian PRA found in Kentucky.

ARTIFACT IV: *Holey Stone*

Most PRA incorporates some of the five basic elements identified previously. The "Holey Stone" from Kentucky employs all five these elements. Different views of the Holey Stone (*Fig 38*) artifact demonstrate many diverse head variants incorporated into the overall shape of a single paleo sculpture. Each position has right- and left-facing images, previously described by the author in a 2020 article in *Ancient Origins Magazine.*[36]

The Holey Stone (named for its hole penetrating the stone) was retrieved from the base of a working gravel mining operation by the author during 2020 at a depth of approximate 15 feet below the surface. The artifact (4.25x3 in. or 10.8x7.6 cm) has a thickness that averages about 1 in. or 2.5 cm. Its most obvious and distinguishing feature is an oblong-shaped hole that connects the two sides, referred to as the "Tunnel." Extensive cleaning has yet to remove all the encrusted patina, yet the Holey Stone is an excellent teaching example for demonstrating fundamental PRA elements.

The adjacent artifact (*Fig. 39*) from Boukoul, Netherlands, is considered to be 4000,000 years old and suggests a continuous artistic tradition when compared to the Holey Stone.

The microlithic sculptures on the Boukoulian artifact, within a Lower Paleolithic context, demonstrate strikingly similar features to the Holey Stone.

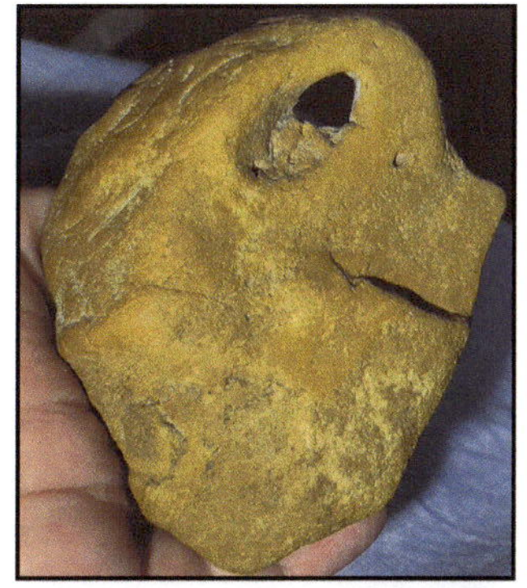
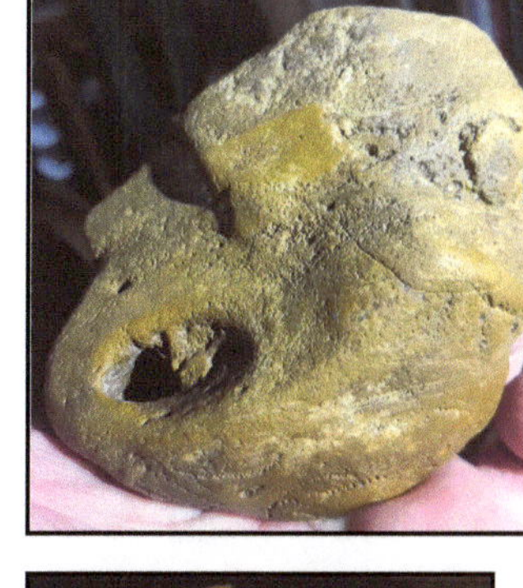
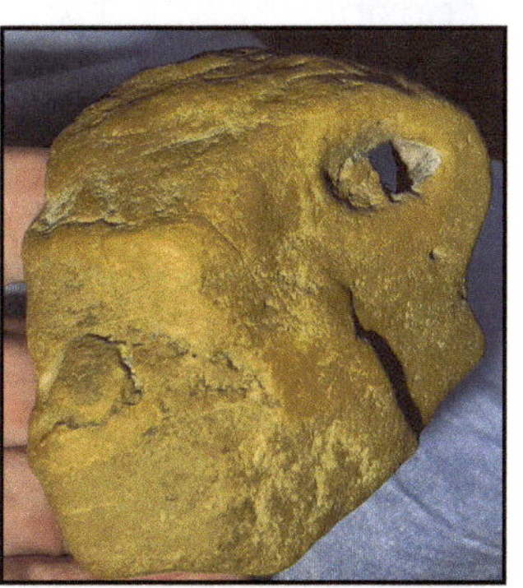
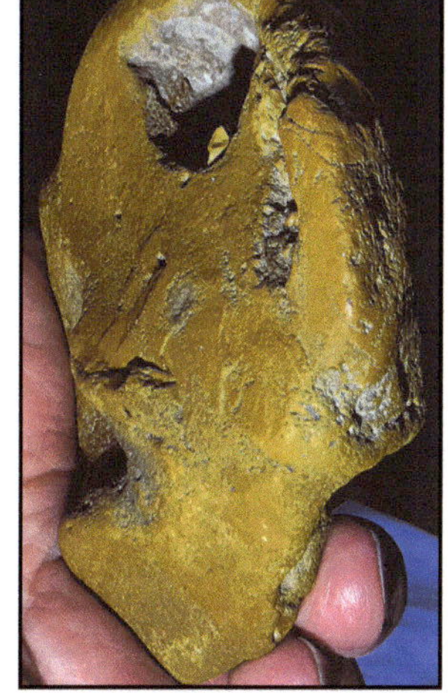
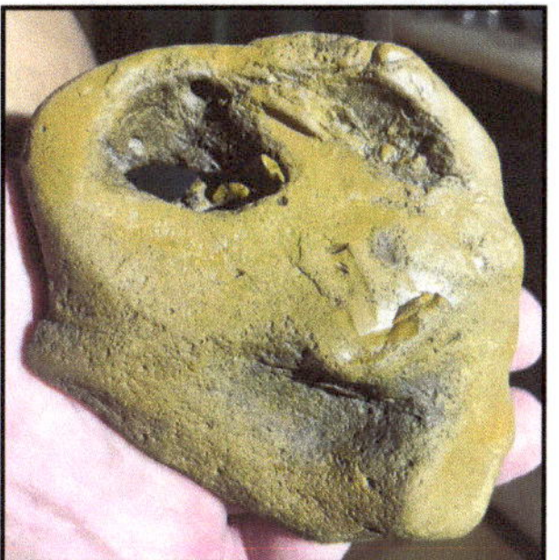

Figures 38: Artifact IV, Holey Stone featuring five of many head variants.

Figure 39: (below), Similar PRA from Boukoul, Netherlands (Jan van Es).[37]

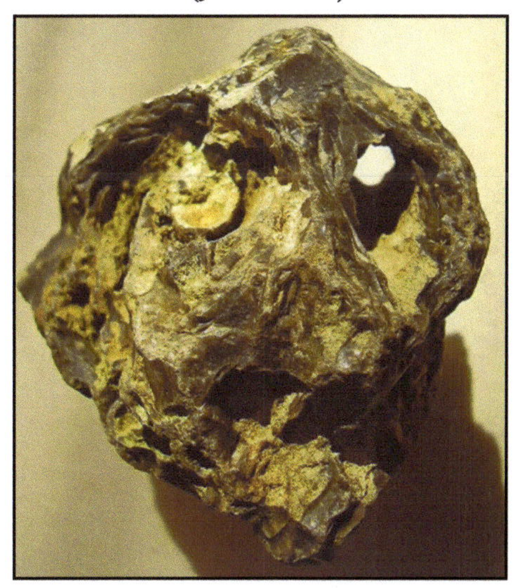

Why Are PRA Artifacts Unrecognized?

There has been and remains unwavering concurrence by the archaeological community that most of what is purported to be PRA is pareidolia, as indicative of Professor Bednarik's critique noted in Part Four. This critique is consistent with the common experience among PRA collectors of being dismissed by professional archaeologists, geologists and academics. For those of us familiar with PRA, it is absolutely incredulous that what is so apparent as artistic embellishments are considered to be solely natural and pareidolia phenomena by traditionalists and "gate keepers."

Gate keepers are those in professional and academic positions of authority who determine what are acceptable archaeological perspectives and topics and who is worthy of holding positions of authority. For example, university department committees who determine which professor receives tenure, or magazine editors who refuse to publish controversial topics.

PRA remains elusive for other reasons, among them our language. Language is key to human perceptions, which have become constrained by what we believe "petroglyphs," "rock art," and "art" encompass. PRA lithic enhancements remain hidden, partially as a result of our language, which has limited our perceptions, disguising intentionally created art in what appear to most as natural surface markings, contours and shapes on common-looking stones.

In other words, the actual language we use can limit our observations, as exemplified by the term rock art itself. For example, a Yale University publication states that rock art appears "...on the sides or walls of caves, cliffs, sheer standing rocks, and also boulders." This definition excludes the most abundant form of ancient artwork, Portable Rock Art. In another example, *Geology.com* states: "There are two basic types of rock art: petroglyphs and pictoglyphs."[38]

To challenge the language barrier, the author

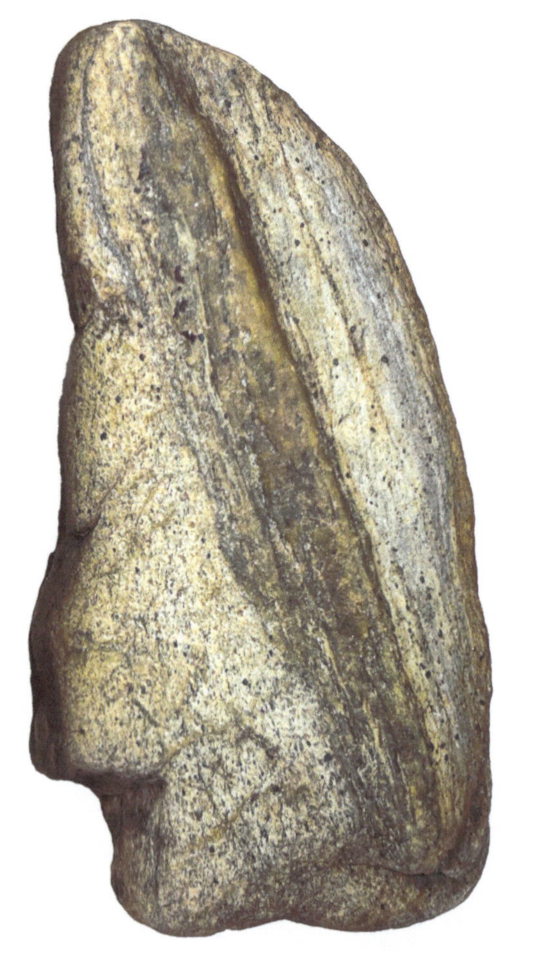

Figure 40: PRA sculpture from Arizona (Carey Bell). Without visible signs of workmanship, this stone can be easily dismissed as "natural."

uses the word ***artfacts*** as a new term to help describe PRA as ancient artifacts and to distinguish them from conventionally understood paleo tools, effigy stones, and fetishes.

The often-subjective nature of seeing art on three-dimensional stones can be unsettling for professionals seeking a fixed image and clear-cut answers to the many unknowns regarding paleo art. Because the Ancients selected and incorporated natural shapes, contours, and lines into their creations, distinguishing human-crafted art from natural contours and shapes can be illusive.

What is disturbing for PRA critics most of all is the idea that PRA is so abundant. However, as the evidence continues to grow, more and more open-minded professionals are beginning to explore the possibility, "We've missed something big."

Another barrier to a broader acceptance of PRA is the lack of validation criteria to distinguish PRA from traditionally understood artifacts, eoliths, mimeotoliths and geofacts. To address the validation issue, the author cites other researchers' methodologies as well as his own approach to confront the central question: can we determine that PRA was intentionally created by the human working of the stone, instead of being a natural stone with no human workmanship?

Validation approaches include advanced photography methods like Reflectance Transformation Imaging[39] to distinguish natural from human-made

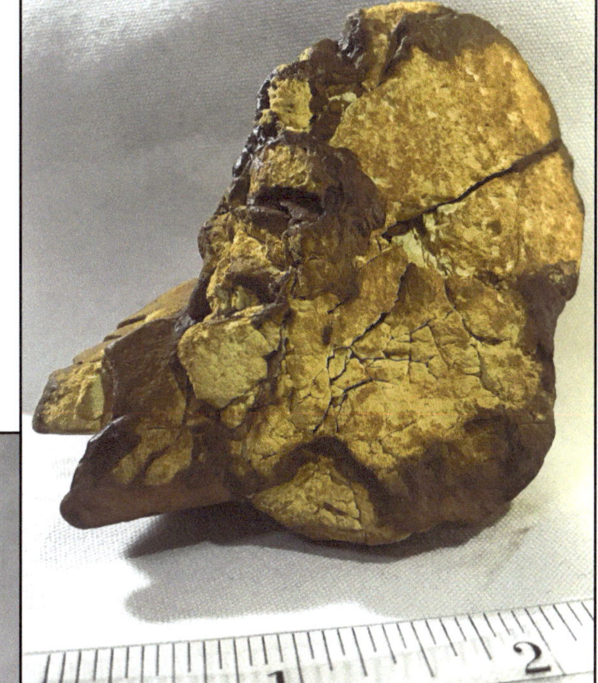

Figures 41: PRA sculpture from Kentucky. Above photo resembles a bird. Photo on the left was rotated 180 degrees and resembles another animal likeness (a snail?) with faces-in-faces imagery.

enhancements. Detailed examinations of PRA by professional geologists and archaeologists using microscopic equipment will be able to identify human workmanship. As more PRA research and authentication techniques emerge, anthropologists, Native American historians and archaeologists will learn to identify, validate, and understand the "moving" petroglyphic features when not-so-plain-old-rocks are properly cleaned, positioned and rotated.

Observing Portable Rock Art

An artifact's shape is a starting point for investigations. The overall form is what observers usually notice first, and the outer outline—even with significant sediment buildup—offers the eye opportunities to seek out profiles of humans, animal shapes, and other anomalies. Turning the object to establish a viewing perspective can offer a glimpse at what was intended to be art. As the PRA candidate is cleaned, eyes, mouth, images on appendages, multi-glyphs and etchings may become recognizable.

One of the most significant tools to aid in observing artifacts is sidelighting, which reveals surface micro-etchings, intrusions, sculpted layers and other workings not apparent when viewing under direct overhead lighting or dull or indirect light. Sidelighting, commonly referred to as *raking light*, brings out the details created by pecking, abrading and etching on rock surfaces, on both fixed petroglyphs and Portable Rock Art.

In Portable Rock Art the sidelighting effect casts surface shadows bringing out details skillfully integrated into the natural rock. The micro details revealed by sidelighting can be seen under natural or artificial lighting as well as firelight and by slowly moving the artifact into the optimum position to evaluate the shape and see any surface embellishments. Figures 43-45 demonstrate sidelighting on PRA using an artifact from Kansas.

PRA often reveals itself in clusters of different minerals embedded within a single stone. Conglomerate rocks (*Fig. 42*) are many different stones bound together in layers/strata to create a singular rock. Conglomerates are sedimentary rocks and are common. The author has found conglomerate rocks with artistic features from Kentucky and Colorado.

In addition to thorough cleaning and employing sidelighting, moving PRA candidates in different directions will often reveal evidence of workmanship and art.

ARTIFACT V: *Conglomerate Rock*

An outstanding feature of this conglomerate rock are faces on some of the smaller stones including a pair of joined head variants, one black and the other white *(inset drawing)*. This interplay between dark and light head variants is a reoccurring theme employed throughout PRA. This artifact also employs a very subtle etching facing up in the basin appendage when it rests naturally on its base.

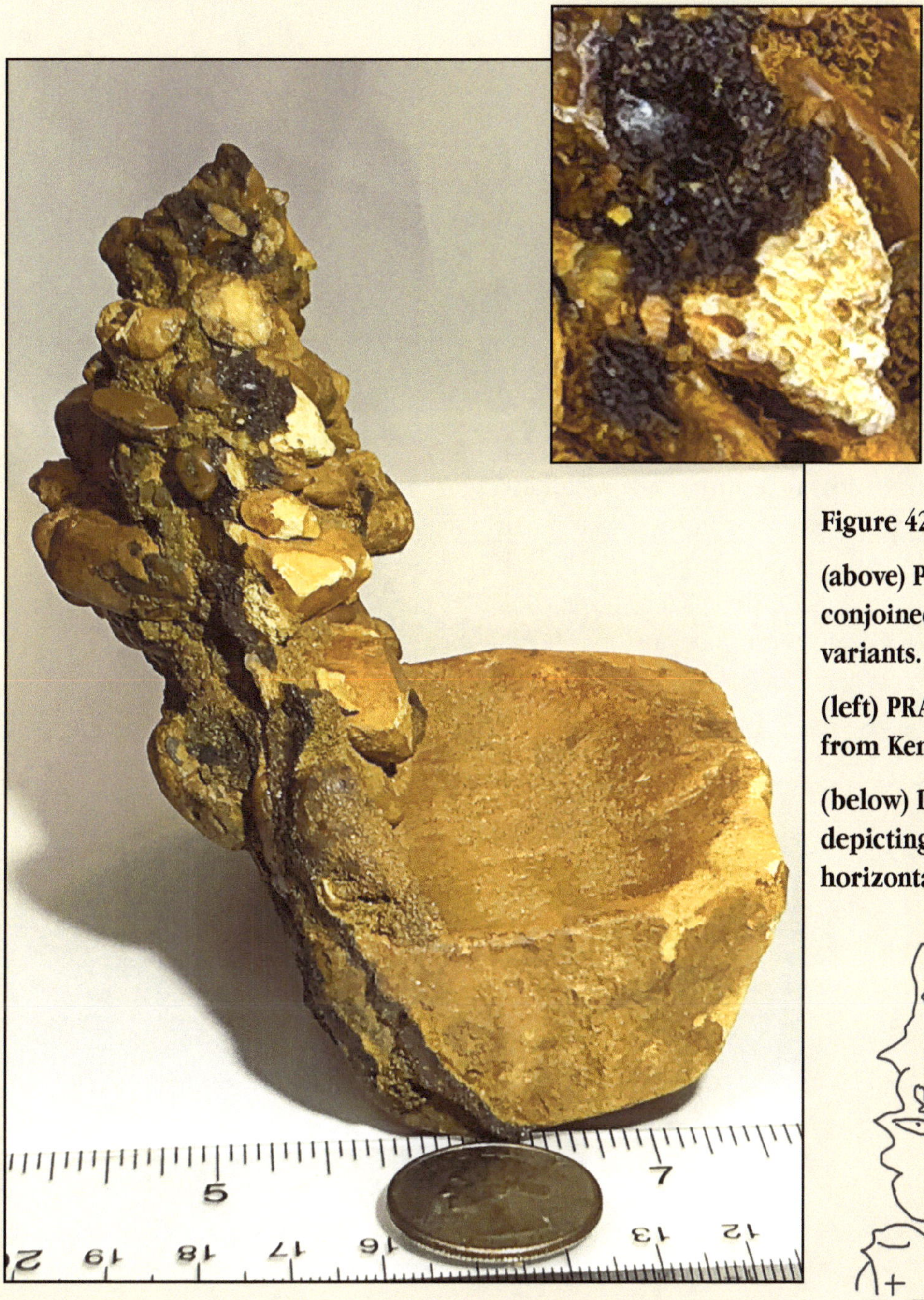

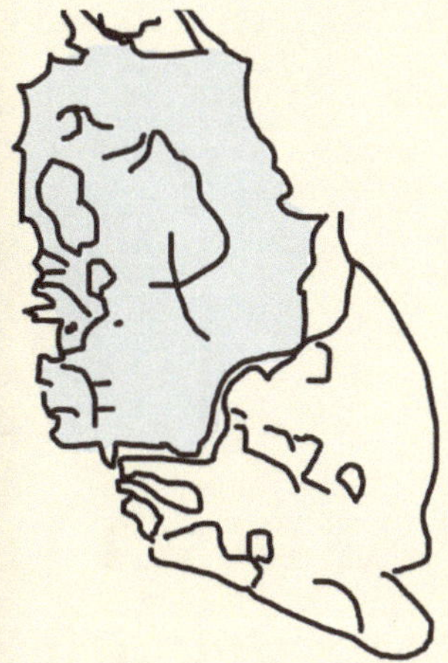

Figure 42: Artifact V.

(above) Pebble detail with conjoined black and white head variants.

(left) PRA conglomerate rock from Kentucky.

(below) Drawing by author depicting a subtle etching on the horizontal surface of Artifact V.

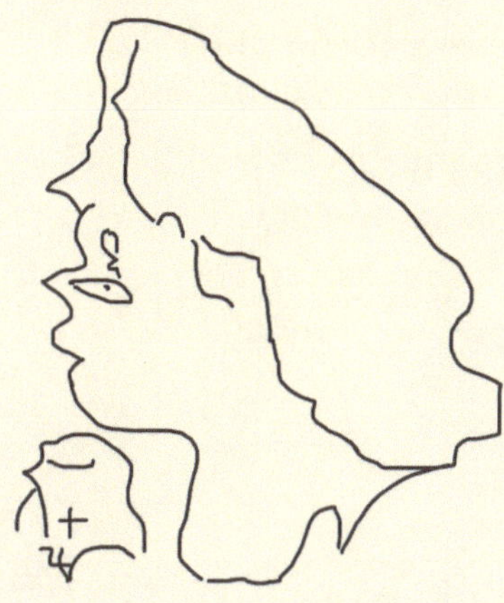

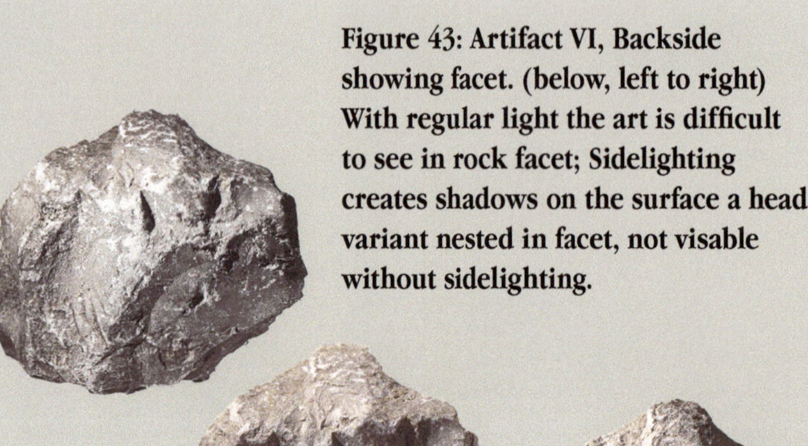

Figure 43: Artifact VI, Backside showing facet. (below, left to right) With regular light the art is difficult to see in rock facet; Sidelighting creates shadows on the surface a head variant nested in facet, not visable without sidelighting.

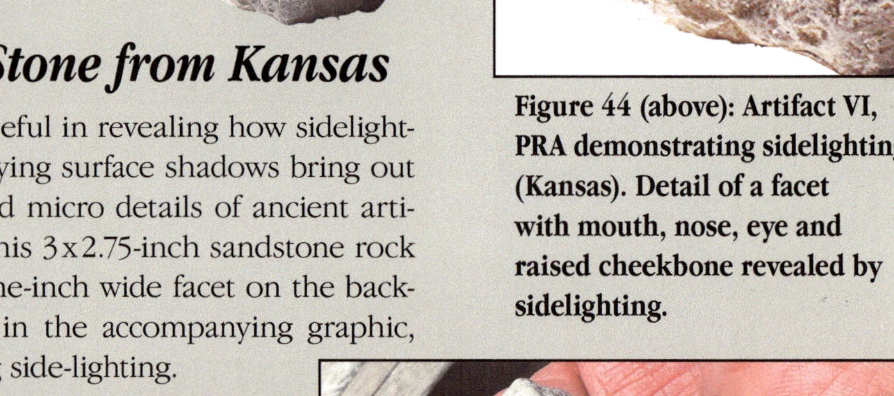

Figure 44 (above): Artifact VI, PRA demonstrating sidelighting (Kansas). Detail of a facet with mouth, nose, eye and raised cheekbone revealed by sidelighting.

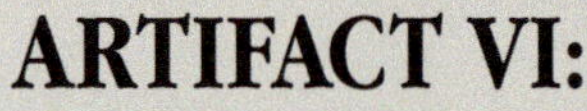

ARTIFACT VI:
Sedimentary Stone from Kansas

Figure 43 (above) is useful in revealing how sidelighting and the accompanying surface shadows bring out fine enhancements and micro details of ancient artifacts. Found in 2018, this 3x2.75-inch sandstone rock has an approximate one-inch wide facet on the backside, which is shown in the accompanying graphic, with and without using side-lighting.

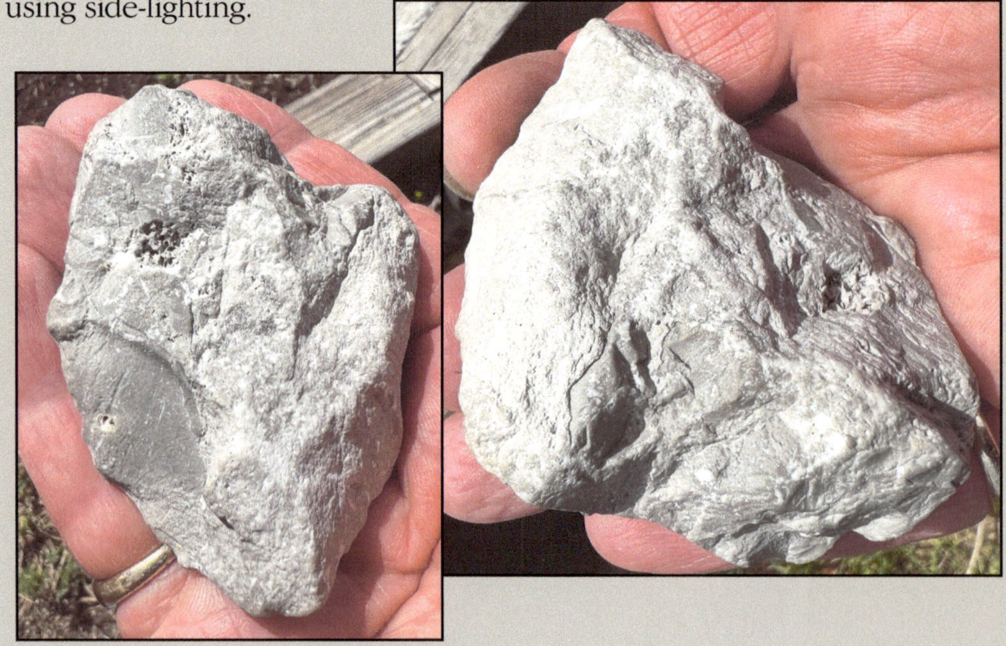

Figure 45 (left-right): Artifact VI, Profiles/ sculptures of whole stones resembling a human and/or animal.

PART IV

GRAND ARTISTRY OR PAREIDOLIA?

Distinguishing PRA from Pareidolia

The phenomenon of "seeing faces in rocks" is common and generally referred to as ***pareidolia***–the perception of significant patterns or recognizable images, especially faces, in natural, random or accidental arrangements of shapes and lines. The word is associated with the faulty perception of seeing patterns in random details of rocks and natural features, often referred to as apophenia according to Merriam-Webster et al.

Pareidolia is also associated with ***mimeotoliths***, rocks that mimic recognizable forms through random processes of formation, weathering and erosion. The term ***simulacrum or simulacra*** (plural) is also often used in referring to natural landscapes, geological features and objects appearing to have organized attributes that are unreal, usually resembling faces.

The inability for most Moderns to distinguish PRA from pareidolia and simulacrum phenomena is the single greatest barrier to its acceptance. There is no easy answer to this objection by nearly all professionals who comment on PRA objects. Nevertheless, to help move beyond the veil of two-dimensional perception, there are techniques to comprehend this newly (re)discovered, ancient artistic platform.

Archaeological artifacts include early stone tools classified by their utilitarian application, era of use, locale and/or type of workmanship. The earliest of these artifacts were often referred to as ***eoliths***. In the nineteenth century these items were considered the original chipped tools created by early humans, but later came to be seen as natural, or ***geofacts*** (nature-fact). Today, the term "eolith" is often used to dismiss the unknown or unrecognized features that exist in artifacts or rocks and

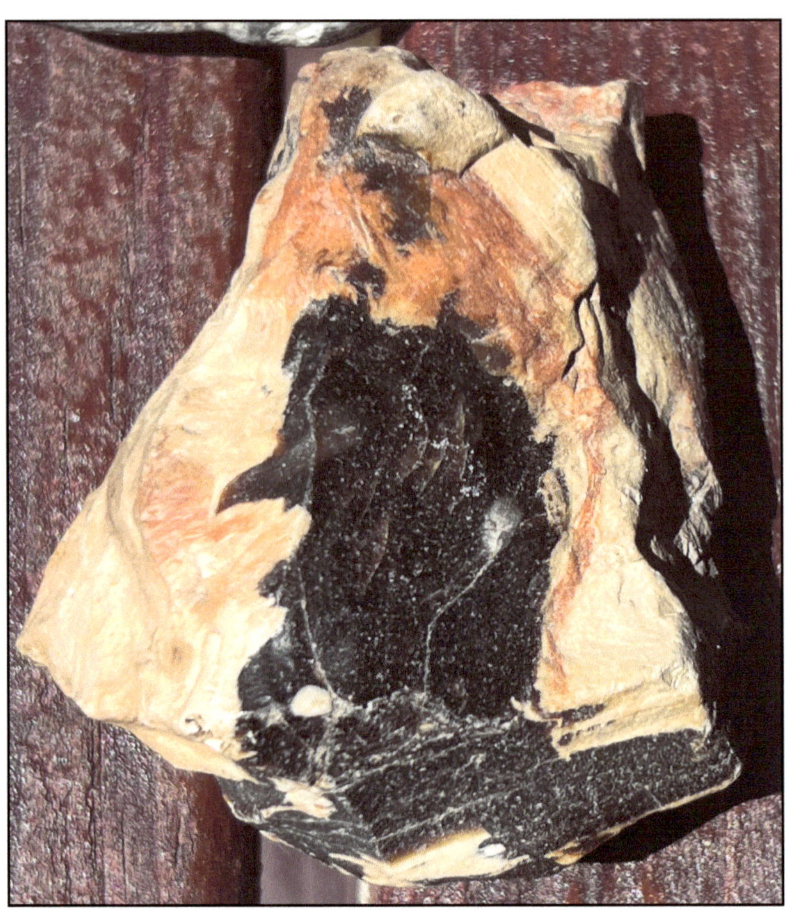

Figure 46: Natural rock with beak-like appearance.

instead crediting them as natural occurrences. Others still use the term to describe Figure Stones.

Robert G. Bednarik has written extensively on rock art and pareidolia, including *Rock Art Science: The Scientific Study of Palaeoart.*[40] An Australian prehistorian and cognitive archeologist, he has expertise in the fields of rock art and paleolithic portable art. His research focuses on the origins of the human ability to create constructs of reality. Bednarik is a chief proponent of the notion that nearly all suggestions of seeing facial features in rocks are pareidolia. He contends the formation of consciousness is based on an unreliable visual system where internal subjective images are confused for reality.

In a 2016 article entitled "Rock Art and Pareidolia,"[41] Bednarik writes:

> *Thus, pareidolia is an integral part of the visual system's operation, being attributable to the need of identifying visual stimuli much faster than proper discrimination and processing would require: "first impressions" are matched with information stored in the brain, i.e. data derived from previous experiences forming what is called an "internal model": a rendered simulation. In visual*

pareidolia a figurative pattern is detected where no representation actually exists, be it two dimensional or three dimensional.[42]

Bednarik documents several cases where the pareidolia seen by one person is transferred to an entire group, who ended up seeing the original beholder's designs where none existed in eroded petroglyphs or weathered rock surfaces. This revelation is important for PRA collectors to understand. One person's imaginary representation can lead to becoming established patterns of faulty perception by others.

Professor Bednarik has written:

The first relevant observation is that in the case of rock art, it is particularly easy to transfer an anticipation of seeing a specific design to others, because motifs are often hard to detect, especially due to weathering. When viewing eroded petroglyphs the visual system of the beholder tends to supplement the sensory data "creatively," i.e. by drawing more than usually on the imagery memorised in the visual centre, allowing it to overrule the information provided from the retina. The differences between the rock art recordings of different observers also illustrate this point.[43]

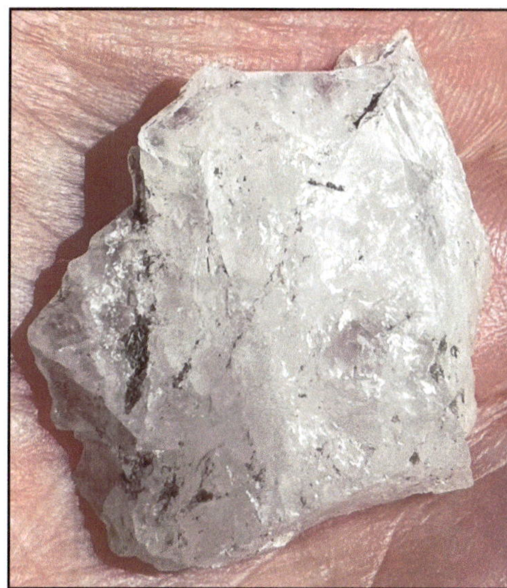

Figure 47: Crushed stone PRA tool look-alike.

He also questions the ability of Moderns to understand the conceptual world of the Ancients, contributing to pareidolia.

Bednarik suggests that we never see the world as it is because there are no direct connections between what the brain internalizes and the real world. As a result, Figure Stones are for the most part pareidolia experiences.

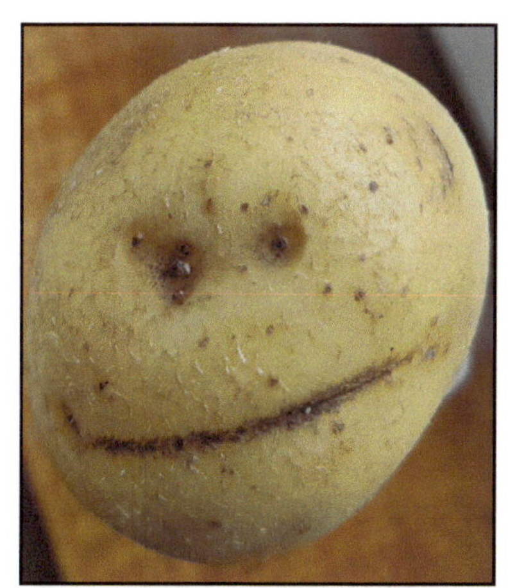

Figure 48: Happy Potato demonstrates pareidolia. (Andy Mabbett)[45]

Bednarik has made significant contributions to understanding rock art and the mechanics of pareidolia. Admittedly, what is often presented as PRA are actually occurrences of natural likenesses, similar to the description of the Indian Head Penny at the center of cut agate mentioned in the Preface.

Nevertheless, the author believes validation approaches can and do demonstrate workmanship, artistic embellishments and head variant designs. Contrary to Bednarik's contention that Moderns do not have the ability to conceptualize or see what the Ancients saw, the Author contends by documenting workmanship and identifying head variant patterns we are able to substantiate intentional imagery in a 3-D context.

Another view on pareidolia comes from Dr. James Harrod, who observed "…'art' is preceded by 'paleoart' and 'paleoart' begins with 'pareidolia and curation.'"[44]

The Makapansgat Pebble (*Fig. 49*) exemplifies a natural artifact. Found in 1925 in South Africa among bones of a forerunner to humans who lived three million years ago. The jasperite 7-centimeter wide pebble bears a resemblance to a human face.

It's a natural, rather than carved, resemblance to a human face and its being carried twenty miles by the *Australopithecus* human predecessors connects pareidolia and paleoart. From the beginning our ancestors used their subjective imaginations, combined with a rock's natural features, to recognize what we refer to as art.

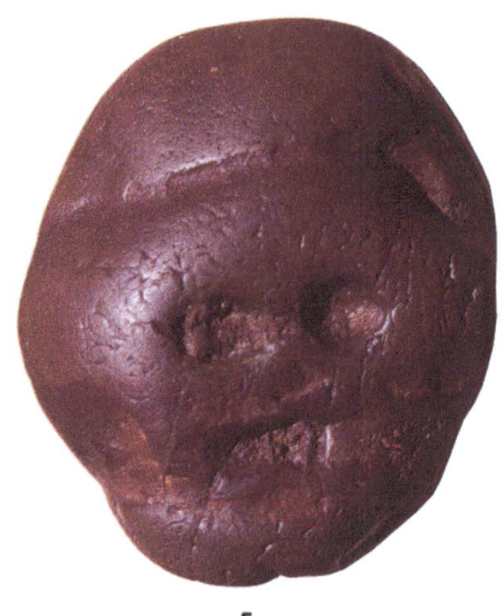

Figure 49: Makapansgat Pebble (Robert G. Bednarik, Wikipedia.)[47]

Along these same lines, author Frank Hamilton Cushing disclosed in his booklet *Zuni Fetishes*, the most sacred figurines are not carved sculptures, but are all natural figurines made by the creator with only a vague zoomorphic resemblance (*Fig. 50*). Cushing wrote:

> *... any person who may discover either a concretion or natural object or an ancient fetich calling to mind or representing any one of the Prey gods will regard it as his special fetich and almost invariably prefer it, since he believes it to have been "meted to" him by the gods.*[46]

(Refer to Figure 58 for examples of fetishes, along with additional insights by Cushing.)

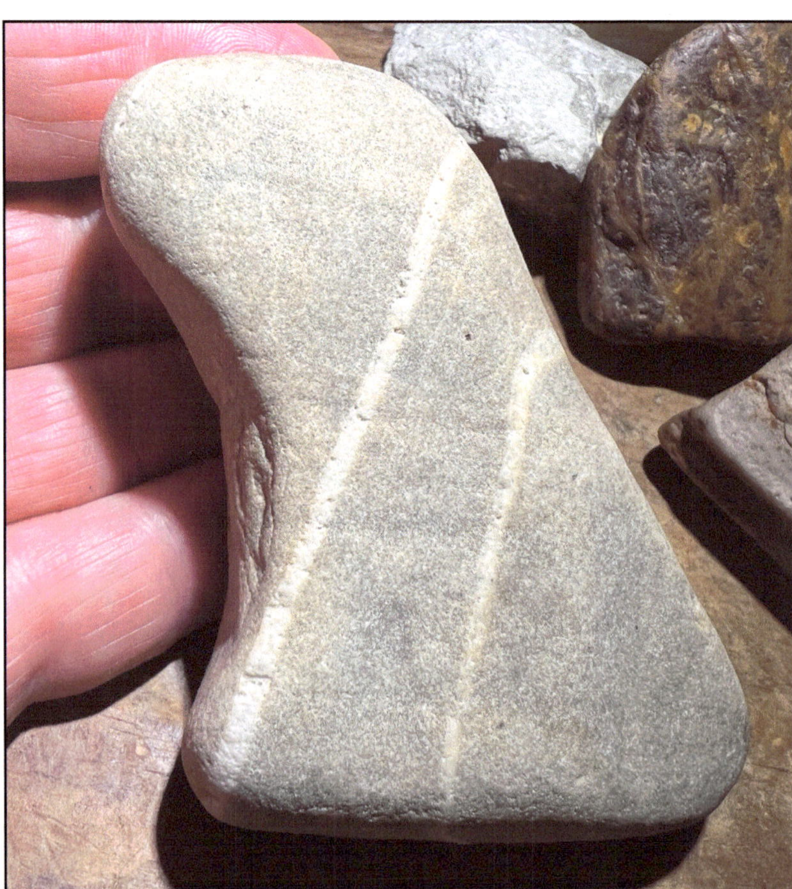

Figure 50: A natural stone with zoomorphic resemblance.

Subjectivity vs. Recognizing Intentionality

Portable Rock Art intentional enhancements are often integrated into natural features, creating collages unfamiliar to modern day viewers. This multi-faceted, three-dimensional art style often requires imagination to see. However, imagination is a double-edged sword. Recognizing and distinguishing what the artist intended from one's own imagination involves objective validation, for example evidence of workmanship. Thus, the key to distinguishing PRA from natural rocks is observing and determining intentionality with some measure of affirmation that the human-crafted enhancements were intended and not random or pareidolia.

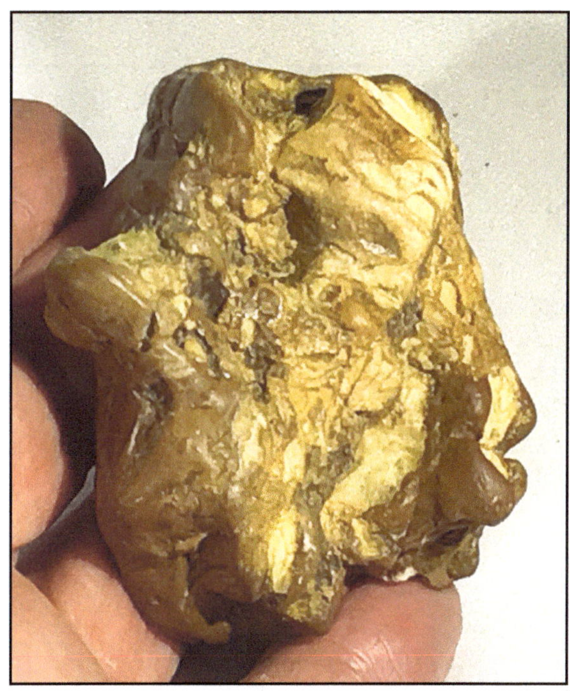

Figure 51: Natural shapes and layers interwoven with paleo sculptures. Once cleaned and the built-up patina removed, paleo sculptures become more apparent (Kansas).

Even using validation criteria, it is often not possible to eliminate pareidolia phenomena, in part because ancient stoneworkers integrated these natural likenesses into their art. It took the imagination of the creator, projected onto the natural rock, as the starting point.

A PRA artifact could have originated as a stone tool and evolved into PRA with slight additions along the way, over time becoming more symbolic than utilitarian. Conversely, PRA can be all artistic and non-utilitarian. In each case, it took the imagination of an ancestor to transform a natural rock into art.

Determining intentionality is a fundamental starting point for evaluating PRA, beginning with eliminating or confirming pareidolia and simulacra phenomena. Specific to petroglyphs, scientific methods, including microscopic examinations, can distinguish between natural and intentional markings. But without this validation, the human eye most often cannot recognize the difference, especially if the prospective PRA hasn't been thoroughly cleaned.

In examining prospective PRA, it is common for natural rocks to appear as intentionally created PRA, while conversely, the best artifacts may appear to be all natural, especially at first sight. This is particularly true when evaluating "X's." The author contends X's are perhaps the most recognizable symbol accompanying PRA head variants. These include both etched and natural X's.

Figures 52 and 53 show stones with X's, one with all natural markings and one with significant artistic enhancements.

Natural X's are common, but before one totally dismisses a prospective find, one should be mindful that natural rocks bearing

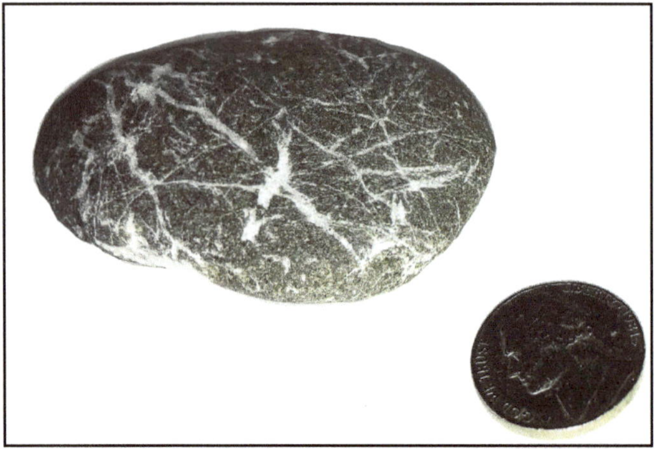

Figure 52: Smooth stone, unworked by humans, with notable and natural "X".

familiar resemblances like an "X" could be integrated into a PRA artifact. It is also important to keep an open mind that a unique petroglyphic inscribed artifact can be easily dismissed with natural scratching and normal wear until the piece is properly cleaned and positioned for examination under optimum lighting conditions.

We are all prone to subjective overlays when viewing art, especially PRA. Since visual perception varies from one person to another, a consensus among PRA viewers can be illusive. Making matters even more difficult are cases of false petroglyphic images being transferred from one researcher to another and being made available to the general public,[48] as mentioned previously.

These barriers to recognizing intentionally created rock art emphasize the importance of identifying workmanship, proper cleaning, as well as how to hold and move artifacts for the best viewing perspectives.

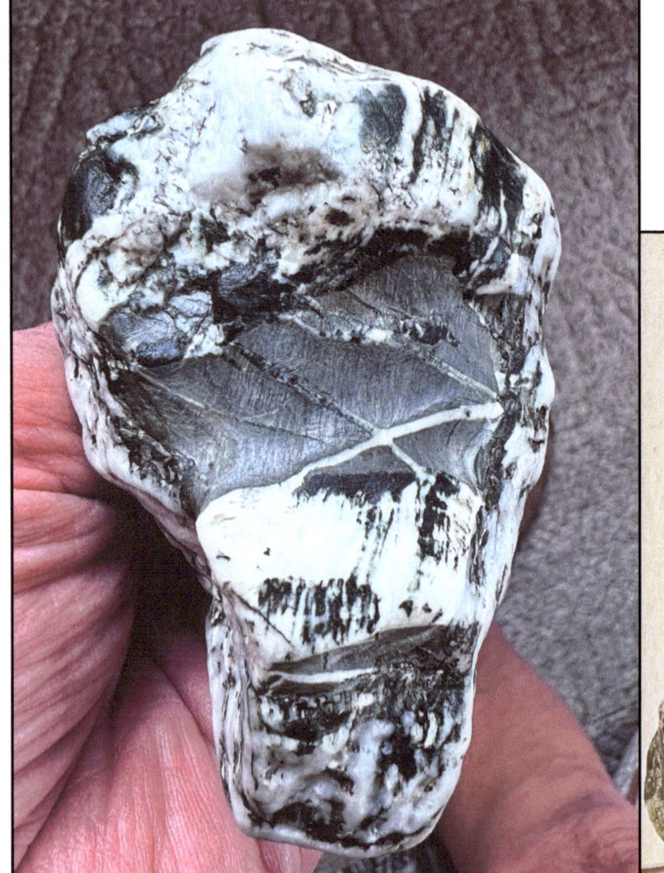

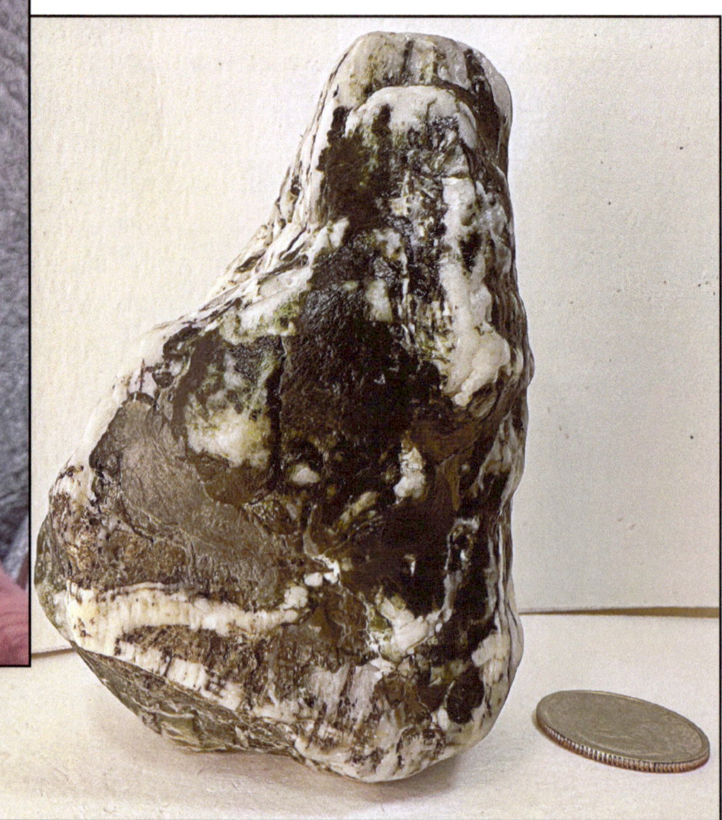

Figure 53: PRA with "X". Front (above) with skull-like features and "X"; back side flipped 180 degrees with left-facing head variant.

Demonstrating Workmanship, Determining Intentionality

Learning how to recognize and differentiate incredibly detailed, subtle, yet complicated artistic enhancements on stone from natural phenomena including pareidolia is a challenge for anyone engaged in PRA investigations.

Since the Ancients employed their imaginations to create PRA artifacts, the viewer likewise needs imagination to comprehend the phenomena.

While we seek to distinguish PRA artifacts from pareidolia, it can be difficult to come to a consensus on what was intended. The challenge and discipline is to see what was intended and not merely project one's imagination onto intentionally crafted PRA. This can be accomplished with experience, familiarity with lithic workmanship, techniques, and head variants.

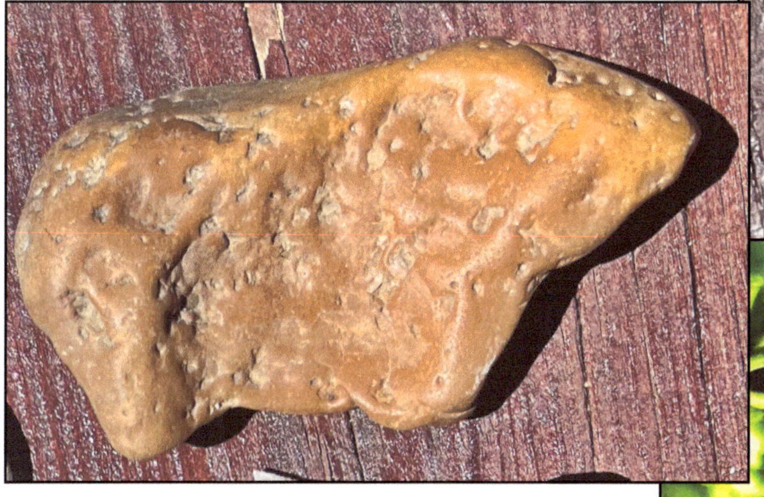

Figure 54: Natural or human crafted stones? (above) Natural rock with natural pits and indentations or a bear image? (upper right) Stone with natural lines resembling workmanship. (right) Multi-tool from New Mexico with sharpened edges, natural lines and PRA likenesses.

Validation Approaches to Determine PRA Intentionality

Of primary importance to validating PRA is identifying human workmanship. This is why stone tools exhibiting art are among the best validation candidates. However, many artifacts do not appear to be obvious tools or otherwise utilitarian. Also, ancient artisans integrated images, shapes and creations into the naturally occurring layers, holes and edges of ordinary rocks, thus challenging traditional validation approaches used solely for documenting paleo tools.

Among rock art readers, there is not a universal call for validation. Some believe systematic approaches limit the experience of interacting with PRA. These encounters include working with PRA to help unlock one's imagination. However, for any measure of scientific credibility, much less a greater acceptance and understanding of this 3-D artistic platform, a confirmation of what was intended is required to eliminate purely pareidolia look-alikes.

Dr. James Harrod has provided a great service to those interested in PRA through his detailed articles and documentation addressing different aspects of the broader paleo art arena. His research includes classifying groupings of paleo art, known as **taxonomy** (*Fig. 55*). Included in his 2014 article, "Paleoart at Two Million Years Ago,"[49] Dr. Harrod lists his criteria for determining intentionality in paleo art, which is especially applicable to distinguishing human-made art from pareidolia.

This systematic approach is rooted in an archaeological and scientific context, providing an in-depth perspective on manifestations of paleo art. These classifications of human behavior relate to paleo art, which include but are not limited to PRA.

In another publication, "Categories and Principles of Proto-Art: Hypotheses on Early and Middle Paleo Art, Symbols and Religion,"[50] Dr. Harrod categorizes early, proto-art objects by their demonstrated intentions, including symbolic places, ritual art, rock art, sculpture along with other non-utilitarian and/or aesthetic objects as summarized in Figure 56.

These categories of intentionality are especially useful for scientific investigations, for validating rock art, and may also be beneficial to the casual collector.

In my own efforts to establish objective criteria to identify PRA and distinguish them from pareidolia, Figure 57 presents a methodology and a rating system for identifying and categorizing Portable Rock Art. Ratings #4–#10 are designated as PRA. This approach has limitations but it offers a simple method for documenting *artfacts* while seeking to distinguish PRA phenomena from natural stones.

SYMBOLIC BEHAVIOR—TAXONOMY

From "Paleoart at Two Million Years Ago" (James Harrod, 2014)

1. **Curation of exotic objects**—manuported non-local crystals, fossils, shells, stone with "pareidolic" or "aesthetic qualities."
2. **Making a trace**—making a mark on a surface that leaves a trace; intent is the trace.
3. **Color pigments**—hematite, limonite, specularite, charcoal, etc.
4. **Adornments**—perforated beads, pendants, ornaments of shell, stone, bone, raptor wing feathers, etc.; may have status, body-adornment, ceremonial or other function.
5. **Geometric shaped artifacts**—artificial circular discoids, spheroids, triangles, rhomboids, pentagons, hexagons, etc., whether marked or not.
6. **Incised, serrated or notched objects**—bone, stone, ochre, eggshell, wood; seriated or repetitive patterns, alternating sets or groups of marks, "tallies," which may suggest numerosity, arithmetic sets, etc.
7. **Rock art, non-utilitarian anthropic markings on rock surfaces made by reductive (petroglyph) or additive (pictogram); or engraved or sculpted portable art (including figurines)**—may be non-iconic (e.g., cupules, grooves), or iconic, including geometric, zoomorphic, anthropomorphic or abstract design motifs. "Glyph-like motifs"—which might be "signs" or otherwise function in some sort of language system.
8. **Regional tool styles**—indicating distinct cultural identity.
9. **Exotic tools**—made using exotic or "aesthetic" materials or features, special degree of workmanship, etc., possibly exchange or status goods. Decorated tools—exotic tools apparently decorated with geometric or iconic figuration.
10. **Mortuary practice**—defleshing, bone modification, cannibalism, depositions, burials with or without grave goods, ochre, ritual objects. Placement in Environs.
11. **Stone/bone arrangements**—intentional heaps of stones or bones, petroforms, cairns, geoglyphs, altars, deposition of stone/bone in special places.
12. **Symbolic landscapes/settings**—unusual or numinous landscape features associated with an archaeological site, which may or may not be signaled by stone placements, etc.
13. **Astronomical markers**—intentional arrangement or alignment of stones or other material on landscape to mark astronomical events.
14. **Musical instruments or locations with special acoustic features.**
15. **Gesture, mime or dance forms**—dance floors, footprints, etc. circumstantial evidence.
16. **Spoken or protolanguage**—only indirect circumstantial evidence possible.

Figure 55: Demonstrated Symbolic Behavior (Harrod)[51]

CATEGORIES OF DEMONSTRATED INTENTION
1. Engravings or notches on stone, bone, ivory, wood, etc., having symmetry or other qualities suggesting aesthetic, decorative, or other intent;
2. Items apparently collected for their exotic or unusual properties, such crystal prisms, fossil casts, unusually colored or shaped pebbles;
3. Articles possibly used for body adornment, including pendants or beads of eggshell, shell, teeth, ivory, wood, vertebrae, bone fragments, or stone;
4. Red ocher and other pigment crayons and remains;
5. Utilitarian objects that show characteristics clearly in excess of what technology and function would demand, and thus seem to have aesthetic dimensions such as engravings or notches on stone, bone, ivory, wood, etc., suggesting technological capabilities.

Figure 56: Demonstrated Intentionality Summary (Harrod, 2001)

As more scientists become involved, validation approaches will become increasingly available to confirm PRA objects were intentionally created and are not merely natural stones. Advancements will include protocols to efficiently clean these ancient relics so the imagery is more identifiable. Technologies that integrate effective lighting, microscopic equipment and photography will facilitate validation. Applying existing analytical equipment, facial recognition computer programs, and state-of-the-art photography techniques will speed wider acceptance of this unrecognized ancient art platform. Until then, gaining the necessary experience to identify workmanship and artistic enhancements while holding and viewing well cleaned artifacts is the best approach to a better understanding and appreciation of PRA.

Figure 57: Author's Rating Criteria for Establishing Intentionality.

PRA RATING CRITERIA FOR ESTABLISHING INTENTIONALITY (AUTHOR)		
0	Natural rocks	Natural
1	Natural rocks, simulacra features, no apparent workmanship	Simulacra
2	Worked/tools without apprent art	Worked
3	Singular carvings, "Effigies," beads	Worked
4	**Stone tools with artistic enhancements**	**Paleoart**
5	**Overall shape resembles image/multi-shapes**	**Paleoart**
6	**Macro images on planes/facets**	**Paleoart**
7	**Multiple head variants/animal shapes**	**Paleoart**
8	**Etched/carved glyphs/images**	**Paleoart**
9	**Holes, shallow areas with enhancements**	**Paleoart**
10	**Extraordinary art, sculptures, connected imagery**	**Paleoart**
11	Traditional stone artifacts, Chines/Mayan jade carvings; sculpted art for adornments, ceremony, memorializing, etc.	Conventional artifacts

What Distinguishes an Artifact from a Fetish?

PRA is sometimes compared with fetishes, which are usually small stone carvings of animals believed to be imbued with magical power. Fetishes are generally singular in form compared to the multi-forms of PRA.

In his *Zuni Fetishes* pamphlet (1881) Frank Hamilton Cushing described the origins of fetishes among the Pueblo peoples. He noted that animals were frequently made into representations to serve as mediators between humans and "the more mysterious and remote powers of Nature." Cushing wrote:

> *"It follows that the special requirements of (his) life or of the life of his ancestors should influence him to select as his favored mediators or aids those animals which seem best fitted, through peculiar characteristics and powers to meet these requirements."*[52]

In the introduction to the eighth edition to ***Zuni Fetishes*** (1988), Tom Bahti noted:

> *Concretions, plant or animal material and of course carvings in shell, stone or wood can all be used as fetishes but their purpose remains the same: To assist man, the most vulnerable of all living creatures in meeting the problems that face him during his life. Each fetish contains a living power, which, if treated properly and with veneration, will give its help to its owner. . . . Because the power of a fetish is regarded as a living thing it must be carefully tended and ceremonially fed, usually with corn meal. . . .*[53]

Bahti noted that Zuni artisans create animal and bird representations that are not fetishes.

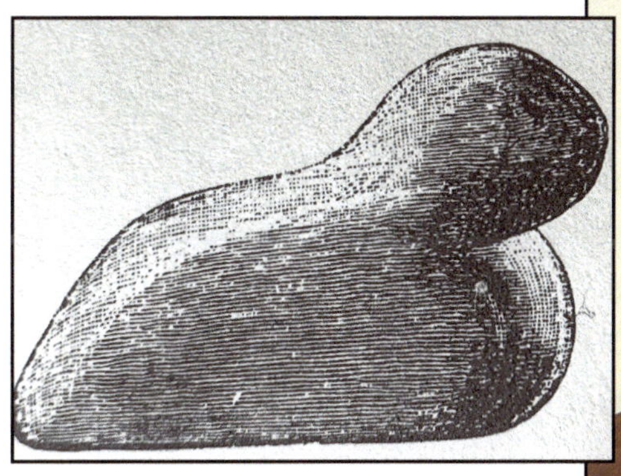

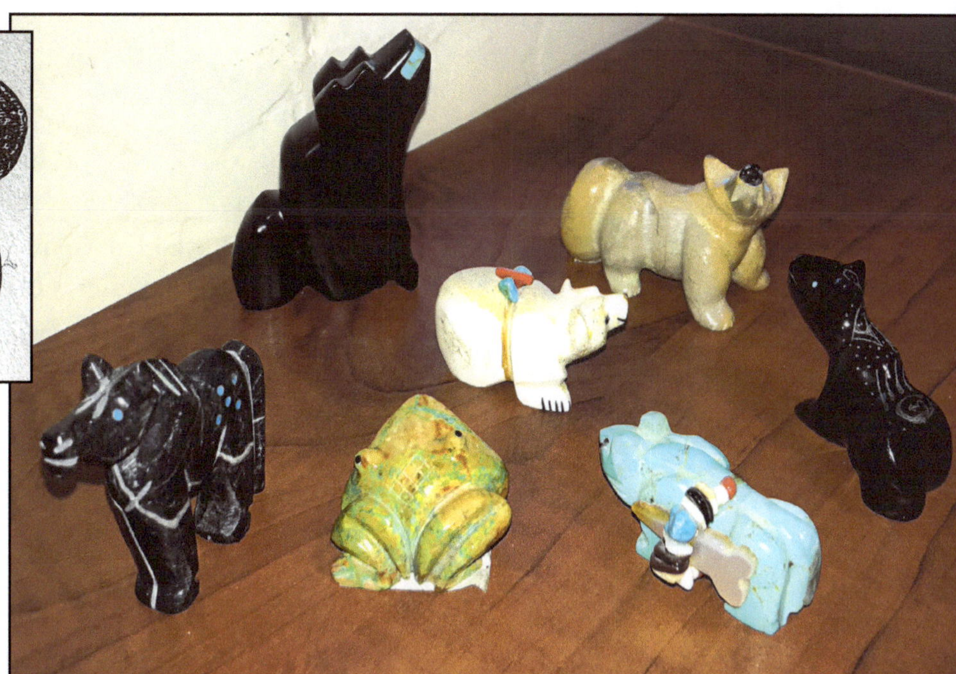

Figure 58: Examples of Fetishes. (above) Authentic, nearly natural Zuni fetish representing the White Eagle (Cushing, Zuni Fetishes); (right) Modern fetish examples.

These insights by Cushing and Bahti paint an intimate picture between fetishes, those that honored them, the mediator animal(s) and Nature.

The tradition of old fetishes representing animals as the mediators between humans and Nature may be directly applicable to understanding PRA. While fetishes are distinguishable from PRA, there is a connection in the author's view. Fetishes are considered imbued with power and the same was likely true with Figure Stones. Perhaps a greater understanding of the mythologies and characters represented in the old fetishes of the Zuni and other Pueblo peoples can teach us more about PRA.

Comparing PRA to a Mayan Jadite Celt with Glyphs

In looking at the different PRA head variants and attempting to differentiate them, Mayan glyphs and artistic traditions offer some insights. The Mayans relied on head variants to convey specific meanings in their art and writing.

Generally referred to as a ceremonial artifact or a greenstone axe head, the pictured Mayan celt is *portable,* made of *stone* and has *artistic enhancements.* The highly polished jadeite

Figure 59: Mayan Ceremonial Celt. The ten distinct glyphs on one side of this five-inch long jadeite celt describe the succession of a king and identifies both the old and new kings.

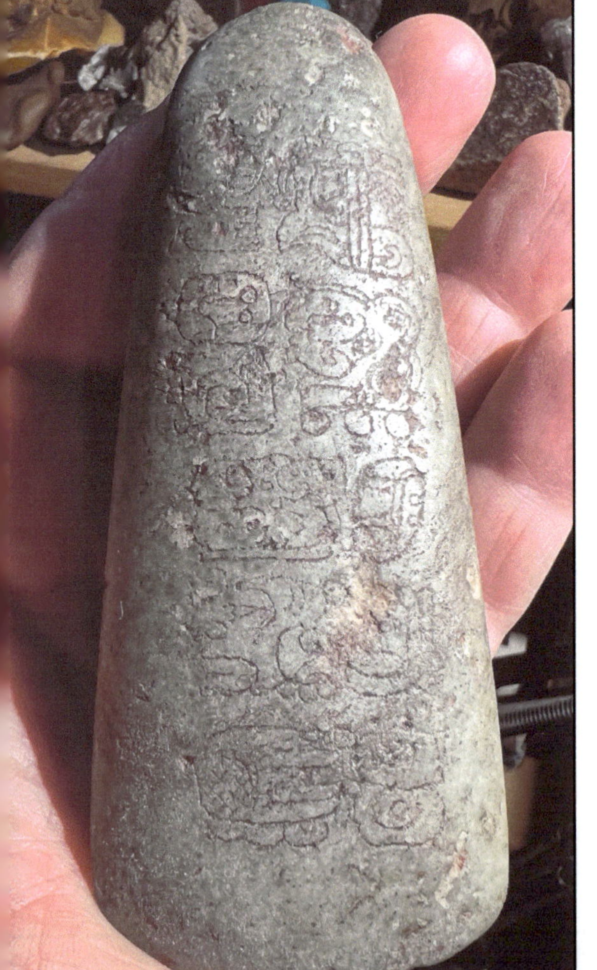

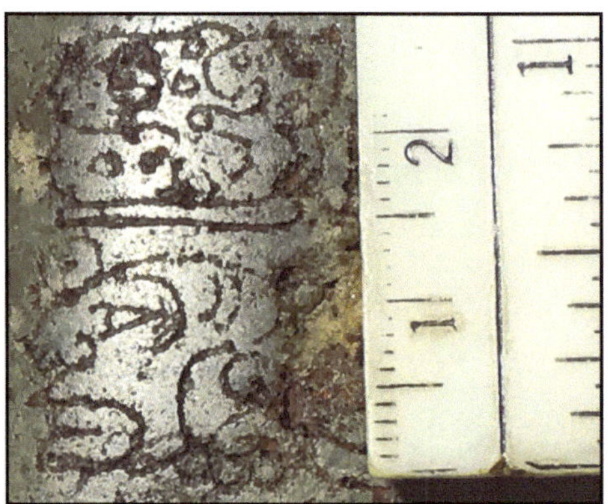

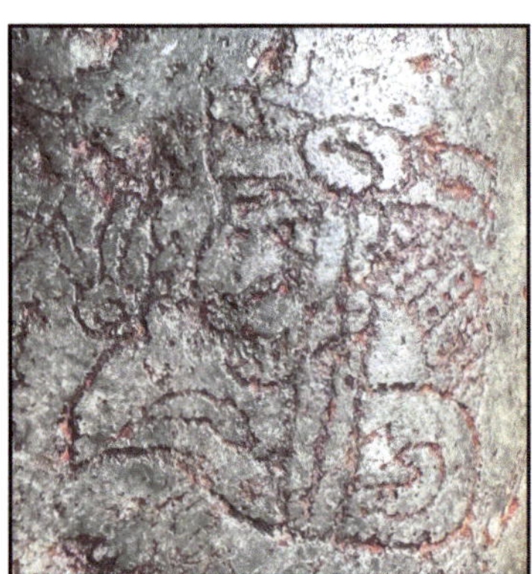

Figure 60: Mayan Celt Glyph Details. (upper left) The top glyph represents a jaguar and is likely part of a king's name (Ben Jaguar). The lower glyph is a profile likely representing Ox (Ux), a Mayan rain god also associated as the god of the number three, distinguishable by the circular head ornament, large nose and three dots for earrings. This interpretation suggests the glyph represents part of the name 3Ahua, a king mentioned in the inscription. (right) The vulture glyph, when combined with the prefix symbol to its right, suggests "the ascension of a king."

celt bears etched designs and glyphs. This object, estimated to be 1500-2000 years old, contains glyphs, which are symbols intended to denote unique characters that collectively convey a written meaning or message.

The author and Mayan scholar Martin Brennen spent years studying this artifact to propose the meaning of the glyphs.

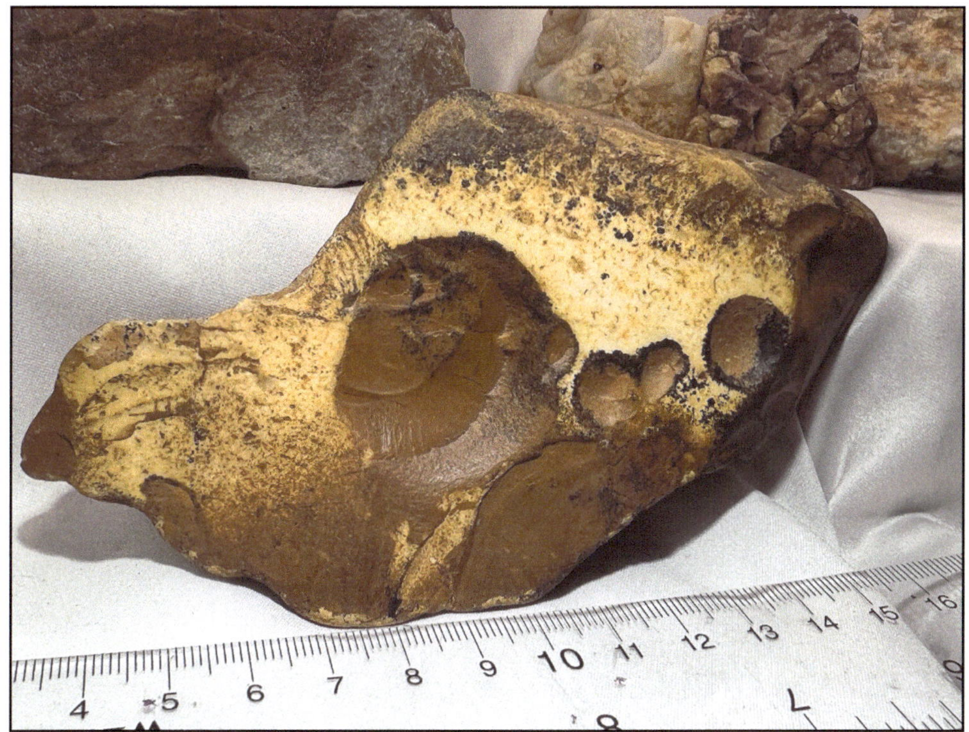

Figure 61: Artifact VII, Bird-Shaped PRA. The design of the beak is the key differentiator in PRA bird variants. (*Refer to Fig. 68 for additional photos.*)

Many birds are distinguishable in Mesoamerican art including quetzals, macaws, guans, pelicans, eagles, owl, and vultures. These are prominent and have numerical, mythological, cosmological and calendrical meanings. However, in most cases only someone familiar with the iconography of the Maya can distinguish the difference between the bird images and their meaning.

Mayan head variants can also display phonetic meanings in addition to mythological, historical, and calendrical references. By extending a nose, adding a tear or an "X" or a particular headdress, a head variant becomes a specific number. The accompanying chart of Mayan head variants designates numbers (*Fig. 62*). Each head figure has a distinctive enough characteristic to identify it as a number and distinguish it from others. More common than using head variants was using a series of dots and bars with each dot representing one and each bar representing five.

Principally ceremonial and used in sacrificial rites, Aztec bifaces demonstrate another version of the Mayan celt. The overall images

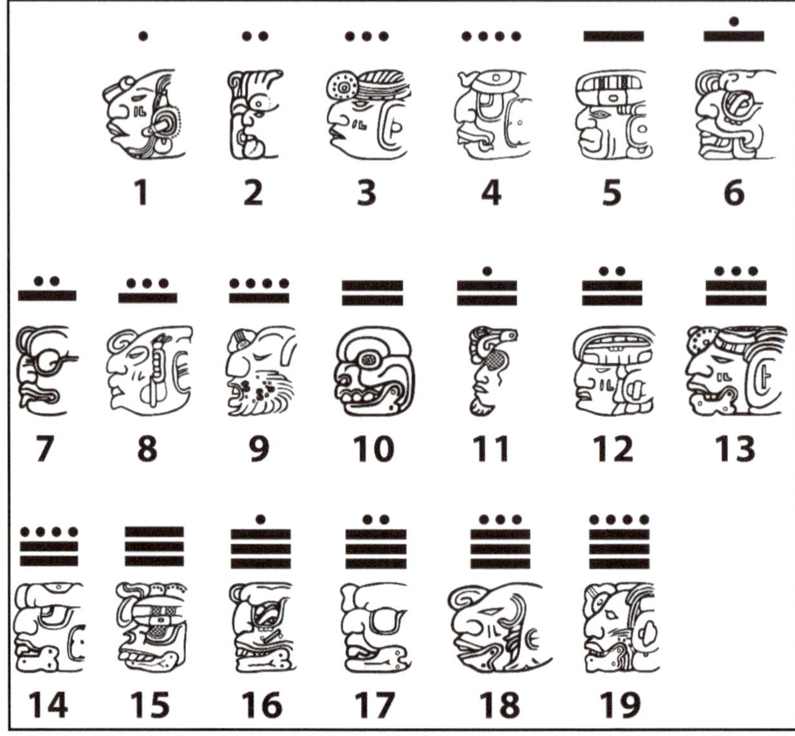

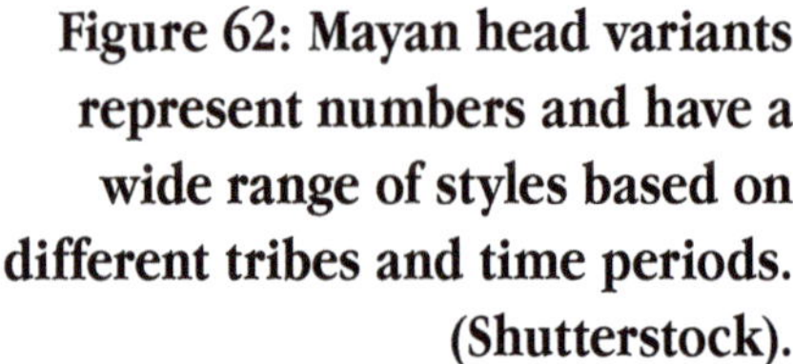
Figure 62: Mayan head variants represent numbers and have a wide range of styles based on different tribes and time periods. (Shutterstock).

resemble a glyph representing the Aztec ritual calendar day called "flint knife," a personification of the Aztec god Tezcatlipoca. In the PRA world, there are stone tools with similar shapes to celts but are crude and unrefined in comparison.

Compared to Mayan head variants *(Fig. 62)*, PRA head variant distinctions are less clear and it is premature to suggest universal meanings for specific head variant shapes. However, there are sufficient examples of PRA head variants from many locations to suggest similarities and prospective universal head variant symbols. For example, a bearded man, the Pointy-Head Guy, the skull man, the serpent, etc., all which could be key differentiators among PRA heat variants. This also applies to the many different varieties of birds.

Mayan and Aztec "artifacts" can and often are "fakes," created in modern times

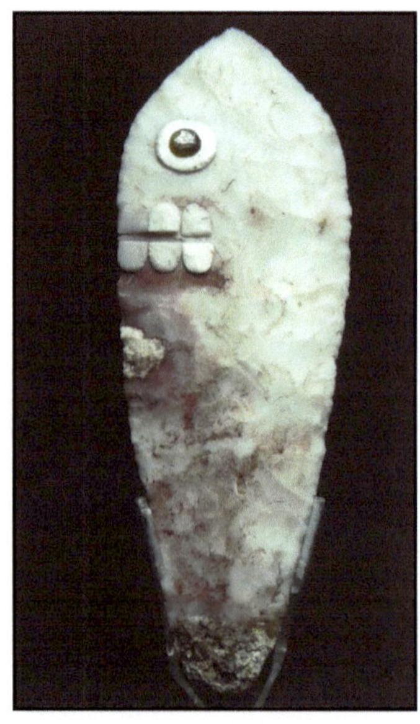
Figure 63: Aztec flint sacrificial knife, Museo del Templo Mayor, Mexico City. The overall image resembles a personification of the Aztec god, Tezcatlipoca. (Wikipedia).[54]

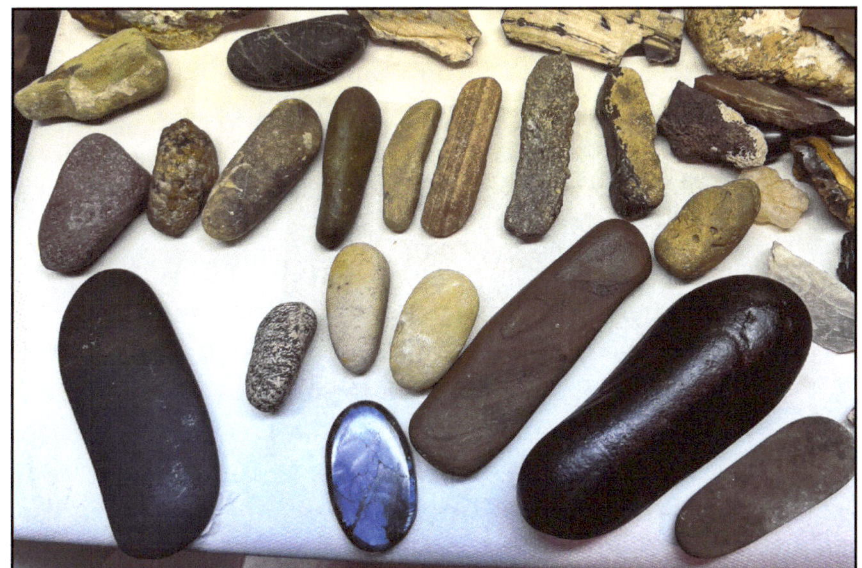

Figure 64: A variety of tools and celt-like stones from the Arkansas River Valley, Colorado.

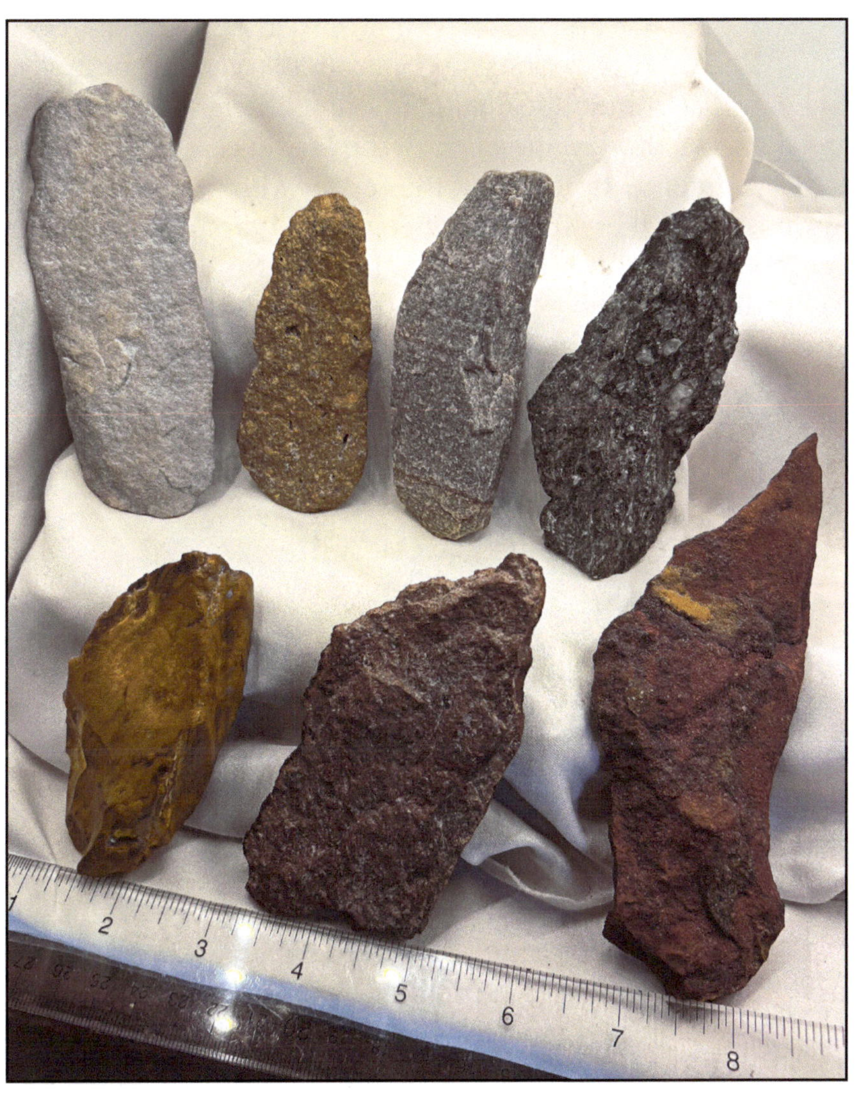

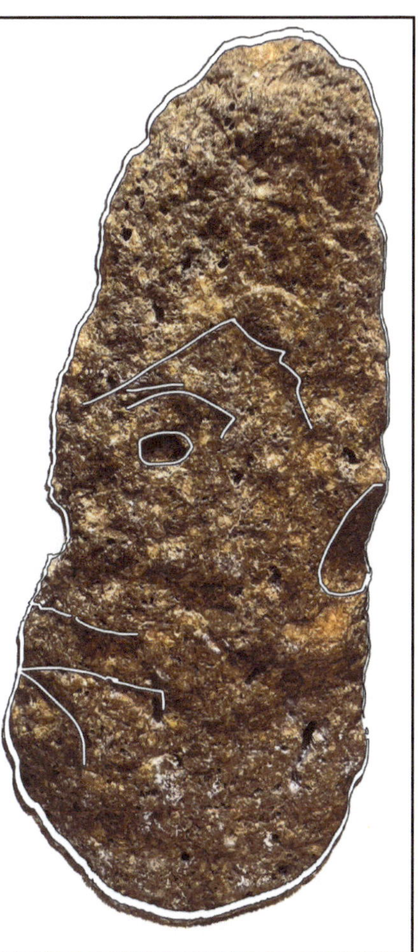

Figure 65: (left) Celt-like tools from the Western U.S. with apparent artistic enhancements. Top row stones are from Colorado. Bottom row from Colorado, Arizona, and Nevada. (above) Enlargement of top row, second from left stone indicating head-variant art.

to look ancient. PRA is abundant, and there is little reason for Moderns to create fake PRA to sell, although this is regularly done with arrowheads. In addition to Mesoamerican look-alike art found abundantly for sale, there are other types of Portable Rock Art from the Americas subject to imitation. For example, so-called "ancient" stone creations from Mexico depicting extraterrestrials are considered implausible by the author.

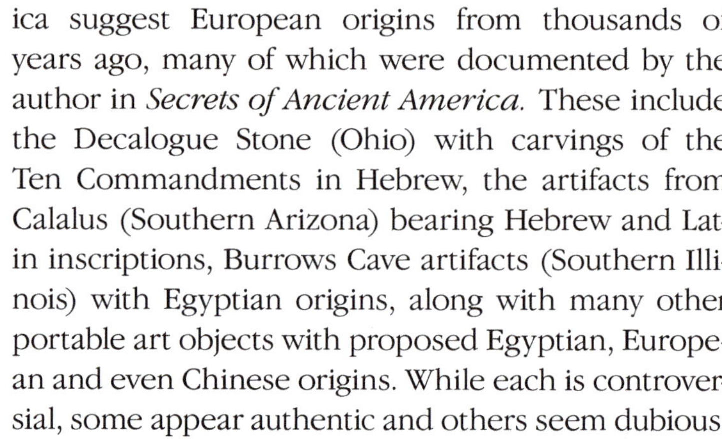

Other controversial portable stone artifacts from North America suggest European origins from thousands of years ago, many of which were documented by the author in *Secrets of Ancient America.* These include the Decalogue Stone (Ohio) with carvings of the Ten Commandments in Hebrew, the artifacts from Calalus (Southern Arizona) bearing Hebrew and Latin inscriptions, Burrows Cave artifacts (Southern Illinois) with Egyptian origins, along with many other portable art objects with proposed Egyptian, European and even Chinese origins. While each is controversial, some appear authentic and others seem dubious.

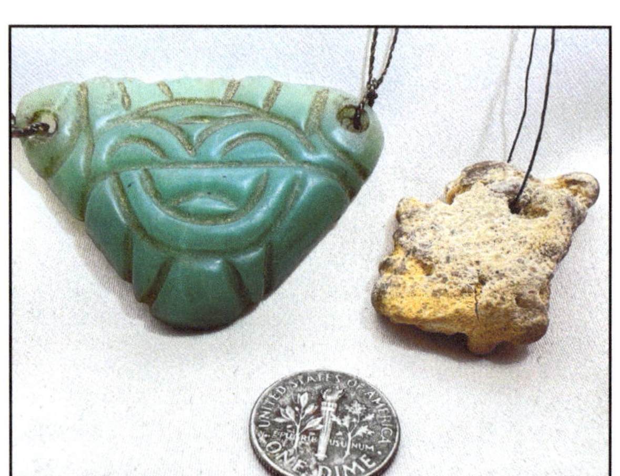

Figure 66: A Mayan jade pendant next to a PRA figurine from Colorado. The jade pendent is carved, highly polished, with beveled holes. The abstract design of a face most likely represents the planet Venus. The canine-like paleo sculpture, worked but rough by comparison, has an eye hole enabling it to be strung. The author contends that both are artifacts.

The introduction of the Mayan ceremonial celt is intended to provide the reader with a perspective of the many dimensions that can be ascribed to head variant petroglyphic features, noting the importance of head variants and their multiple meanings within the context of Mayan culture. Like Mayan iconography, there's more than meets the eye when it comes to 3-D Portable Rock Art.

Is There a Difference Between PRA and Artifacts?

It has been observed that PRA is "crude" by comparison to an artifact like the Mayan celt and pendant. When found in the field, PRA can be nearly indistinguishable from surrounding natural rocks. The recognition of a potential find can originate by the overall shape, sparkles from mica and other metallic components, or unique geo characteristics that make it stand out from surrounding rocks. Tools in particular stand out as a result of worked edges and points. Once recognized, cleaned and viewed under proper lighting, human-made embellishments and shapes emerge in PRA creations. Most human crafted PRA has unique, 3-D artistic qualities, which will become increasingly apparent as PRA becomes more accepted as art.

PART V

PRA TECHNIQUES AND TOOLS

Shape Shifting

Before addressing the tools used to create PRA, a beginning point to understanding how PRA artifacts were created is appreciating the artistic platform itself, which relies on three-dimensional imagery interlaced with contoured, natural shapes, micro-sculptures and etchings.

As noted throughout this book, PRA combines the natural along with pareidolia to mimic animal and human imagery. Thus, the primary "tool" used to create PRA was the imagination of the creator focused on the overall shape, whether it be for a utilitarian or non-utilitarian artfact.

In some cases, this involved significant modification of the stone to create or modify surfaces for making and enhancing points, sharpened edges, and smooth surfaces via well understood lithic workmanship techniques including pressure flaking and indirect percussion using a hammerstone to create a tool.

What is less understood is how the Ancients created the finer PRA paleo sculptures and imagery described in this book. Among these mysteries is how they created art on such a micro-scale? Certainly, better eyesight was required, perhaps along with smaller hands and use of specialized engraving tools, mentored by generations of a story telling tradition within a cultural context.

When examining any single PRA example, keep in mind the creator conceptualized the interconnected imagery while crafting the stone. Multi-glyphs along with interconnected faces and shapes were designed to be viewed while rotating in one's hand. Thus, allowing each singular petroglyph to become connected to a greater spectrum of appearances.

One must also consider the quality of light. The only illumination available beyond sunlight came from a flickering campfire which cast both direct and indirect light on stone, analogous to a strobe light. When artifacts are positioned at the optimum angle, indirect and flickering light casts shadows on surfaces, which could have aided in crafting PRA.

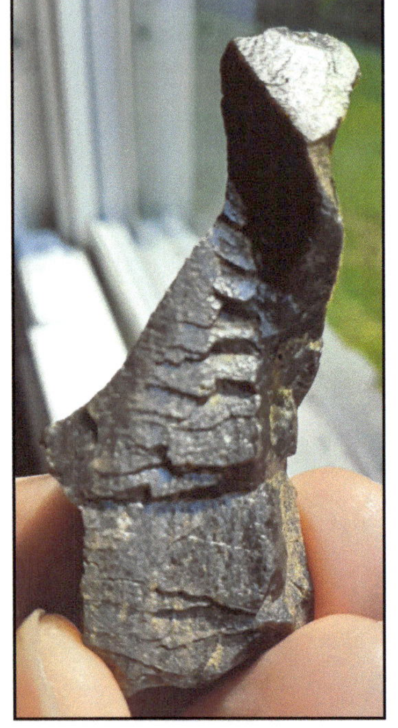

Figure 67: PRA layers in a multi-tool. The use of layers is a key aspect of lithic artistic techniques (George L. Davis).

Layers, Contrasting Colors and Glitter

In addition to the overall shape of the object, among the secondary techniques employed in PRA are the ***use of layers, contrasting minerals/colors*** and incorporating ***glitter***.

Layering employs the stone's natural layers to create 3-D sculptures and images. Among layering techniques, head variants and series of head variants were carved along the edges and borders of natural layers.

Another technique used was chipping or scrapping away a top layer, referred to as the "cortex" layer, to reveal a contrasting color underneath. Artifact VII, the bird stone from Kentucky, shows black patina on the surface interconnected to lighter color images.

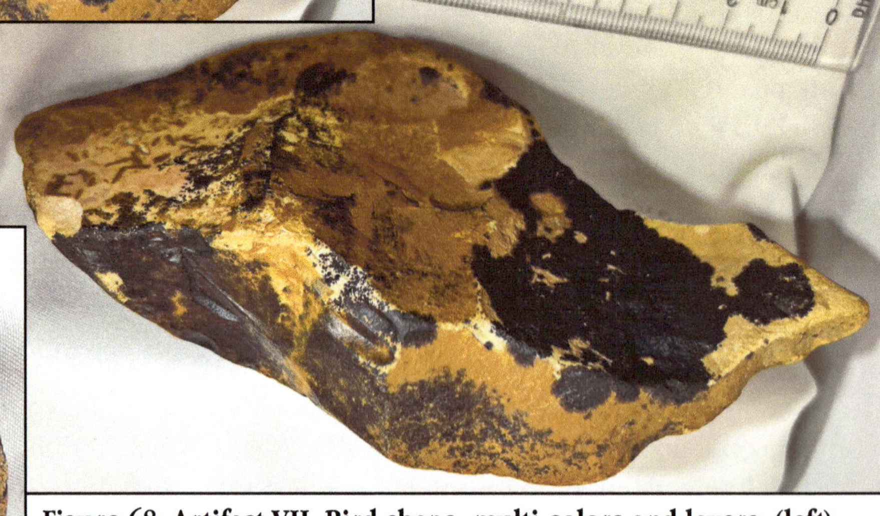

Figure 68: Artifact VII, Bird-shape, multi-colors and layers; (left) Detail of natural rock colors and etchings; (above inset) Shows offset of black and white layers to create a left-facing head variant in black. (*See Fig. 61 for front view.*)

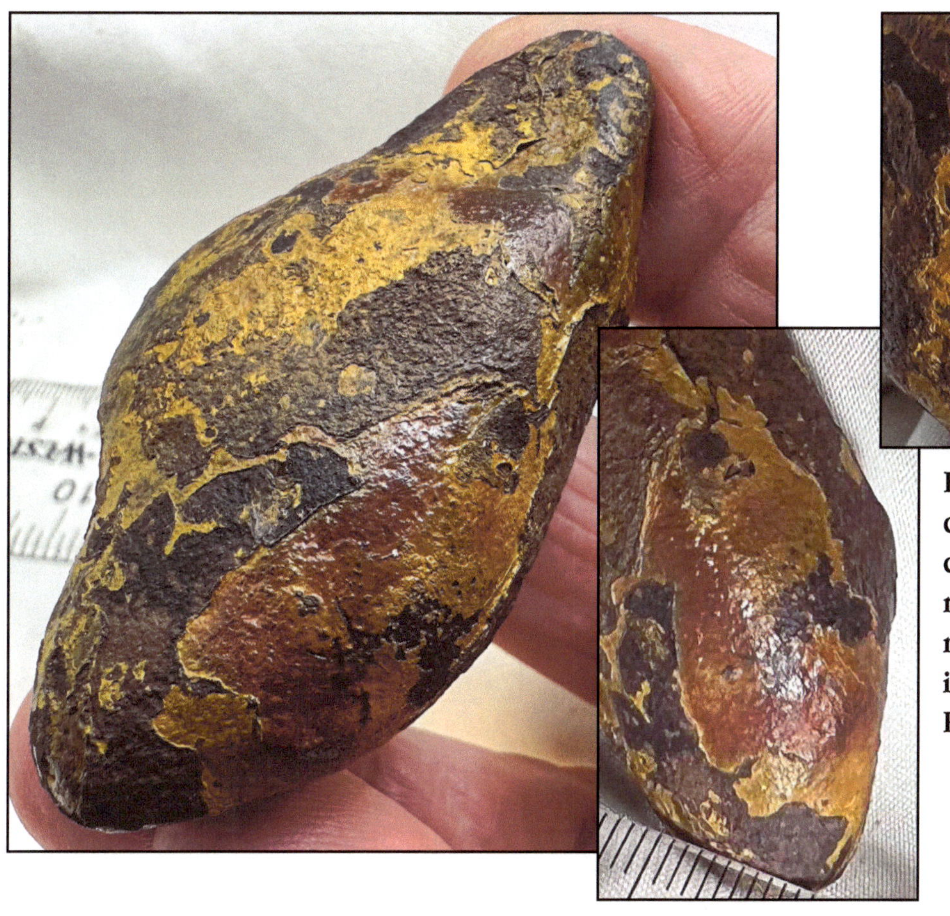

Figure 69: Layers and natural colors integrated into PRA. A colorful jasper from Colorado reveals how both layers and natural colors are integrated into head variants and other PRA imagery.

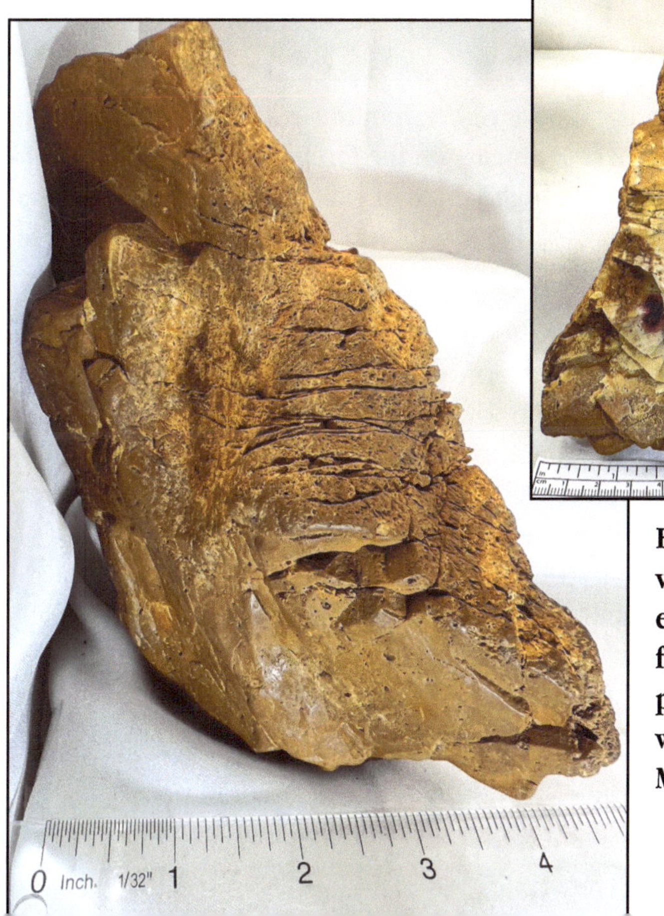

Figure 70: Artifact VIII, Inscription Rock (front and back views), a multi-mineral PRA artifact from Kentucky, exemplifies how the Ancients used colors, layers and facets to create rock art. The multitude of head variant patterns and etchings suggest a sophisticated artifact with intentional art in many of the surface facets (Clay Mathis).

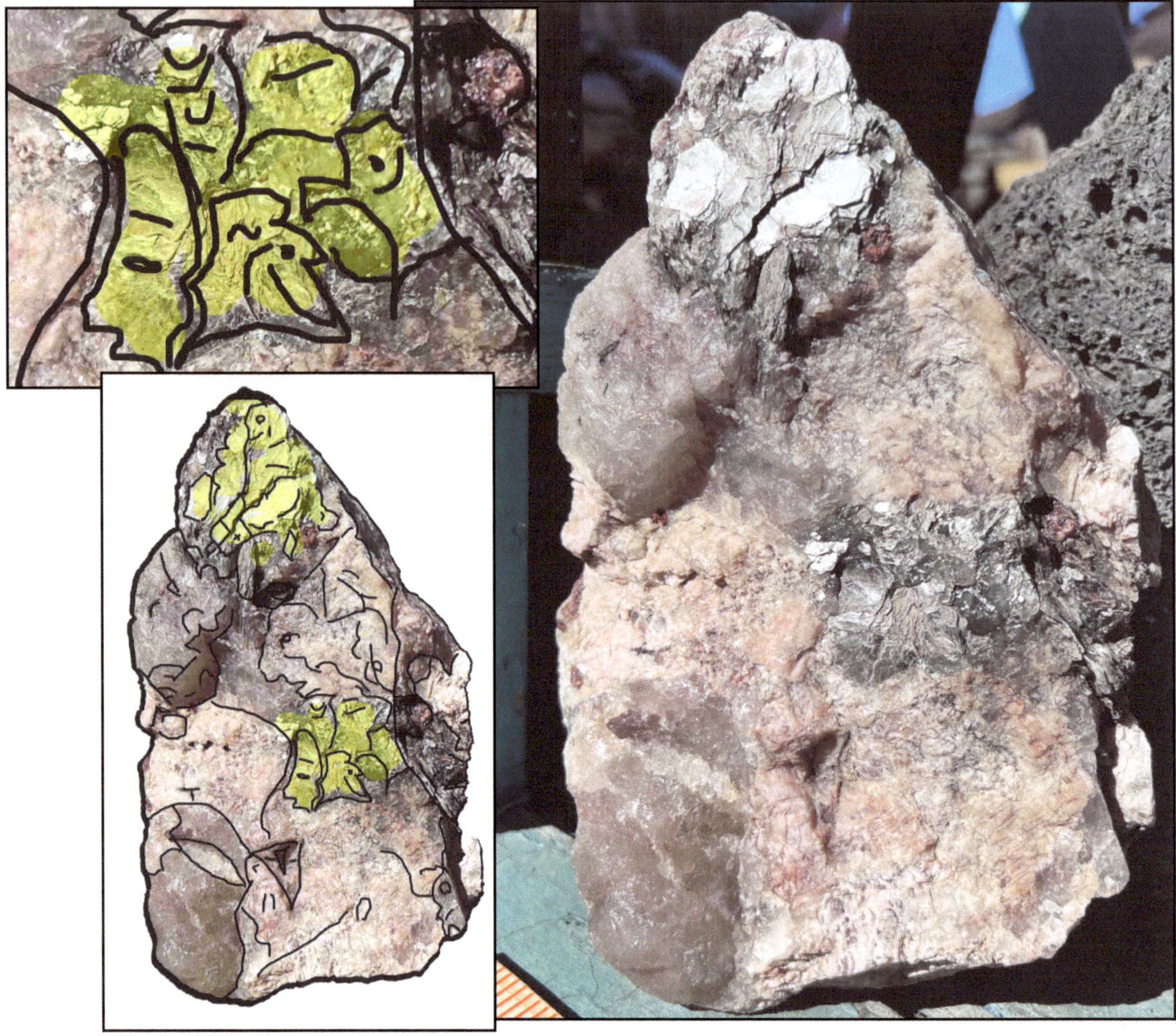

Figure 71: The PRA sculpture (above right) from the Arkansas River Valley in Colorado, sports reflective mica adornments on the forehead and cheek of a left-facing head variant; (above right) Mica highlighted in yellow; (top) Offers details of sculpted mica micro-sections representing small head variants in the cheek area.

Where mica and other reflective layers of stone were available, PRA appendages were often fashioned to emphasize natural layers of glitter. The Ancients carved smooth mica surfaces to create images punctuated with head variant etchings. To see these micro-images the artifacts must be thoroughly cleaned to remove finely compressed surface sediment built up over time.

A twinkle of glitter can often be a sign of a prospective Figure Stone. "Glitter" also includes metal, crystalline and semi-precious stones presented in Part VII, Recognizing Petroglyphic Features.

The following glitter stones attracted the author's attention as a result of the "twinkle" and each proved to be an artifact.

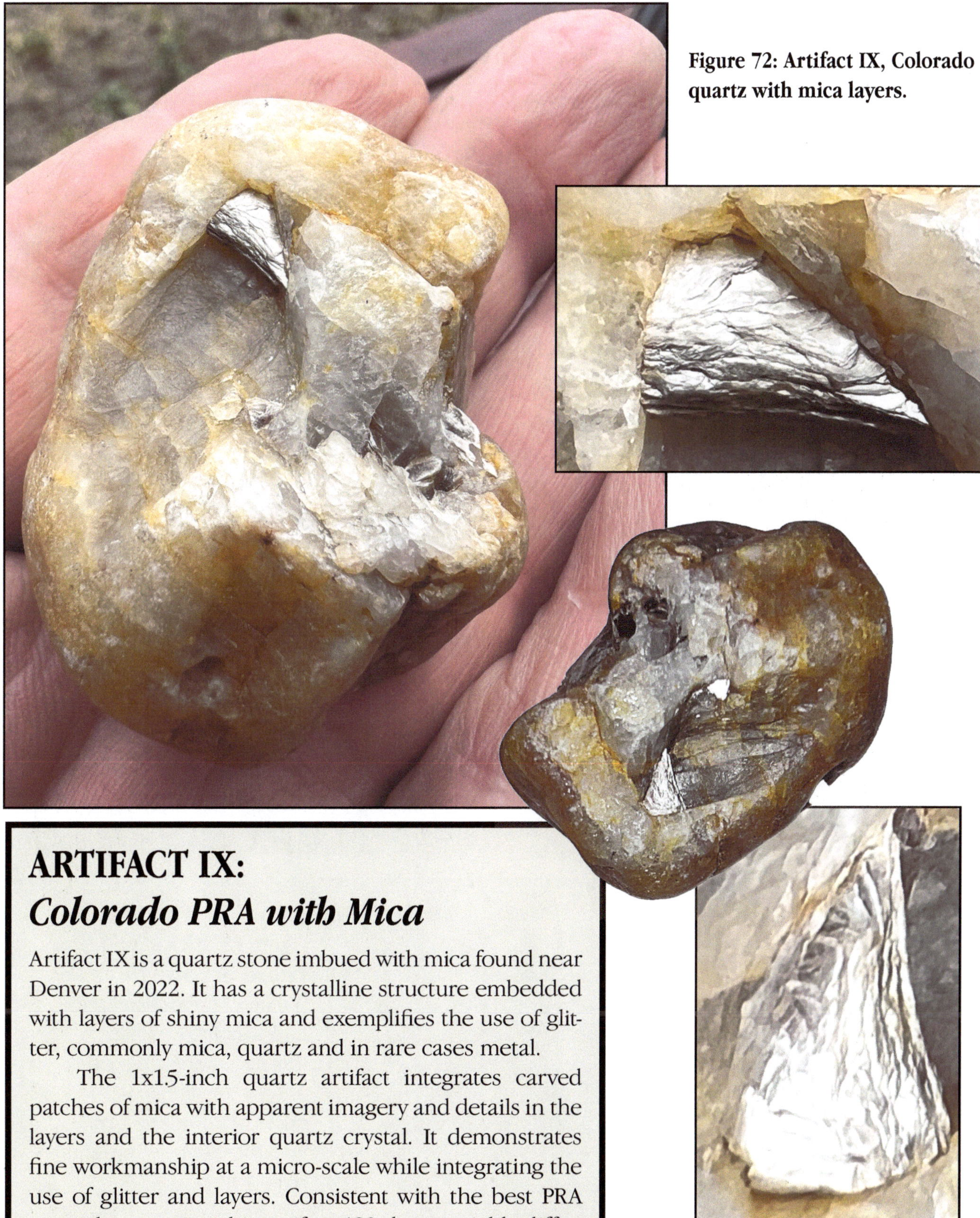

Figure 72: Artifact IX, Colorado quartz with mica layers.

ARTIFACT IX:
Colorado PRA with Mica

Artifact IX is a quartz stone imbued with mica found near Denver in 2022. It has a crystalline structure embedded with layers of shiny mica and exemplifies the use of glitter, commonly mica, quartz and in rare cases metal.

The 1x15-inch quartz artifact integrates carved patches of mica with apparent imagery and details in the layers and the interior quartz crystal. It demonstrates fine workmanship at a micro-scale while integrating the use of glitter and layers. Consistent with the best PRA examples, rotating this artifact 180 degree yields different artistic configurations.

Glitter from the Colorado Front Range

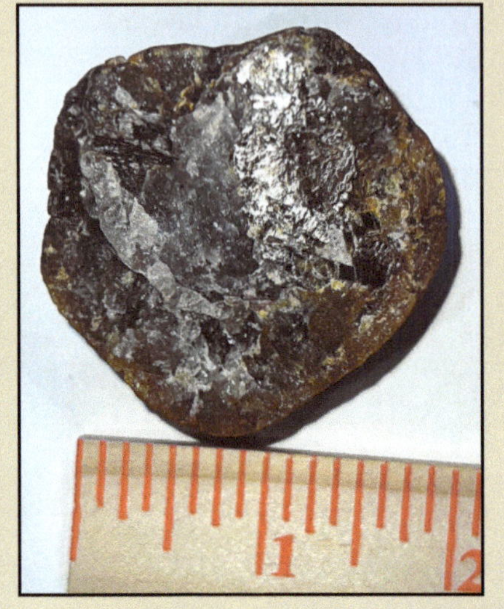
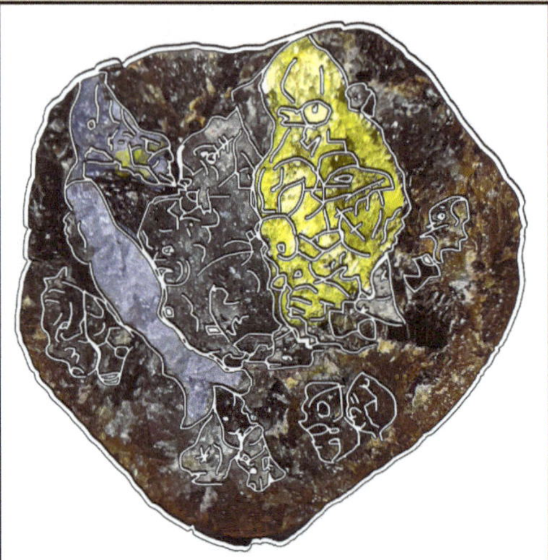

Figure 73: Artifact X, Mica glitter. The "shimmering" mica of the right image has the shape of a head variant (yellow). The carved serpent (blue highlight) on the left side incorporates mica. Separating them is a quartz head variant.

Figure 74: Pebble with shiny golden layer. The 0.8-inch-wide pebble has a streak of gold resembling a head variant. The details are emphasized in the reflective quality (right). An apparent "X" is positioned on the nose of the golden image.

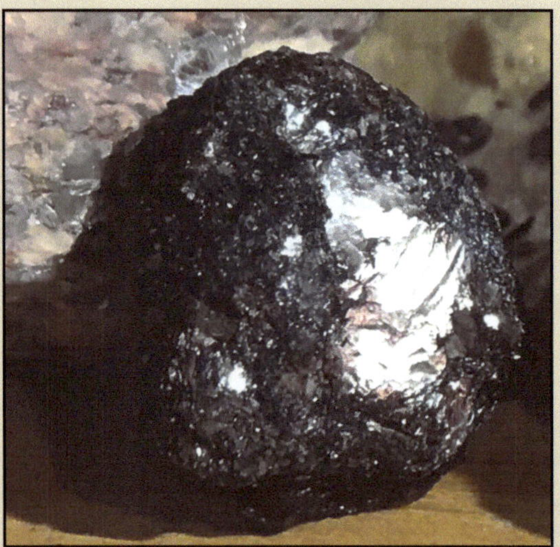
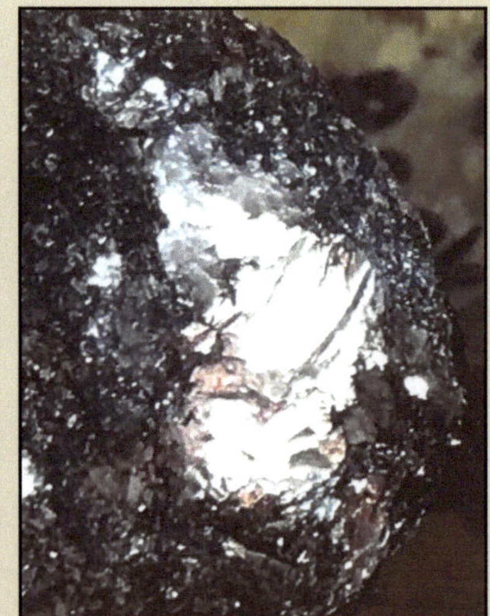

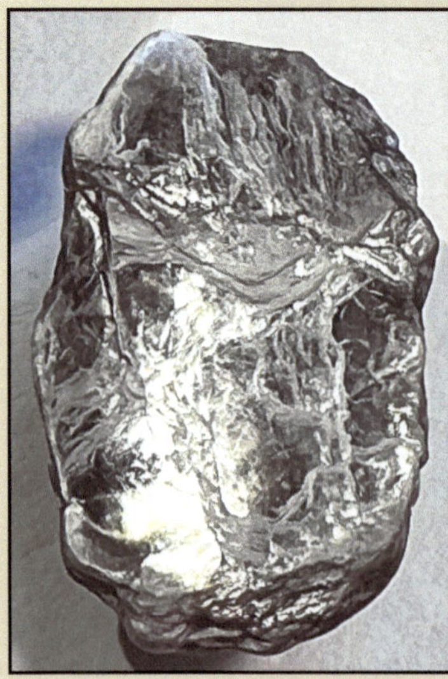
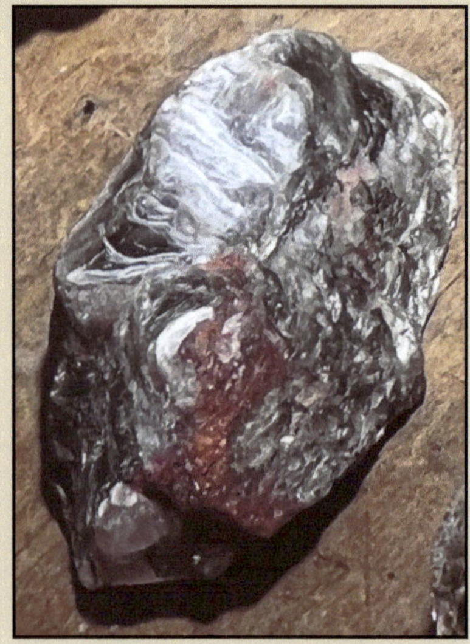

Figure 75: Mica nugget with prospective art (Colorado). Front and back, 1.2 inches long, this nearly pure nugget of mica appears to have micro workings to form a metallic-like head variant sculpture.

PRA Tools

To achieve 3-D artistic enhancements, specific tools and techniques were employed to modify natural color gradations, layers, natural holes, edges and existing indentations to emphasize desirable aesthetic qualities. Of great importance and contrary to contemporary archaeological thinking, many paleo tools are endowed with artistic features.

Archaeological research posits that most lithic tools were used for crafting shaft-style tools, including spears, digging and throwing implements, as evidenced by Oldowan stone tools from Africa. Little research focuses on the tools used to create handheld paleo sculptures as exemplified in the following informative summary extracted from a Cambridge University Press publication authored by John J. Shea:

> *Stone tools are shaped mainly by fracture and abrasion. . . . In lithic technology, the objective piece is called a core or a flake-tool. Force, or load, is transmitted by a hammerstone. The fracture products are called flakes or collectively, débitage (French for "waste") . . . Bipolar reduction for butchering probably preceded chopper-like core reduction and provides a key link between primate nut-cracking technologies and the emergence of more sophisticated lithic technologies leading to the Oldowan.*[55]

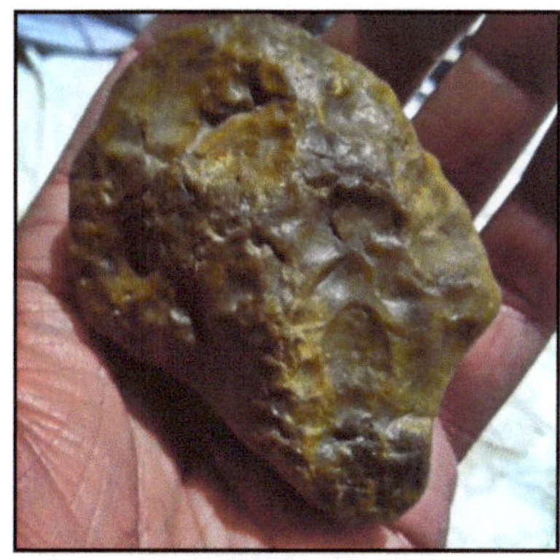

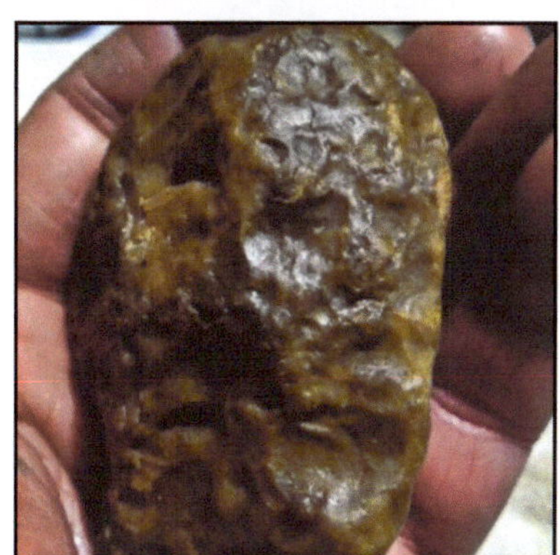

Figure 76: Example of indirect percussion (Tim Banninger). With indirect percussion, a hammer and chisel would have been used to create eyes, mouth, and chin of the profile.

Missing from this and most lithic technology descriptions are the techniques and tools used to create art on rocks. Dr. James Harrod and Mary Leakey, among others have documented artistic enhancements on both utilitarian and non-utilitarian stones from the Oldowan era. It is now clear from observing a multitude of PRA creations that adding artistic enhancements went beyond conventionally understood fracturing and includes chipping, grinding, hole drilling, pecking, and etching in addition to use of abrasion tools.

While traditional lithic technologies (fracturing whole stones and shaping them into tools via pressure flaking) were employed, we must consider that fashioning paleo art involved many different implements and techniques to create 3-D imagery, including indirect percussion using a combination of stone hammer and chisel as suggested by overlapping flake scars.

Using a hammerstone, a prospective rock was fractured, creating an inner and outer side along with sharp edges. The smooth outer side would be handheld and the edges fashioned as sharp cutting or scrapping implements. The exposed inner side of the fractured stone offered opportunities to fashion art, as demonstrated by two examples (*Figs. 77-78*), the oval shaped scraper and a split core with apparent art on the interior side.

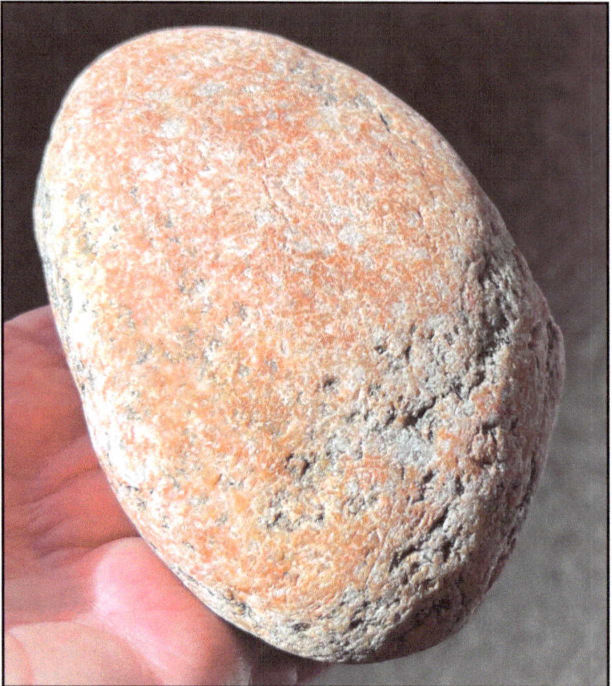

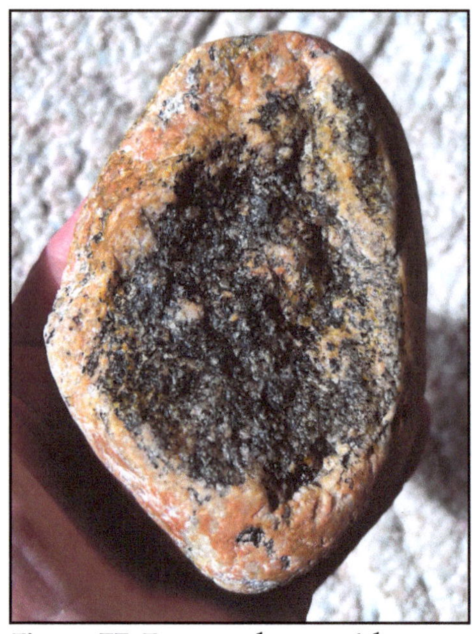

Figure 77: Fractured core with prospective interior art, Colorado.

Figure 78: Handheld Scraper (right) with Art, Colorado. A fractured quartzite, bi-polar flake has different head variant shapes, functional edges, a smooth outer side for comfortable hand holding and an inner side with opportunities for artistic enhancements including micro-sculptures. Scraper shown in two positions: vertically emphasizing a left-facing head variant and horizontally showing a likely mastodon image.

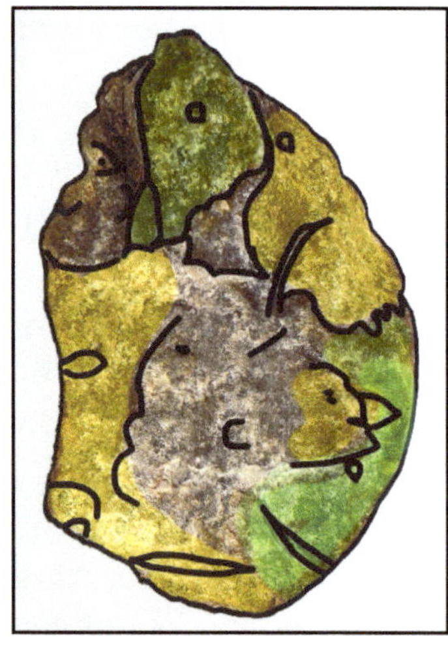

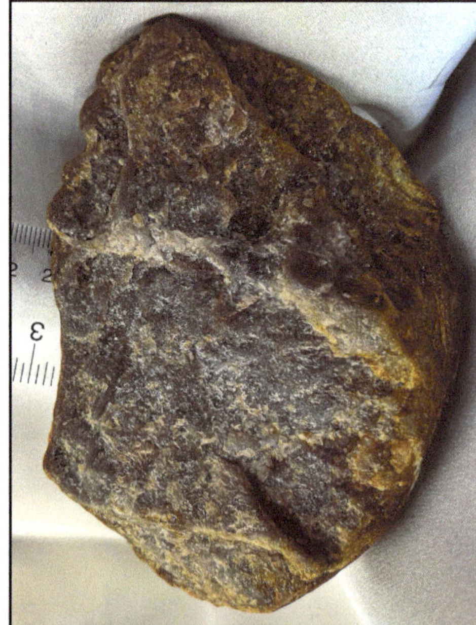

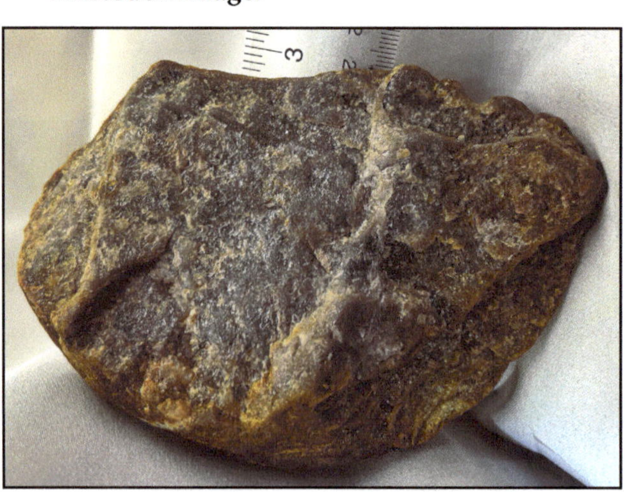

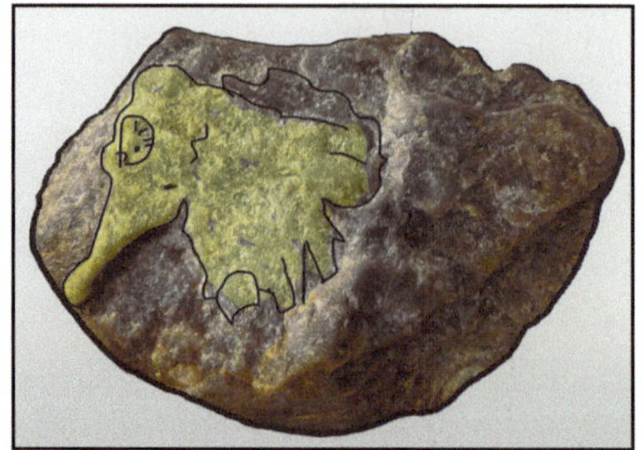

Most stone tools had specific functions in daily tasks like preparing hides. Once a stone was modified, mainly by fracturing and pressure flaking, an important tool for creating PRA included a class of stone implements referred to as *burins*. Burins have been around since humans began creating specialized tools and are among the stone age tools used to create PRA.

Sometimes the terms *graver* and *burin* are used to describe the same tool. Gravers, from the word to engrave, were metal or stone tools with sharp points or *spurs* used to engrave surfaces and to create fine petroglyphs. Authors from Europe often refer to burins as gravers, while American authors consider gravers to be stone tools created by pressure flaking and created to have functional points.

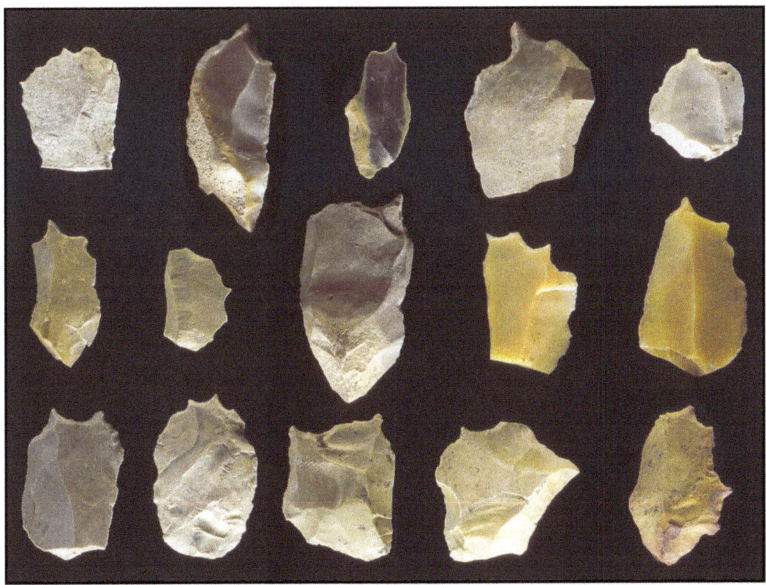

Figure 79: Single and Double Spurred Stone Tools.[56] Photo from a private collection from the Olive Branch Site, Alexander County, Illinois, an early archaic Dalton habitation location. The fifteen single and double-spurred tools were discovered during excavation and were used by Early Archaic Dalton people approximately 11,000 years ago. About half of them have two spurs or points. Most spurs are located on the ends of the flakes. Some have spurs on a side of the flake (Peter A. Bostrom).

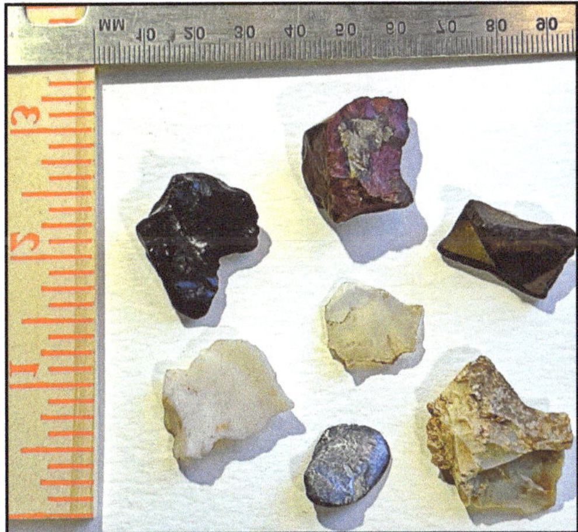

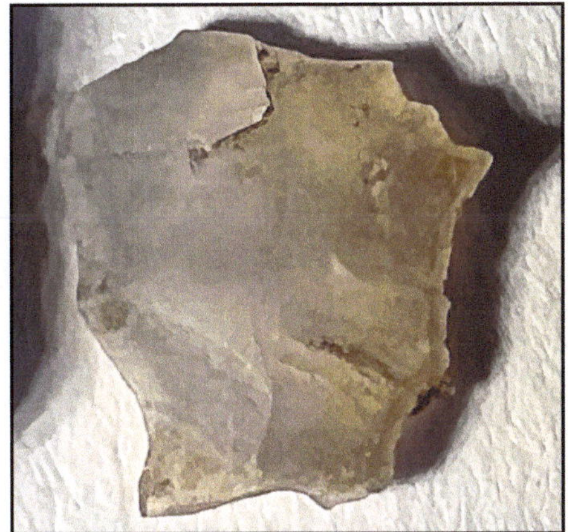

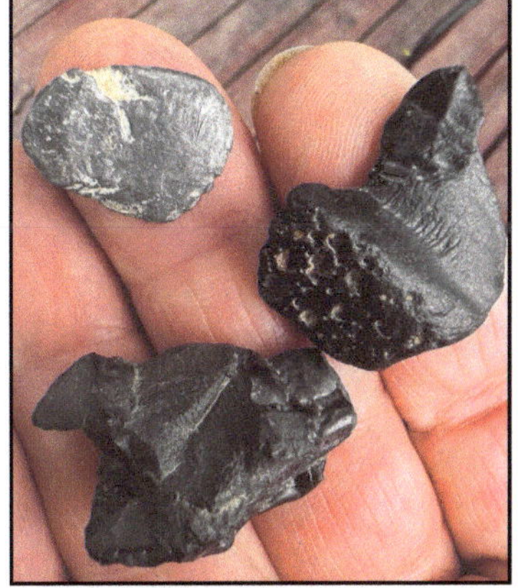

Figure 80 (left): Graver tools. Figure 81 (center): Quartz graver. Figure 82 (right): Top object is a fine metal tool with sharpened worked edge; black artifact on right side is a small knife; and tool at the bottom is a sharp graver tool; all three paleo tools are from the Front Range of Colorado.

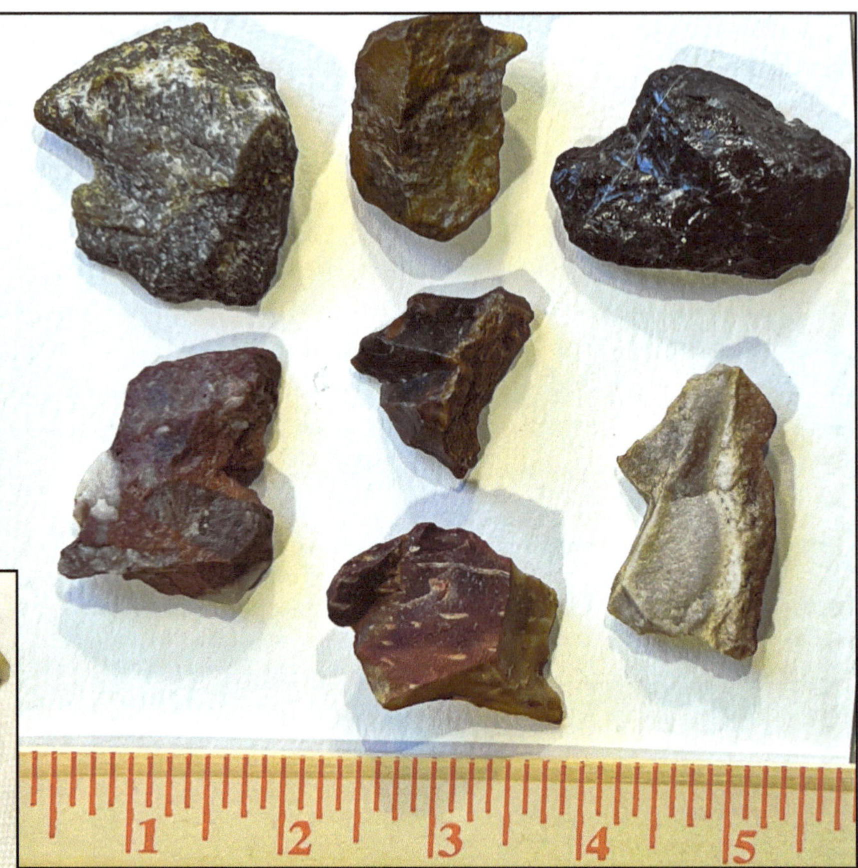

Figure 83: Small tools with PRA likenesses, Colorado and Kansas.

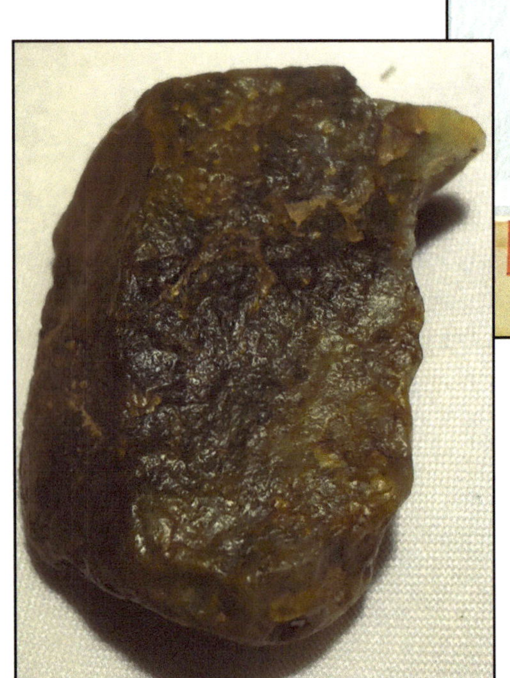
Figure 84: Agate graver with bird likeness, Kansas (Tim Banninger).

The following is an excerpt from a book regarding burin/graver identification by Jean M. Pitzer of the Center for Archaeological Research:

> *Burins are perhaps the most interesting and complex of all of the tools of prehistoric man and they continue to be objects of considerable interest to archaeologists. As Noone writes (1950:186), the burin "may be said to be the first specialized working tool of all man's artifacts." No other tool was made in such a variety of types, yet burins, which are consistent in form and design, are found in many different cultures. Burins were first recognized in Paleolithic assemblages in Europe as tools, which had been made with great skill and precision for the performance of specific but multiple types of tasks—tasks that were soon identified (in Europe) by experiment and replication (Movius 1966, 1968).... More recently, burins have been found in widely separated sites in the New World. The number of sites has risen steadily as students have learned to recognize burins in an increasing number of lithic assemblages.*[57]

Only a minority of bruin/graver tools contain artwork but looking at the shape of the graver itself can offer clues to artwork. Once a familiar shaped head variant or animal shape on the tool is identified, finding a prospective eye and mouth in the form of chips, natural irregularities, and worked marks can help determine if the stone is a complete head variant or animal shape, or if it is solely a tool.

Stone Tools with Artistic Enhancements

Paleo tools include a wide range of utilitarian objects including stone knives, multi-tools, awls and scrapers. Tools are identifiable in the field by beveled and/or worked edges, extrusions coming to a point and also how they fit in one's hand. Finding stone tools with artistic qualities is fortuitous because they demonstrate human workmanship, a significant PRA validation criterion. Was the recognizable image the original shape of the stone or the crafted intent of the creator? In either case, the result is a tool with an animal likeness.

Arrowheads, a broad term used to describe different size and shaped hunting points, range from small bird points to larger spears and represent a small fraction of stone age tools. It is much more likely to stumble upon a multi-tool (*Fig. 85*), scrapper, or chopper than an arrowhead.

There are countless stone tools and arrowheads in public and private collections worldwide, some with artistic features that remain unrecognized. Nevertheless, arrowheads with intentional art are rare but can be identified, as Figure 86 suggests.

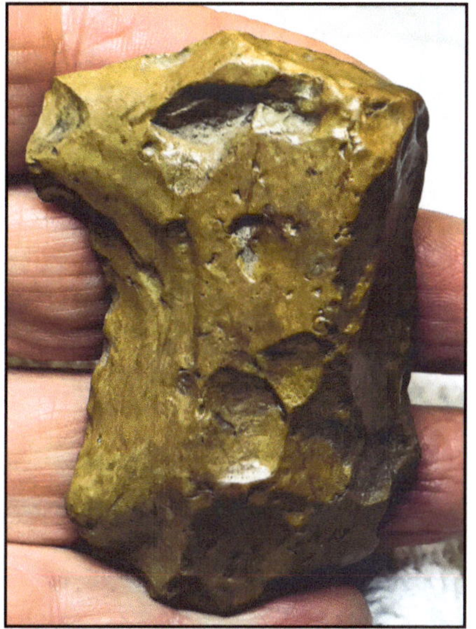

Figure 85: Kansas multi-tool (Tim Banninger).

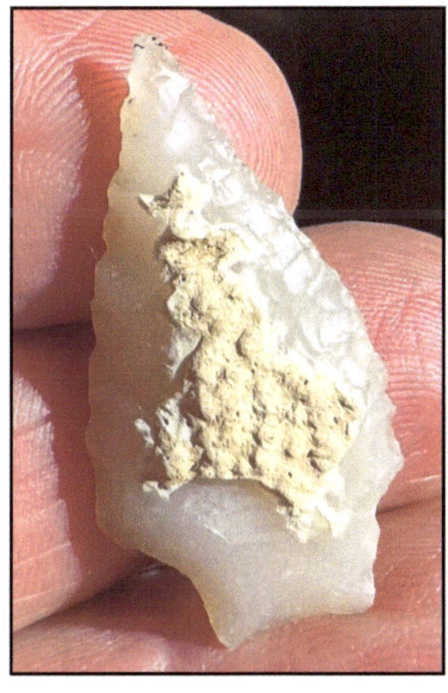

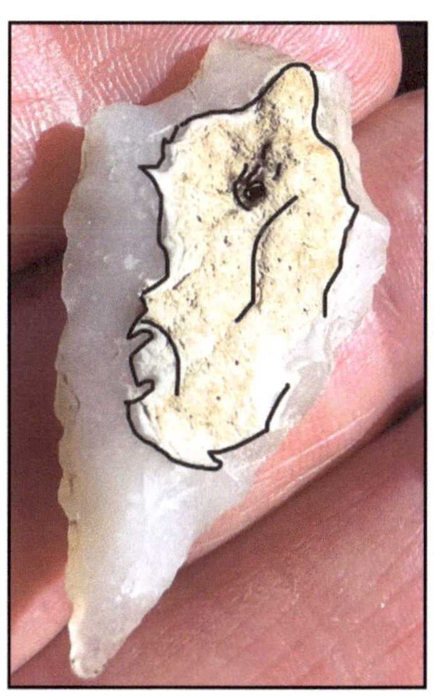

Figure 86: Arrowhead with fashioned outer layers: This quartz arrowhead from California has a cortex with apparent carved images. Front (left) and back with black outline added.

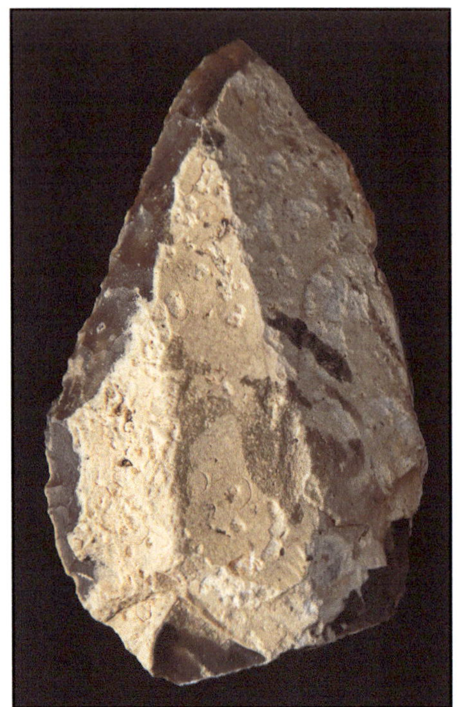

Figure 87: Quartzite spearhead, Acheulean culture, Sahara Desert (Shutterstock).

Excluding arrowheads and points, other types of stone age tools fit comfortably in hand. Thus, fashioning a suitable stone into a hand-held tool required surfaces for comfort while employed in different positions in addition to having a functional edge, point(s) and/or surfaces.

The artistic ingenuity displayed by scores of artifacts collected from Arizona, Kansas, Colorado, California and other locations contradict conventional archaeological dogma that ancient work tools were simply "disposable" and little effort would have been expended on artistic embellishments. As PRA clearly demonstrates, the Ancients had a tradition of bestowing imaginative features on stones, likely going back to the beginning of the human timeline.

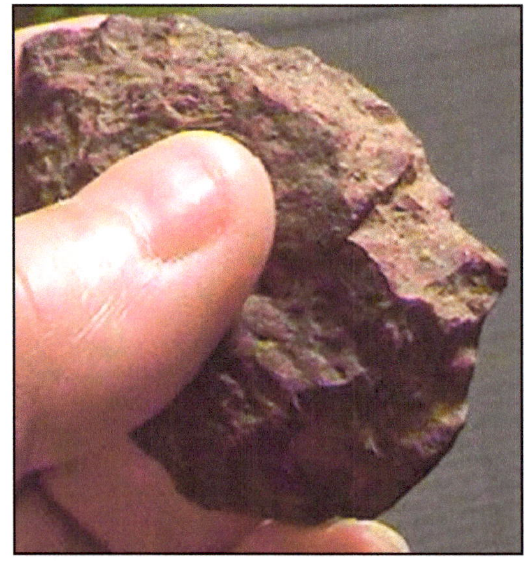

Figure 88: Hand axe with worked PRA likeness, Texas. The significant flake created the eye section of the right-facing head profile (Bill Waters).

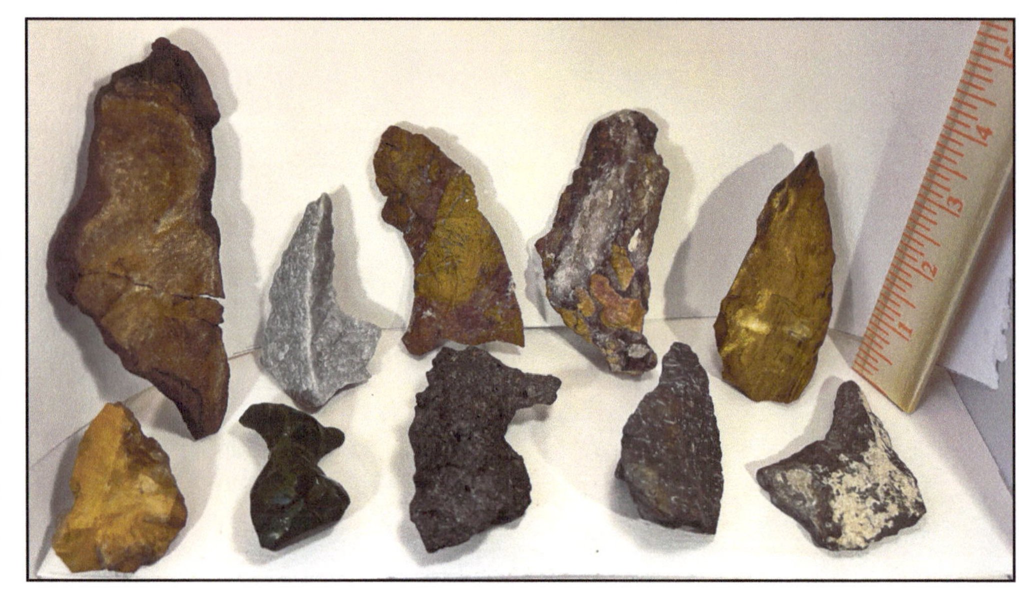

Figure 89: Stone Tools with PRA Resemblances. (from top left) Found in Nevada (damaged and glued), Colorado, Arizona, Arizona, Colorado; (bottom row) Colorado, Massachusettes, New Mexico, Colorado, and Colorado.

The author posits that in the process of making tools, the Ancients identified opportunities for artistic embellishments, perhaps during the initial flaking activity. At some point, while creating them and during their use, more embellishments were added to prized tools. In cases of non-utilitarian PRA, the Ancients identified a likeness in the stone, that they refined and embellished into paleolithic sculptures and art.

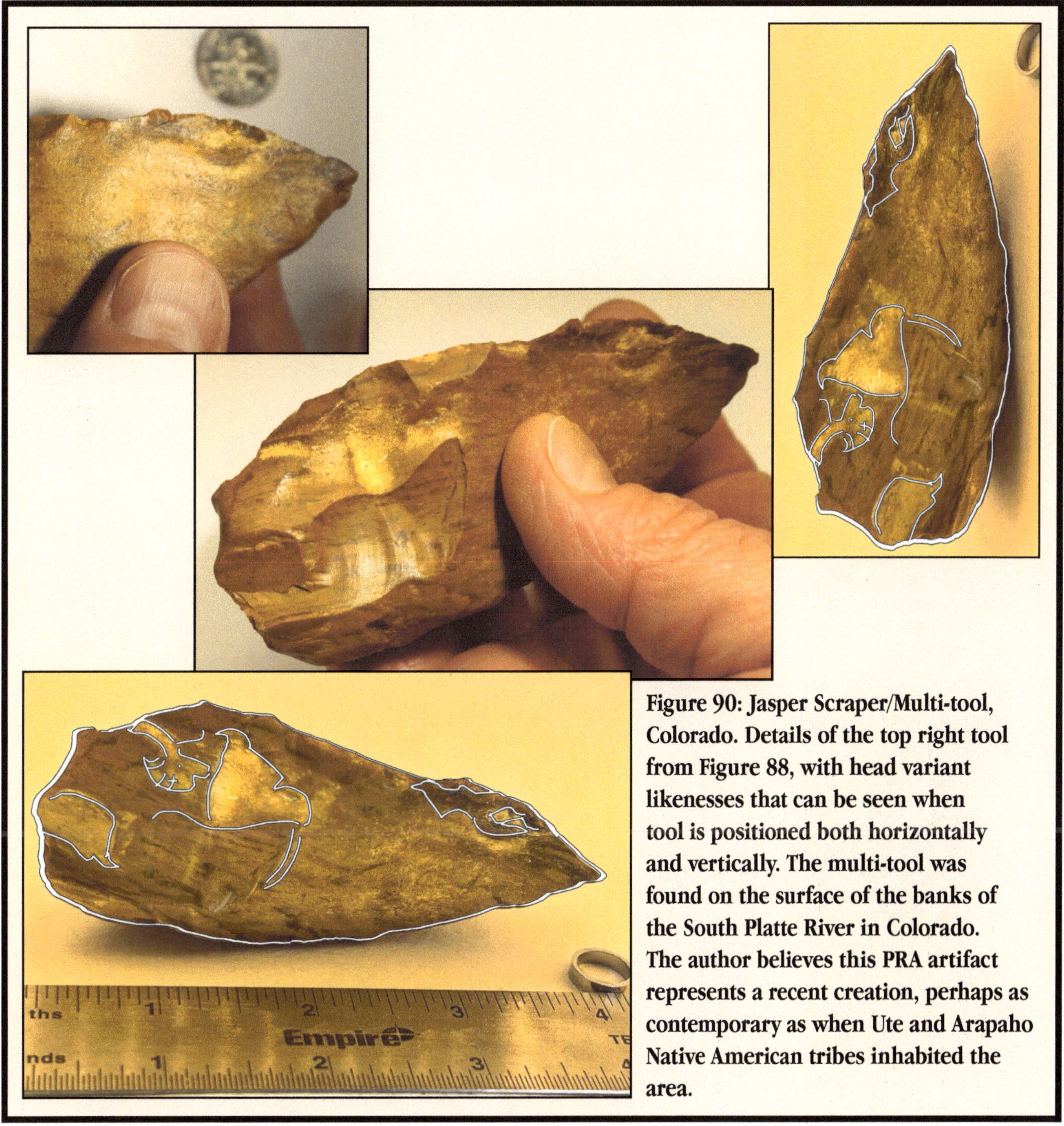

Figure 90: Jasper Scraper/Multi-tool, Colorado. Details of the top right tool from Figure 88, with head variant likenesses that can be seen when tool is positioned both horizontally and vertically. The multi-tool was found on the surface of the banks of the South Platte River in Colorado. The author believes this PRA artifact represents a recent creation, perhaps as contemporary as when Ute and Arapaho Native American tribes inhabited the area.

ARTIFACT III:
Arizona Knife / Multi-Tool

A well-crafted knife with multiple cutting edges from Southern Arizona. It integrates many of the PRA features previously described including color gradiants, head variants on both sides and strategically placed tiny holes. The holes, smaller than a pin head, function as eyes for head variants on both sides.

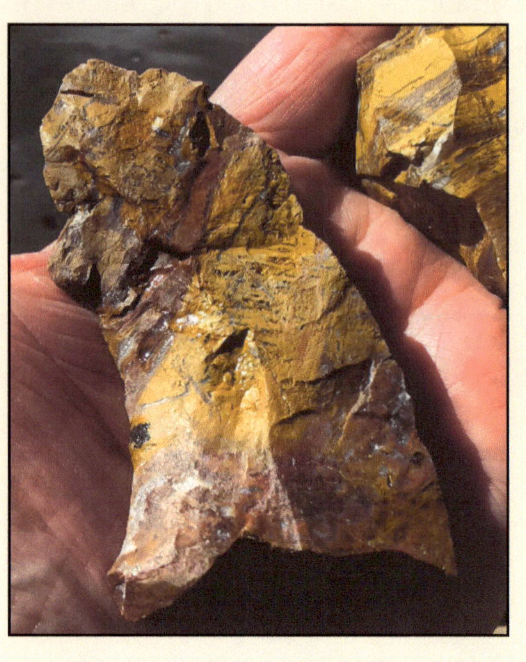

Figure 91: Artifact III, Knife/multi-tool from southern Arizona. **(*See Fig. 36*)**

One can imagine that as common rocks were being chipped from outcroppings, or whole oval and round stones were struck to expose their core, a distinction arose between artful and utilitarian opportunities. In some cases they exhibited immediate potential for a useful implement, which was worked with a particular function or multiple functions in mind. Perhaps along the way to completing a knife, artistic enhancements were made or alternatively during usage, embellishments were added over time to demonstrate the artist's abilities.

It is likely the Ancients would have identified prospective rocks that could be fashioned with art. These included natural stones with flat bases, pareidolia-shaped stones with natural looking resemblances to head variants, conglomeration rocks, stones with natural holes, and specimens with outstanding and unique qualities including crystals (most often quartz), glitter (most often mica), and stones with contrasting layers, colors, and types of minerals.

Clearly a more complete understanding of the tools used to create artifact is required, along with new artistic perspectives enabling an understanding of PRA enhancements.

As more collectors, professional geologists, archaeologists and academics become aware of PRA, some stone tools discovered during fieldwork and some artifacts in existing collections will be understood to have artistic in addition to utilitarian dimensions.

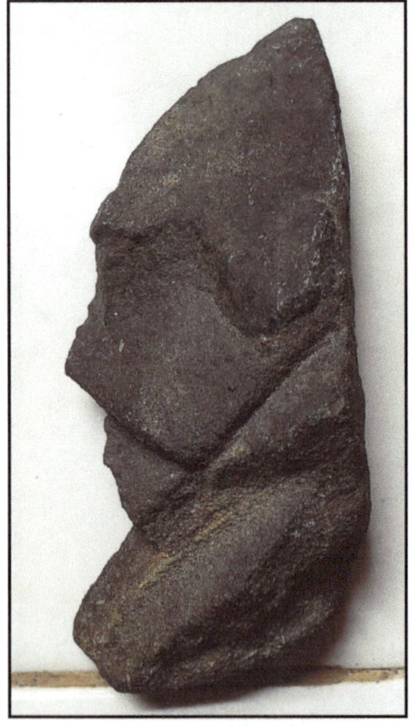

Figure 92: Knife with PRA features, Virginia (Alan O'Hara).

PART VI

HOW OLD ARE THEY?

Earliest Human Art

PRA may be among the oldest crafted art. In all likelihood, it was produced from the earliest beginnings and thereafter continuously throughout human history. This age-old human tradition may have come to an abrupt end at the hands of the conquest of the Americas and the destruction of aboriginal cultures worldwide.

Mary Leakey one of the few accredited archaeologists who identified PRA objects, dated the craft to 1.4 million years ago.

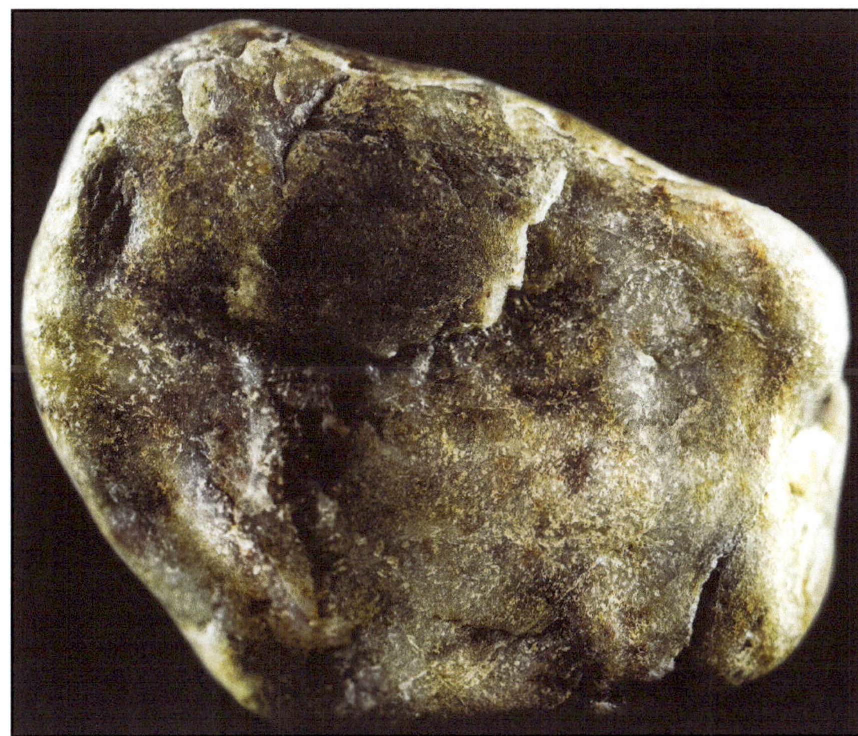

Figure 93: PRA with mastodon likeness, Michigan (Chris Penney).

James Harrod's archaeological investigations suggest that paleo-art became evident around two million years ago, as evidenced in the flaked pebble core technology of Homo *rudolfensis/habilis.*[58] Dr. Harrod's observations are based on eight Oldowan palaeoart objects, seven in stone and one in bone, including non-utilitarian artifacts and tools. He concludes that these artifacts were created around a million years earlier than current dating of the earliest paleoart, noting:

> ... *It would also demonstrate that* Homo habilis/rudolfensis *or a very early* Homo erectus *had substantially more advanced cognitive, design and symbolic competencies than suggested in current theories, and it would constitute a challenge to develop more advanced cognitive semiotic and art-theoretic analytical tools for illuminating the role of such paleo art in hominin cultural evolution.* ("Paleoart at Two Million Years Ago?")

Dating PRA is best undertaken within a "context" or "provenance" that would include an object's complete documented history, including a known location, accompanied by additional archaeological and datable biological materials. When found at a single location in abundance, one can assume the PRA was created by the same culture and during a time period that can be validated. These include massive finds from regions known to be home to the "Mound Builder" cultures encompassing the Southeast U.S.

Even so, it is not easy to reliably date PRA because of their portability. Artifacts could have been passed down through generations. Also, since PRA would have been left behind by migrating cultures, it is quite possible these same artifacts were found and used by different people over time.

Most PRA artifacts found in a natural setting and on the surface suggest their last use occurred in the most recent thousands of years. In rainy regions, one would suspect PRA to be somewhat buried, potentially with an exposed surface. In wind swept areas like deserts and the U.S. Great Basin, they are more easily visible on the surface.

When found in urban settings, PRA caches were excavated by Moderns from far away river beds and sand/gravel mines, scooped up to be screened and delivered as gravel and rock fill to residential and commercial customers in far away locations (*Fig. 135*). With the destruction heaped on the environment by gravel mining and extraction operations, PRA caches and individual pieces extracted from any original context make dating nearly impossible; however, this has created opportunities to find PRA in the most surprising locations, including in urban settings.

Mojave Desert PRA

The oldest known petroglyphs in North America come from the Great Basin region of the Southwest U.S., dating back approximately 10,500 years. Some of these petroglyphs are located on the west side of now dried-up Winnemucca Lake in Nevada on limestone boulders.

While the author is unaware of any PRA research at the Winnemucca Lake site, the petroglyphs and associated rock sculptures offer a glimpse into the artistic style of these ancient dwellers. PRA from a Mojave Desert petroglyph site demonstrate that PRA may be found at petroglyph sites (*Fig. 96*).

The diversity in cultures who inhabited the Great Basin region over thousands of years make it difficult to reliably date and determine the origins of paleo art found on the surface, since more recent Native American tribes may have left handheld paleo sculptures among earlier artifacts at the same location.

Although most PRA cannot be reliably dated unless found within a context, based on Mary Leakey and James Harrod's research we can conclude PRA goes back at least one million to two million years ago.

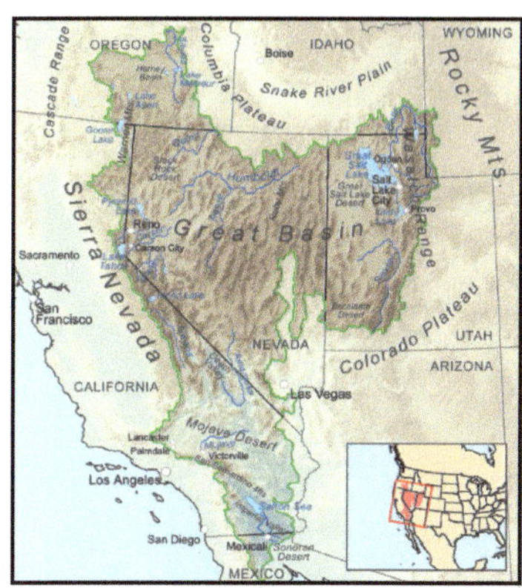

Figure 94: Map of Great Basin, Southwest United States.

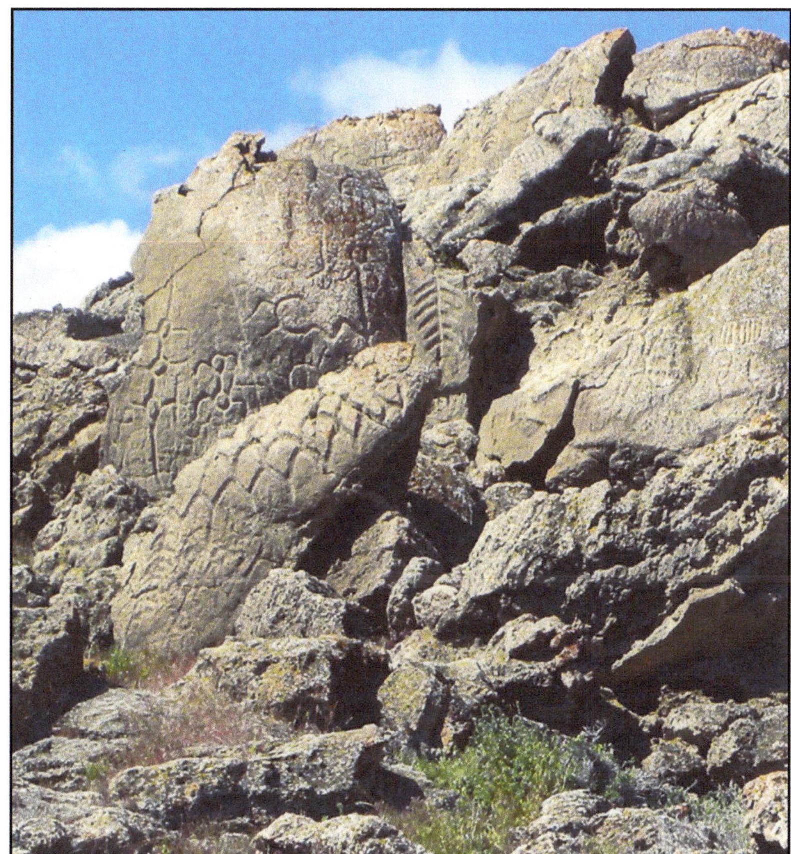

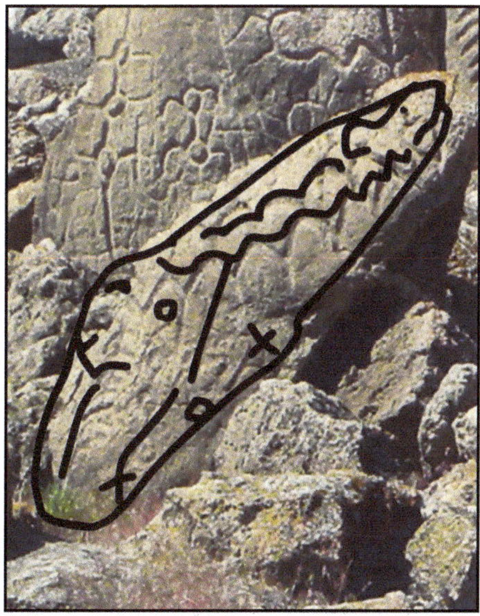

Figure 95: Earliest petroglyphs in North America are located in Nevada. Winnemucca Lake petroglyphs from "Winnemucca Petroglyphs: Oldest Rock Art in North America." (Benson et al., 2013.[59] Drawn insert by author.)

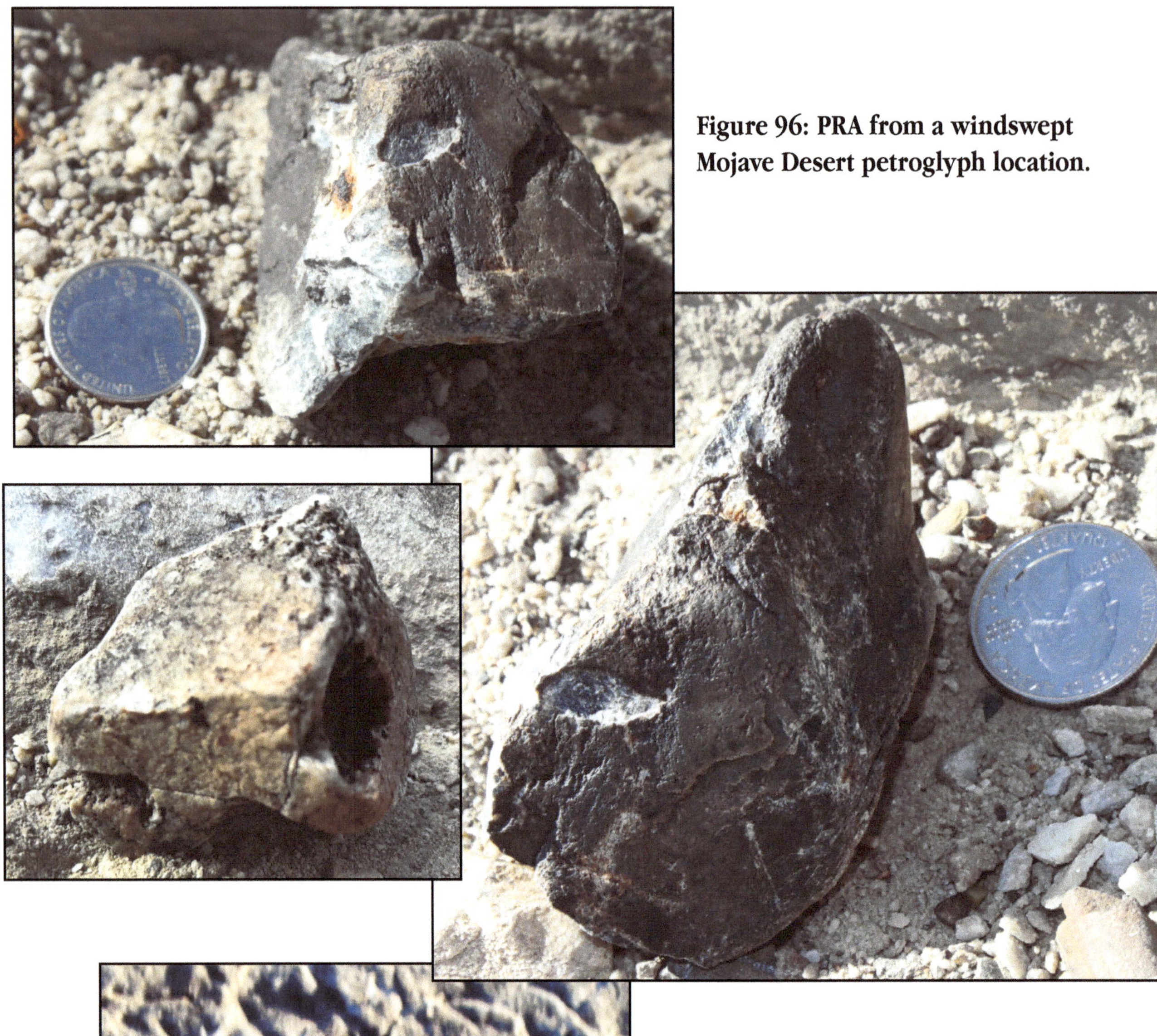

Figure 96: PRA from a windswept Mojave Desert petroglyph location.

Figure 97: SEA petroglyph, Mojave North (*also see Fig. 8*); A common theme among head variants is an elongated, Pointy Head, as demonstrated by the SEA petroglyph at Mojave North and other examples shown above.

Neanderthal Portable Rock Art?

It is likely that PRA may be found at some archaeological and petroglyph sites including documented Neanderthal habitation sites. While the focus on investigating Neanderthals revolves around tools and tool-making, Neanderthals had artistic capabilities, as evidenced by ocher pigment applied to the stalagmitic dome of Cueva de Ardales cave in Spain at least 64,800 years ago.[60]

Supporting the proposition that Neanderthals created art, a 2021 study by Nature Ecology & Evolution documented a decorated bone found in the Unicorn Cave in West Harz, Germany. The Unicorn Cave Bone (UCB) is estimated to be 50,000 years old, made from the phalanx or toe bone of a deer, and was created by Neanderthals, as reported in the *National Geographic* online magazine article, "Were Neanderthals making 'art' in Europe's fabled Unicorn Cave?"[61]

Unlike most stone PRA examples, the UCB, as the name entails, is made of bone and was discovered in a cultural context. A preliminary examination of UCB photographs by the author suggests the UCB exhibits attributes of Portable Rock Art. The UCB photos appear to show a multi-faceted series of head variants with analogous PRA imagery, while the backside imagery suggests a bird-like representation facing left with a short beak.

The *National Geographic* UCB article mentions, "...***tool-shaped stones***...*in the cave,*"[62] an indication the Unicorn Cave is an opportune location for finding other types of lithic workings and paleo art, perhaps including PRA. But if we're not looking for it, we probably won't see it, even when artifacts are in plain sight.

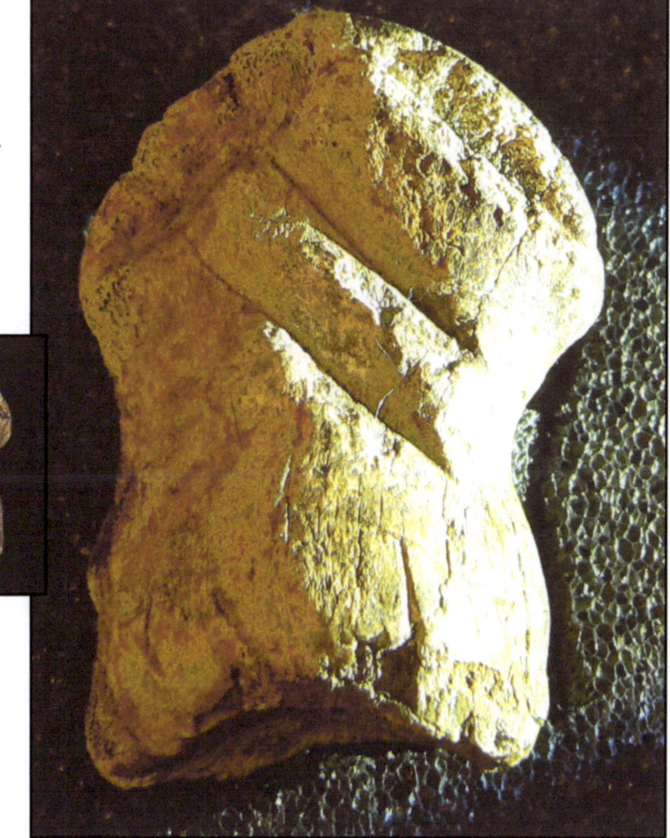

Figure 98: Unicorn Cave Bone; Inset is a drawing by the author showing prospective paleo art elements (Axel Hindemith/ Lizenz: Creative Commons CC-by-sa-3.0 de).

Clovis Culture Portable Rock Art

In the America's, the Clovis cultures are considered among, if not the earliest peoples arriving from Asia across the Pacific "land bridge" near the end of the last glacial period around 13,000 years ago. These peoples arriving from Asia are considered to be the ancestors of modern Amerindian peoples. They brought with them a distinct style of tools found at hundreds of different locations in the Americas, including the first recognized Clovis points near Clovis, New Mexico in 1936.

At a Clovis archaeology site in Anzick, Montana, a human skeleton of a one-year-old Clovis boy, descended from Siberian peoples, is an ancestor of North American Natives based on genetic testing. Dr. Harrod reviewed photographs of artifacts from the Anzick Clovis Site and discovered what may be among the earliest known Portable Rock Art sculptures in the Americas. He reported that least sixteen and up to forty artifacts appear to have fair to good artistic figurations, "depicting zoomorphic, anthropomorphic and therianthropic beings." In the 2022 report, "Portable Art Sculptures from the Anzick Clovis Site, Wilsall, Montana," Dr. Harrod identified different animals with spiritual significance to different Native American traditions including bear and 'Bear-Man,' 'Mask Face with Different Eyes'; Owl; 'Fox/Coyote'; "Frog/Toad'; 'Mammoth'; and 'Vulture (Condor or Turkey) or Raven.'[66]

Among the photos examined by Dr. Harrod was a chalcedony projectile point with significant artistic imagery, that according to Dr. Harrod, are natural images without work traces but are also representational of animals and rituals.

Dr. Harrod notes that of the sixteen kinds of Palaeolithic symbolic behavior/palaeoart (*previously cited in Figure 55, Harrod's Table of Demonstrated Intentionality, Harrod, 2014*), six categories appear to be found at the Anzick site. The Harrod report suggests that the earliest peoples of the Americas created Portable Rock Art sculptures and figurines.

How old is PRA? Based on work by Leakey and Harrod (*cited in Parts III and IV*), Portable Rock Art goes back to humans' earliest beginnings. In the Americas, the Clovis cultures created artistic enhancements at least 13,000 years ago.

Regarding PRA being found my Moderns, dating a specific find is extremely difficult. The exception is when artifacts are found in abundance in small areas like a cache, with the possibility of finding undisturbed organic material for dating purposes and nearby archaeological features that suggest a cultural context and timeframe.

PART VII

RECOGNIZING PETROGLYPHIC FEATURES

Previously, I referred to five basic types of enhancements attributable to PRA. There are other artistic aspects, but these foundational paleo art perspectives help to identify petroglyphic features.

- Profiles and sculptures of whole stone resembling a human and/or animal, the key element and beginning point to identify PRA.
- Sculpted shapes and images on facets/planes/appendages.
- Etched and carved petroglyphs into rock surfaces.
- Multi-glyphs, including faces-in-faces and totem-style imagery.
- Edges, holes and indented or depressed surface enhancements.

It can be challenging for the inexperienced eye to recognize these distinct elements as anything other than "natural" because of a lack of reference and unfamiliarity with 3-D, multi-faceted paleo art.

A fundamental aspect of being able to see PRA imagery is becoming familiar with the 3-D landscape and to look for specific signs of workmanship, head variants, and animal shapes. The human eye is generally not accustomed to seeing micro details in what appears to be random, unorganized incongruous rock surfaces with petroglyphic features incorporated into paleo art. Therefore, proper positioning of the object is critical to perceiving intentional rock art.

Orientation

Unlike petroglyphs on fixed surfaces that provide straight forward viewing, a three-dimensional object has many sides with multiple viewing angles. Is there a "base" on which it rests naturally? This can be a starting point for positioning and viewing. A natural base can establish how it might have been viewed, placed or used in ancient times. Tools with artistic embellishments, including knives, awls and scrappers, generally will not have flat bases and need to be propped up or handheld.

Figure 99 highlights Artifact XI's different styles of petroglyphic features. Figure 100 focuses on a multi-glyph involving the dark varnish on one side, in which the artist used the contrasting colors to create multiple and interconnected imagery.

ARTIFACT XI: *Orientation Is Key*

Multiple head variants are clearly discernable as Artifact XI is rotated. The same is true with previously highlighted Artifact IV, the Holey Stone. Therefore, one's orientation requires the idea that, unlike a painting, there is not one way of seeing PRA. Instead, it is meant to be viewed from multiple perspectives, like rotating on a space ship in outer space to see the 360-degree surroundings.

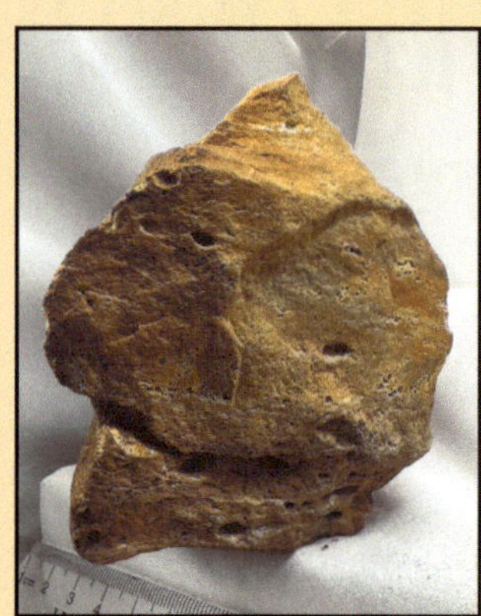

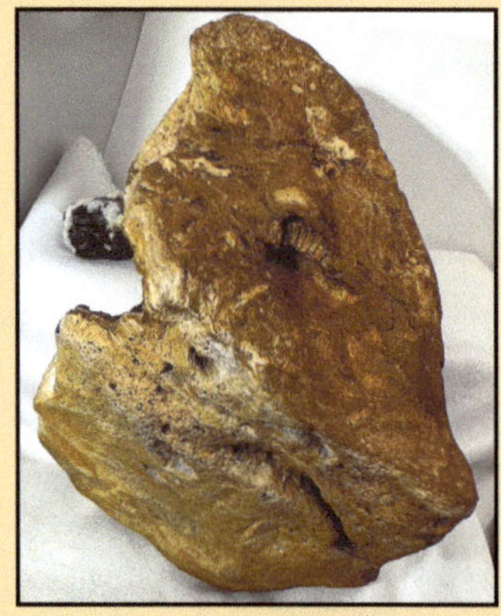

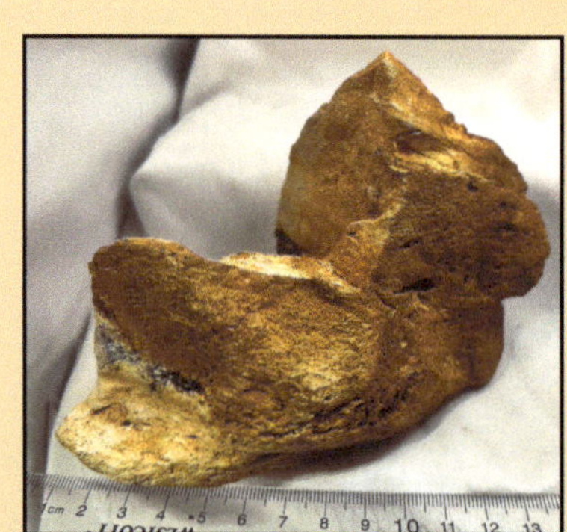

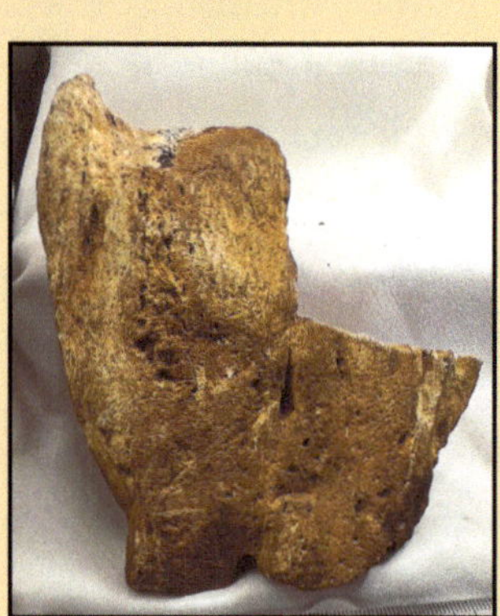

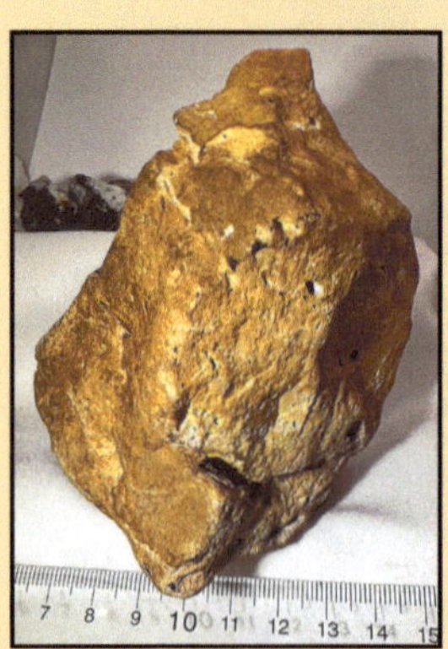

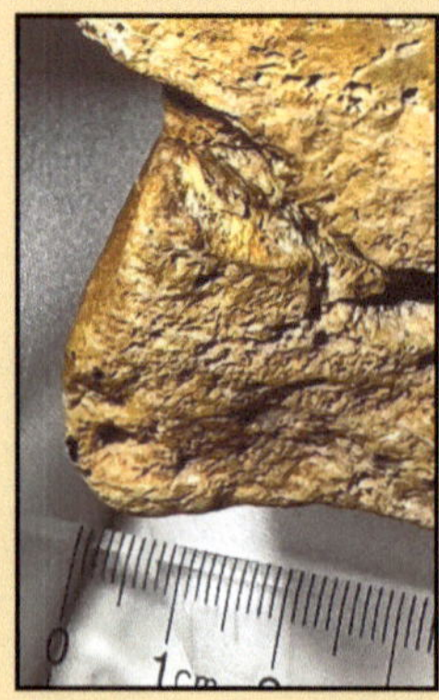

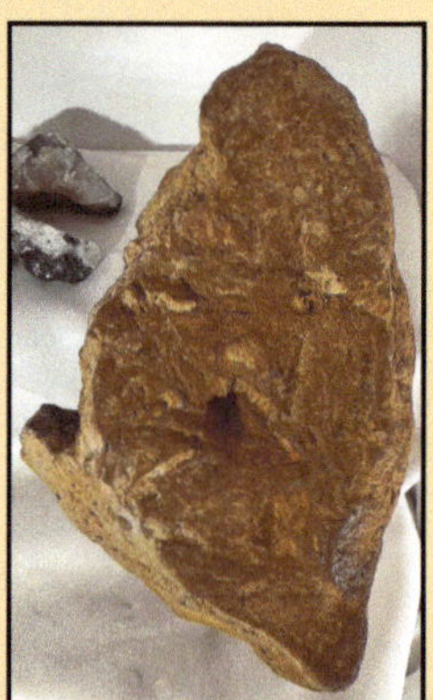

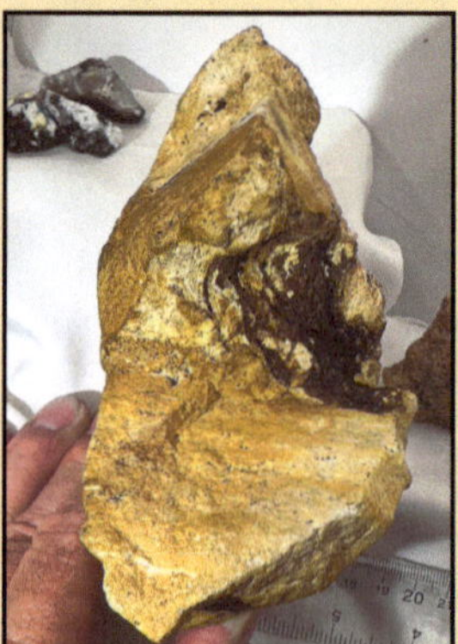

Figure 99: Artifact XI, Different viewing perspectives create diverse head and animal variations. The last photo, indicating white and black elements is further detailed in Figure 100.

Figure 100: Artifact XI, Petroglyphic Features Incorporating Layers. A layer of exposed black varnish is visible on one side. At first the darker color seems without artistic merit, but with greater inspection it brilliantly demonstrates how contrasting colors were used. Head variants were created in black varnish with a white background, as seen on the left side. On the right side a petroglyphic image was created in white with black outline.

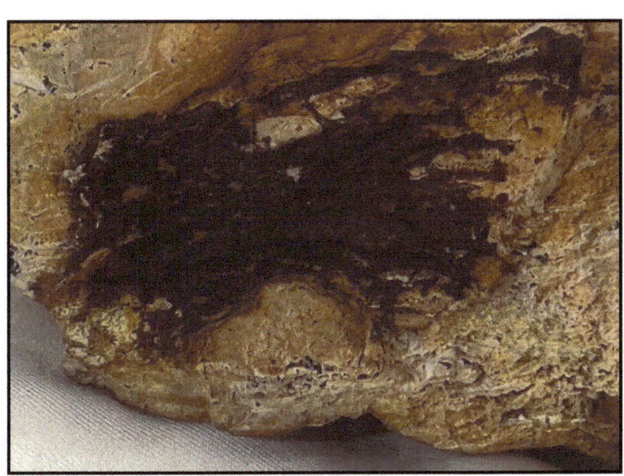

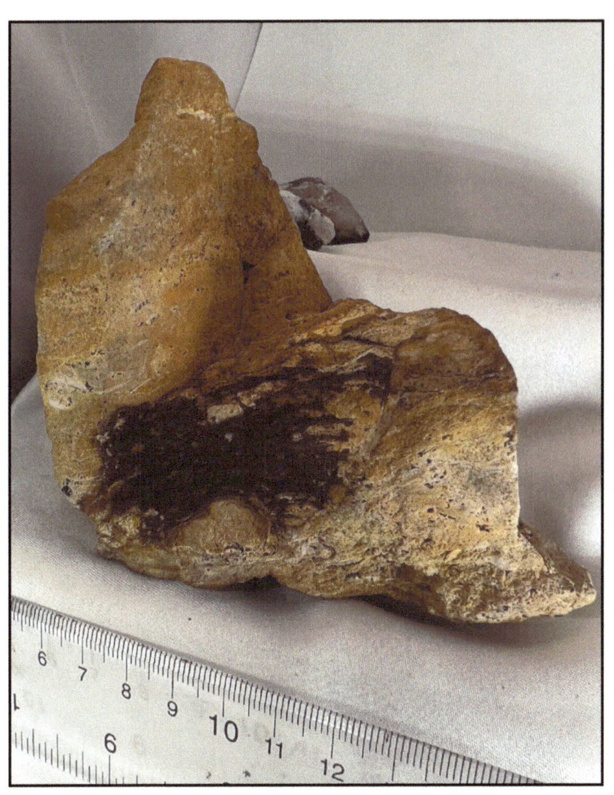

Sculpted Shapes on Facets/Planes/Appendages

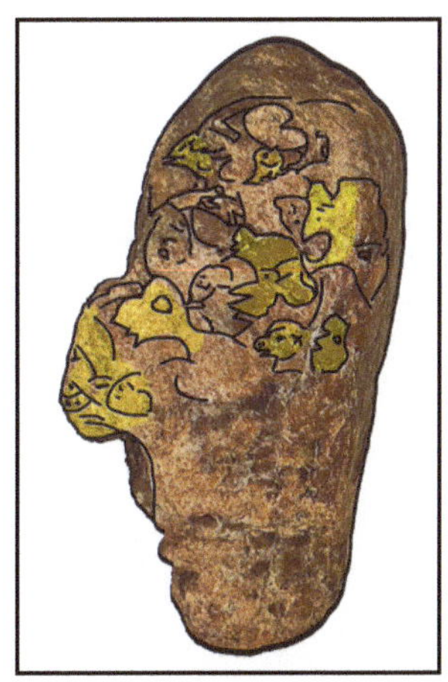

Paleo enhancements were chipped, scratched, and carved to create and enhance familiar looking shapes. When layers of sediment are removed, multiple images can become discernable.

To see sculpted shapes and images, it is best to first focus on the overall shape. Sub-facets/appendages with art are quite often found on edges. As previously stated, finding the eye(s) and mouth of head variants is a starting point, along with the facial outline including the nose, chin and forehead.

Figure 101: PRA Sculpture with Art on Appendages. Figure Stone from the South Platte River Valley, Colorado. This conglomerate stone has many smaller, prospective etching and micro sculptures.

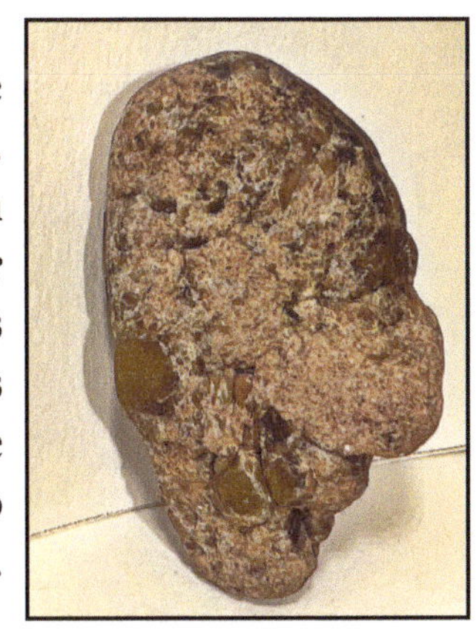

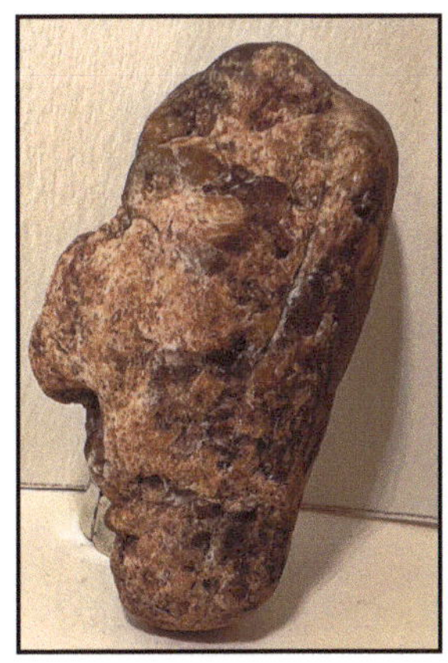

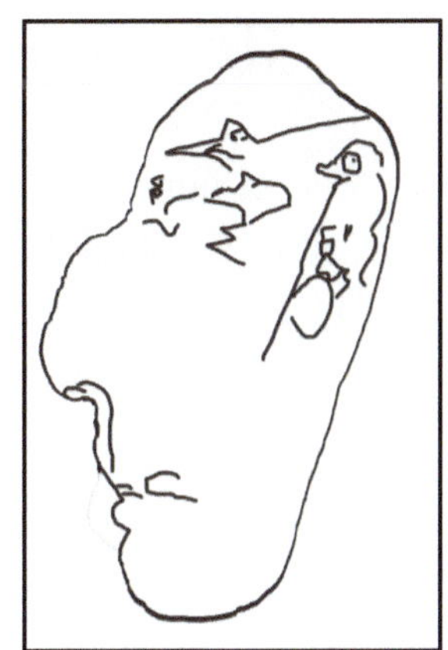

Etched Petroglyphs

Etched petroglyphs are more subtle in appearance. They are elusive because of built-up residue in the finely etched lines, grooves and cracks, leaving the initial impression of looking at a flat surface. Also, etched images are specific to singular viewing positions. They are often integrated with natural parallel lines and cross hatches, which provided the Ancients opportunities for embedding carved micro-glyphs. (*See Fig. 42, Conglomerate Rock and drawing.*)

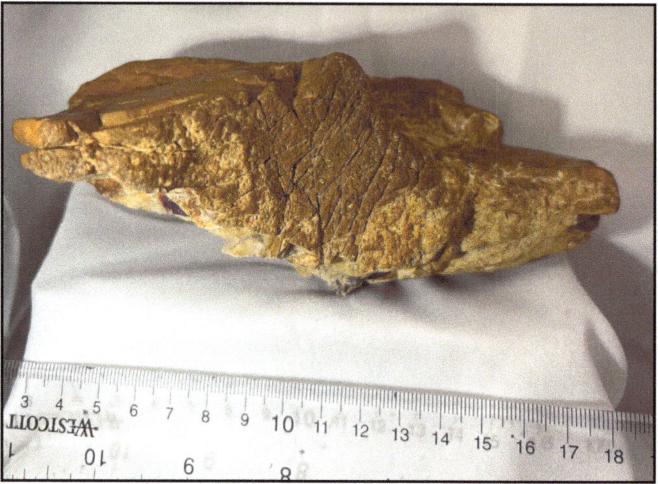
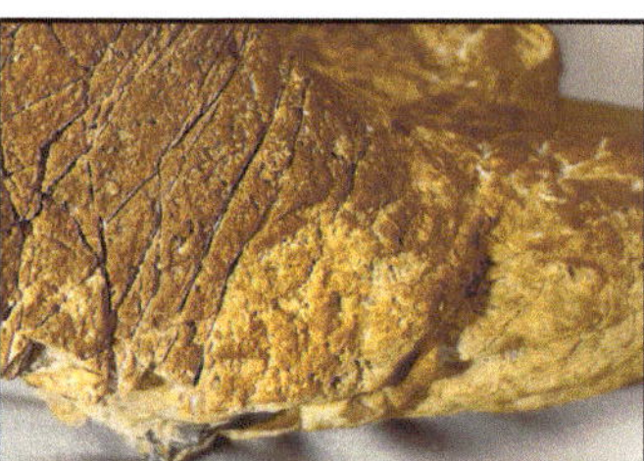
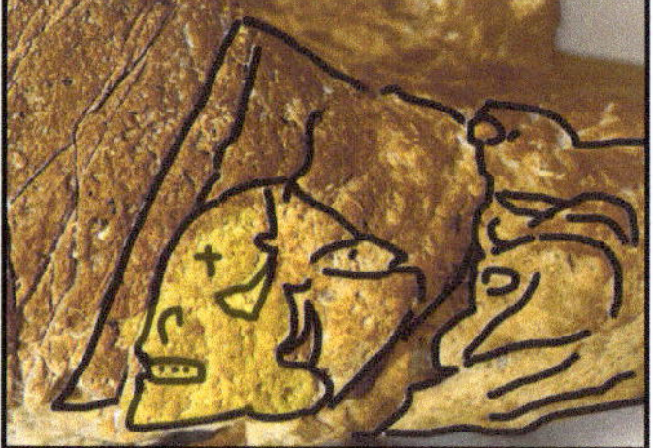

Figure 102: Artifact VIII, side-view head variant details.

Multi-Glyphs, Including Totem Styles

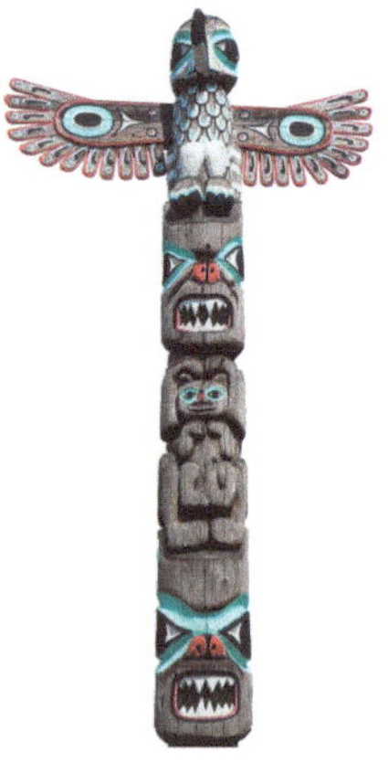

Figure 103: Wooden totem pole, Alaska. (Spatuletail, Shutterstock).

Multi-glyphs incorporate various glyphs and images into a single petroglyph or sculpture. Multi-glyphs include faces-in-faces imagery. Interconnected glyphs appearing in series are a basic characteristic of PRA, as the Ancients connected images both horizontally and vertically. The word "totem" refers to a spirit being, sacred object, or symbol representing a group of people, such as a family, clan, lineage, or tribe. PRA images can appear as stacked, totem-pole style art, but unlike Native American carved totem poles found in the Northwestern U.S., PRA has distinguishable left- and right-facing characters within a single figure.

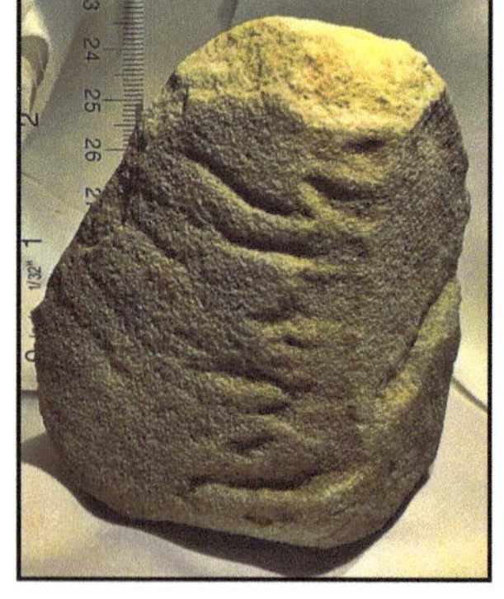
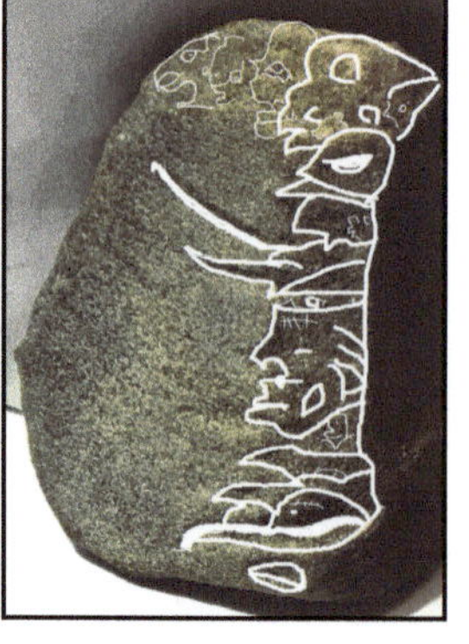

Figure 104: Totem Style PRA. Although severely weathered, enough of the carvings remain to see head variants.

PRA images shown stacked on top of each other most often seem to reference a headdress, predominately animal shapes, which connect the images. Totem style arrangements also include horizontal placements of images. Multi-glyphs commonly are arranged in a collage style, with many head variants appearing within a single appendage, accompanied by faces-in-faces imagery.

The quartz artifact from New Mexico in Figure 105 has a central crystal matrix embedded with stone pebbles. Many of the crystal facets and pebbles appear as PRA head variants. The shiny quartz facets enabled fine detailed creations best seen under direct sunlight.

Multi-glyphs can become apparent when holding and rotating the object in one's hand. These include what are commonly known as the faces-in-faces phenomena and are a main feature of PRA creations. Distinct head variants are often connected by natural or worked grooves. Artifact IV, the Holey Stone, also exemplifies smaller petroglyphic imagery integrated into a larger panorama of stone age art.

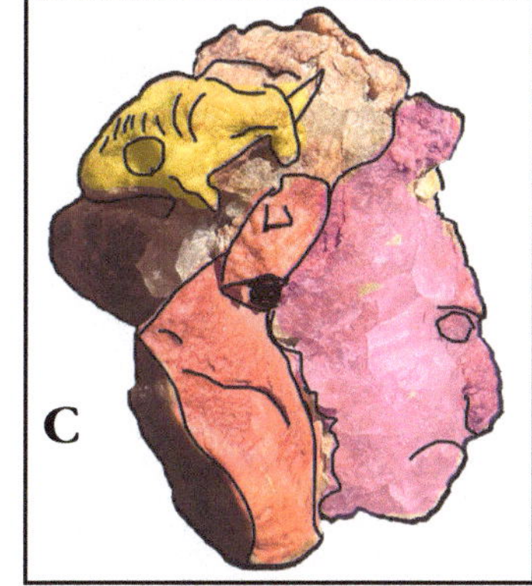

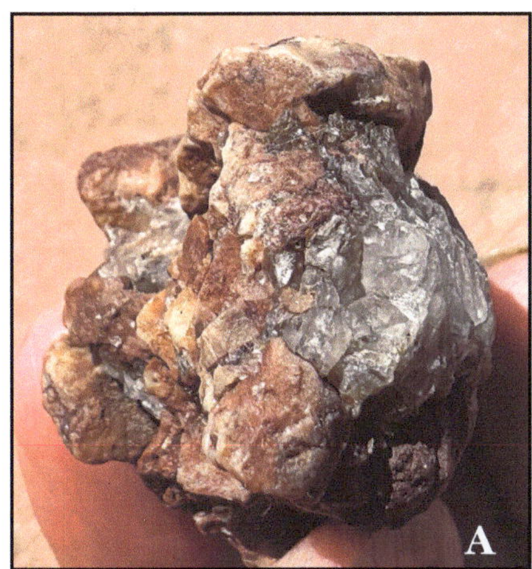

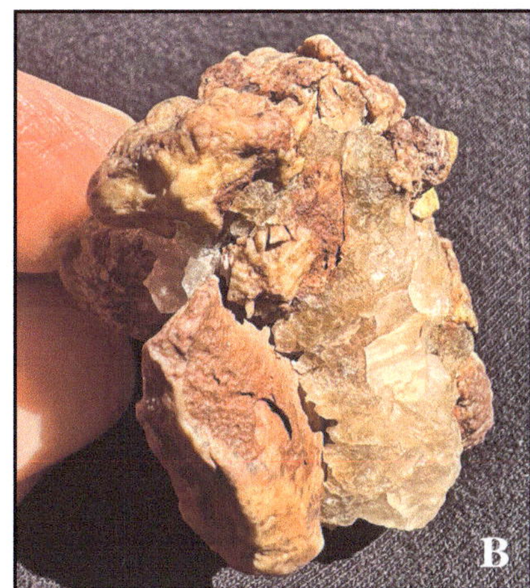

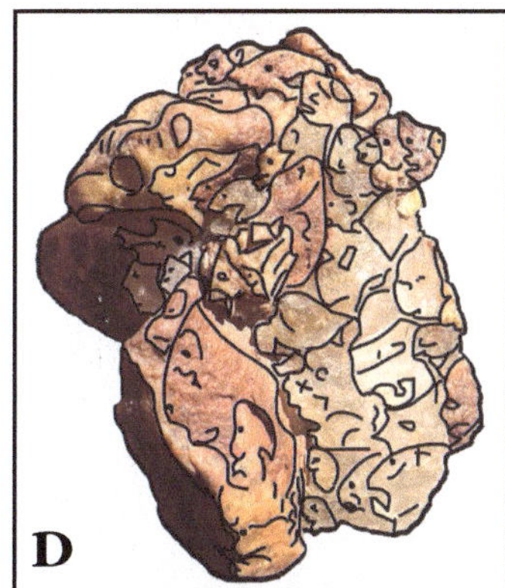

Figure 105: Photo A is a view showing left-facing head variant. Photo B shows another side and the central quartz matrix. Photo C (colorized) depicts primary head variants from Photo B. Photo D depicts level of micro details of etched and sculpted carvings.

Figure 106: PRA with Multiple Head Variants 2, Colorado. This one-inch wide stone was found half buried on a dirt road near the South Platte River. The author's drawings (right) seek to demonstrate how the Ancients connected head variants. The pegmatite artifact has a matrix of quartz and fine detailed sculptures and etchings on all sides.

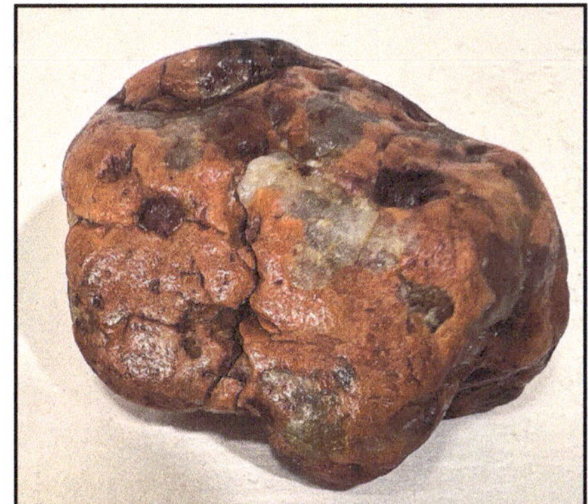

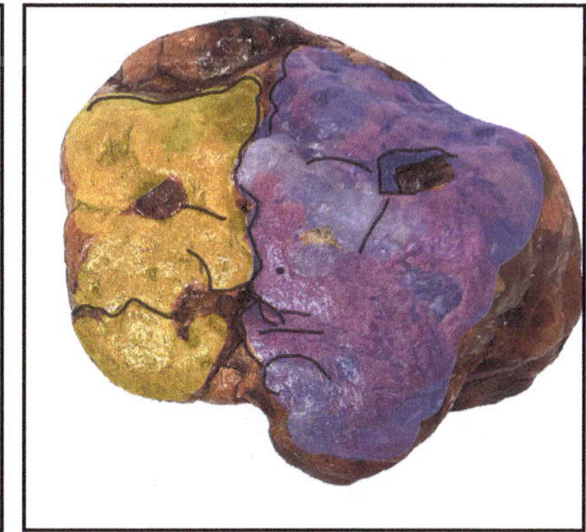

Holes, Indentations and Caverns

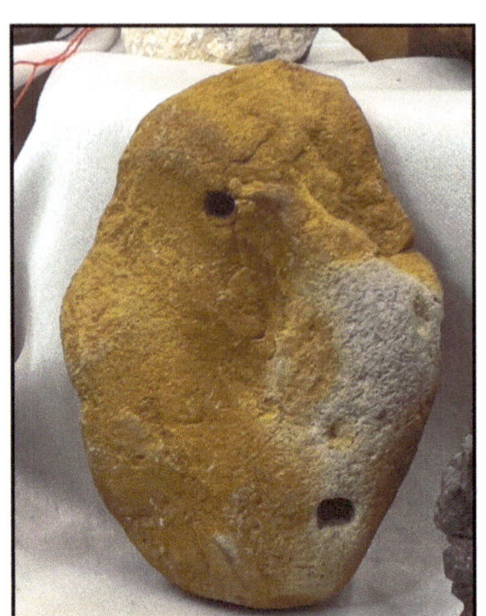

Figure 107: Colorado Artifact with Two Holes. The two holes are positioned to represent an eye and a mouth.

Holes and indented or depressed surfaces are regularly incorporated into PRA micro-sculptures and petroglyphs. The most common application of holes and indentations is as eye and/or mouth placements within head variants.

In many cases the Ancient artists created sculptures around natural and worked holes and indentations. Therefore, when looking for PRA enhancements, locating the eyes and mouth is perhaps the most significant identifier. In rarer cases, holes penetrate the entire stone. To see tiny penetrating holes, artifacts must be cleaned then held up to the light. Some are smooth enough and/or small enough to have been strung and hung around the neck, although this seems unlikely in most cases due to the weight and/or sharp edges.

The previously described Artifact IV, the Holey Stone, exemplifies the intricacies and artistic details found in the best PRA with holes and indentations. Especially in larger artifacts, the holes and indentations mimic caves and cave-like micro-environments adorned with etchings and micro-sculptures.

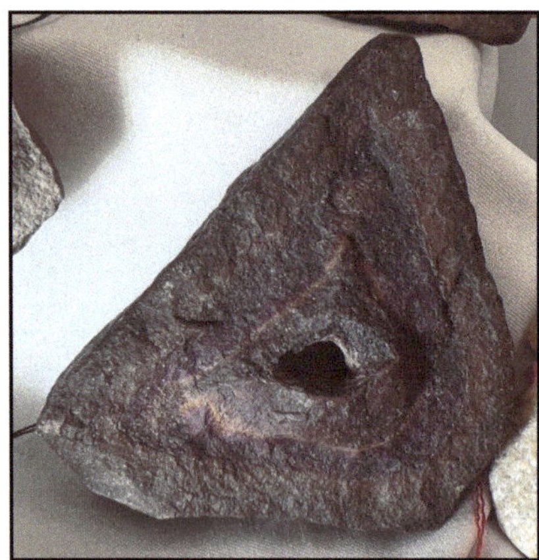

Figure 108: Triangular-shaped rock with a central hole.

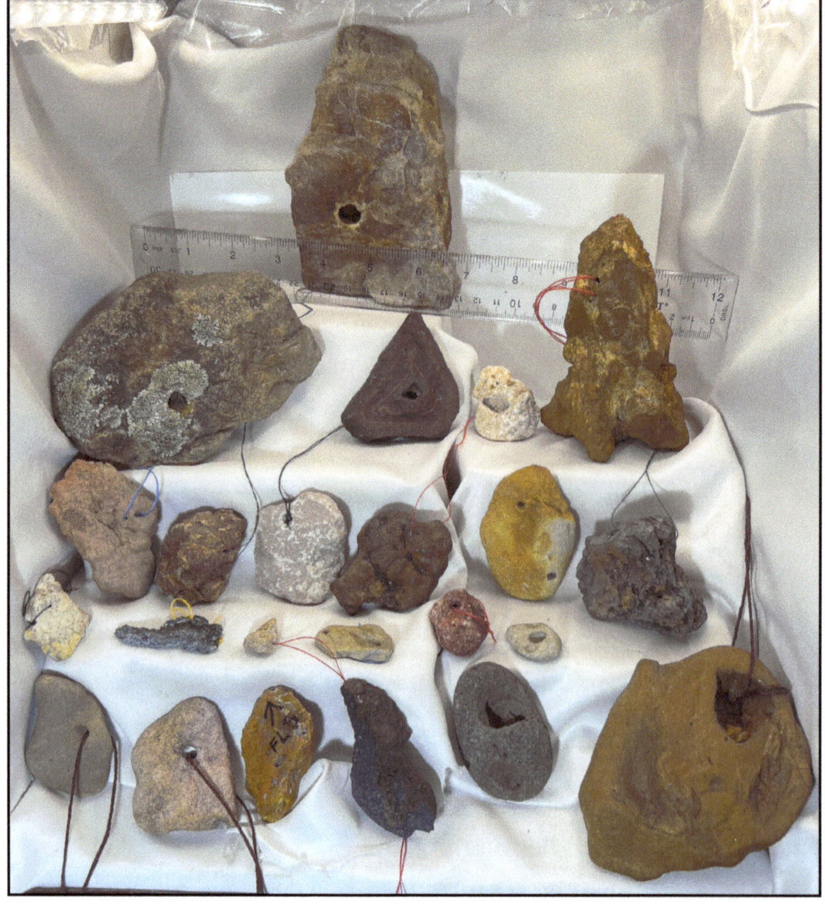

Figure 109: Collection of Artifacts with Holes. This collection includes PRA artifacts with holes that penetrate the entire stone, as indicated by string. In yet another example, Figure 36 (*page 31*) shows a knife with tiny holes that penetrate the artifact.

'Not This, Not That'

Artifact XII demonstrates the limitations of establishing fixed ideas of what a PRA artifact is. It was recovered fifteen feet below the surface at the bottom of a gravel pit in early 2020. At first appearance and taken as a whole, the two prominent features of the 4-inch long, 2.5-inch wide artifact are the hollow cavity and a reddish, smooth bird beak-like extrusion on each side. The hole descending into the chamber pervades the entire interior. The hollowed opening is 0.75-inch diameter, which widens to over an inch as it descends, mimicking a deep cave. Penetrating the hollow cavern on the backside is a pinhole, which is the placement of the eye or mouth position of a petroglyphic head variant.

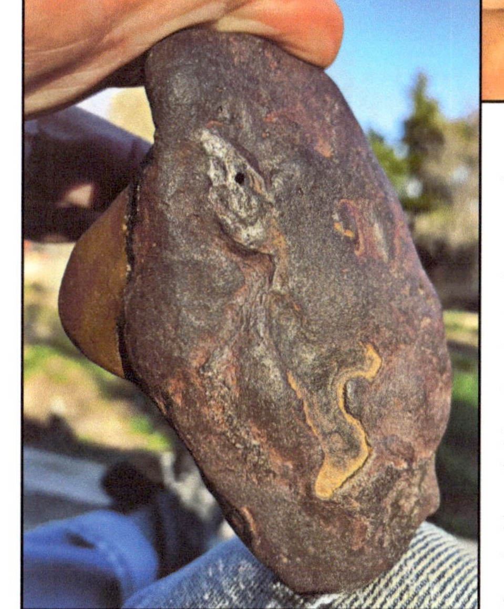

Figure 110: Artifact XII with prominent "beak" on two sides. A bird with rounded "beak" and a hole on top are recognized on the front. When positioned upright, the front bird imagery continues on the back including the "beak," in addition to a pinhole that penetrates into the inner chamber.

There are several petroglyphic features, including the head variant with the pinhole as the eye. This image looks like a Pointy-Head Guy when positioned vertically, but when turned 90 degrees counterclockwise, it appears as a serpent with serpentine-like lines connected to the head. When the cavity is filled with water and positioned horizontally, the "crying serpent" imagery appears (*Fig. 111*).

The connected serpentine line to the head variant reinforces the interpretation of a serpent. When positioned vertically the head variant resembles a crying human as water emerges from the pinhole.

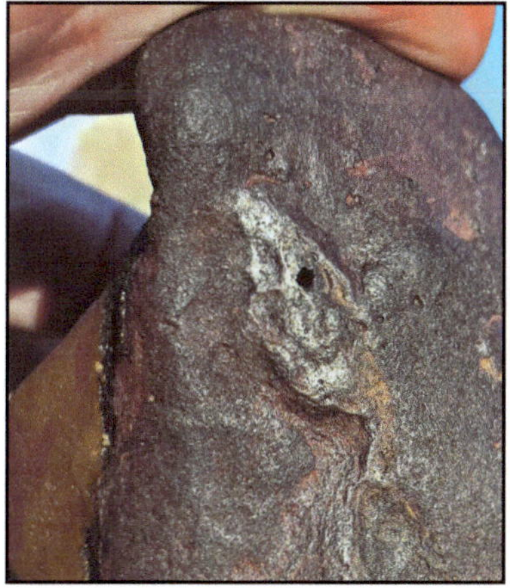

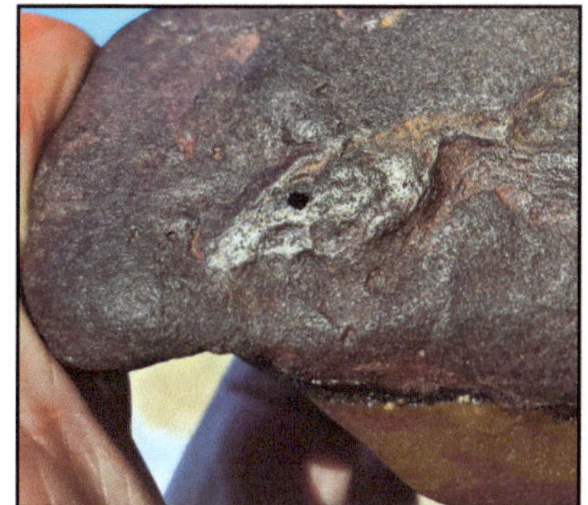

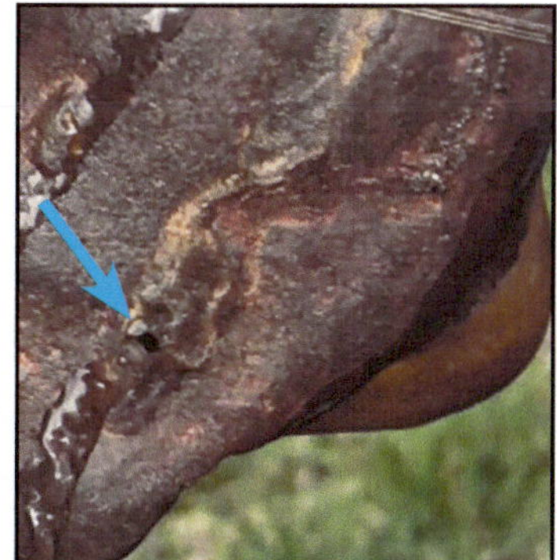

Figure 111: Artifact XII, pinhole details.

When one blows into the water-filled chamber, the oozing water from the pinhole becomes a pressurized squirt.

After removing the compacted sand-like material, small brushes and an electric toothbrush were used to remove the buildup of sediment in the interior. As a result of cleaning, several prospective petroglyphic features became discernable on the chamber's inner lip.

An unexpected feature of this artifact was discovered when blowing across the lips of the chamber-opening causing a high-pitched shrill. Thus, the other identifying name "the Whistle." Do we call this artifact a *bird? The Crying Serpent? The Whistle?* Whatever we choose to call it may limit what it is and what was intended.

'X' Marks the Spot

While the epigraphic aspects and meanings of the art may be speculative, there is at least one symbol found on many artifacts — *"X" marks the spot.*

"Xs" can appear in or around crafted eyes, and thus are valuable in identifying facial images. The "X" placement in an eye, cheek, or mouth can also help to validate a head variant and human workmanship.

The "X" symbol appears in many PRA artifacts and is apparently a

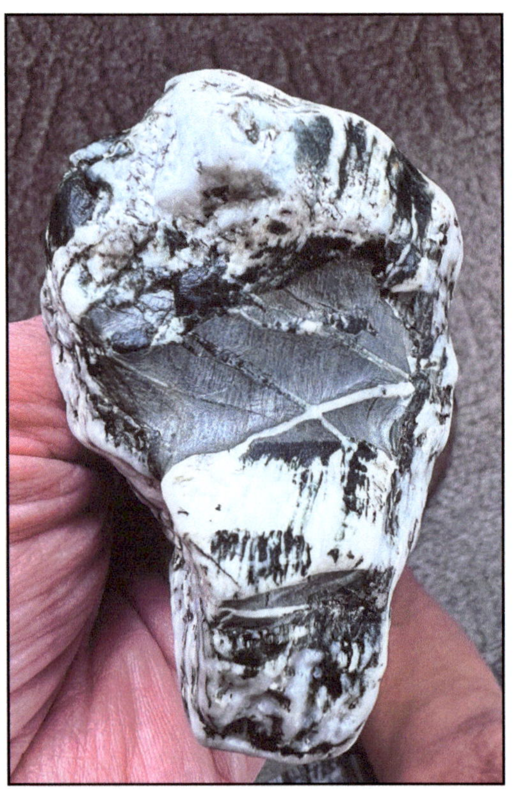

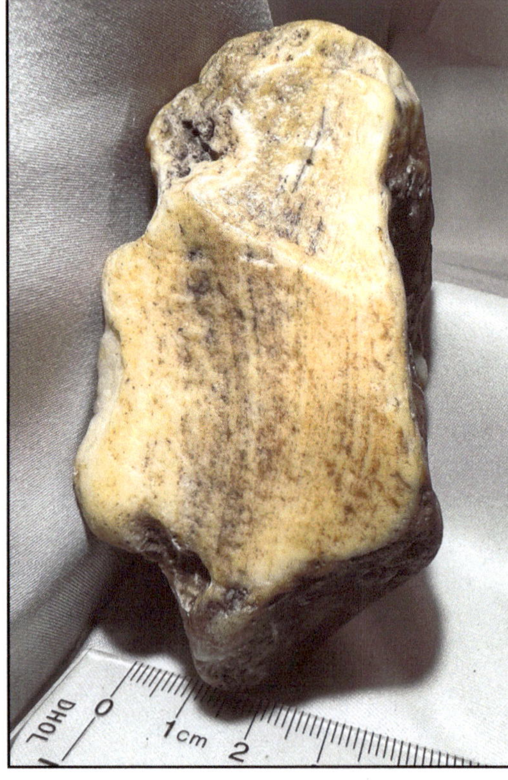

Figure 112: Artifacts with "X".

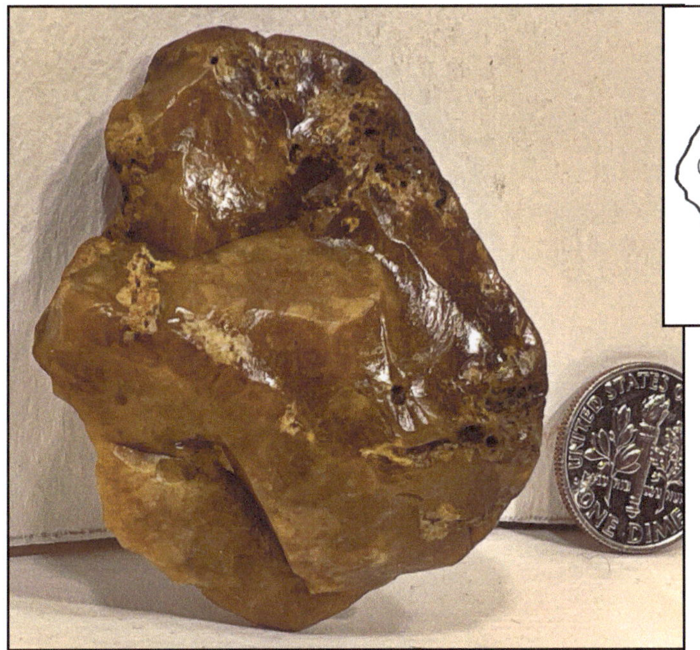

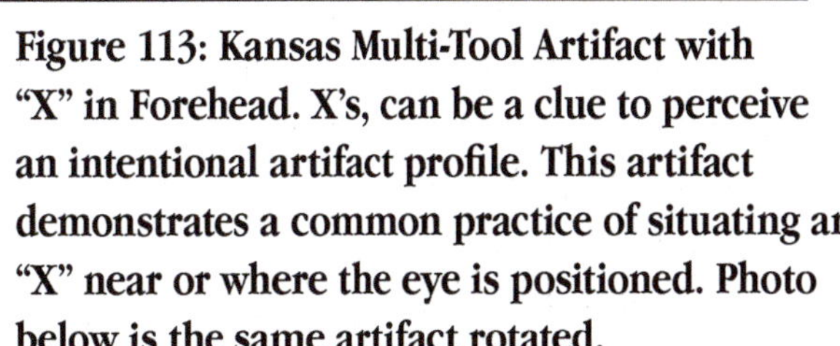

Figure 113: Kansas Multi-Tool Artifact with "X" in Forehead. X's, can be a clue to perceive an intentional artifact profile. This artifact demonstrates a common practice of situating an "X" near or where the eye is positioned. Photo below is the same artifact rotated.

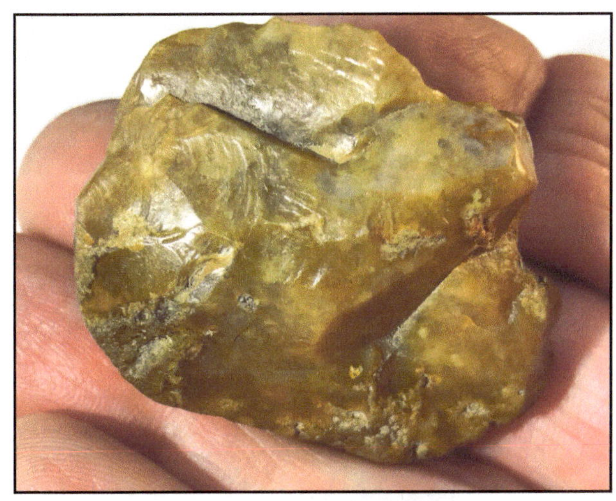

universal symbol. "X's" may be finely etched into the eye or other placements, and also may dominate the stone with larger sculpted "X's". However, not all "Xs" are carved and many configurations utilize natural lines and cracks that are "X"-shaped. Some "X's" are entirely natural, but nevertheless are integral to PRA features.

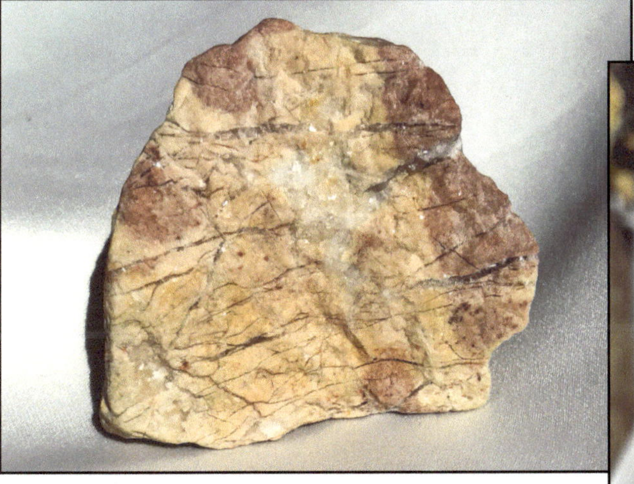

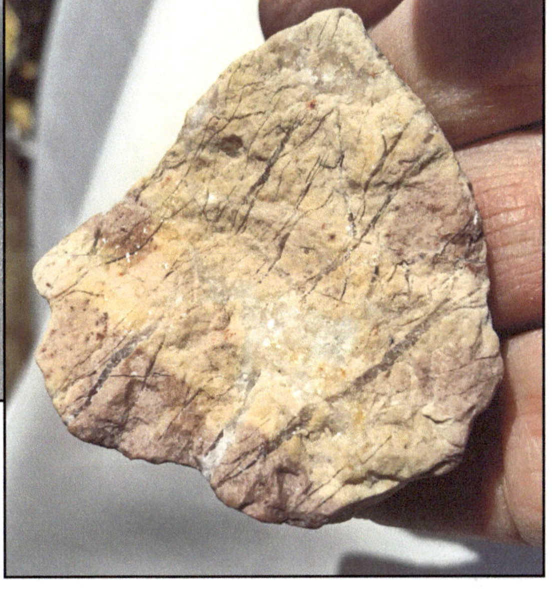

Figure 114: Artifact with Natural and Apparent Worked "X's". A 2 x 2-inch artifact with quartz crystal interior from the Colorado Front Range area. Natural and etched "X's" appear on both sides.

Bird Imagery

Among head variants and petroglyphic imagery, human and bird shapes dominate the PRA landscape in the author's view.

Practically speaking, the reasons birds appear so often is the shape of the beak, which could be employed as a tool. The different beak shapes allow one to suggest specific types of bird.

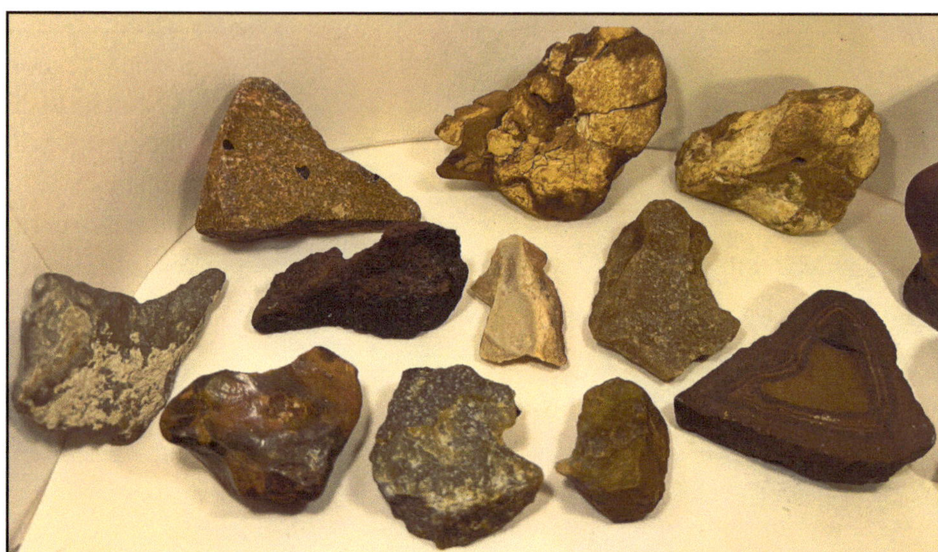

Figure 115: Collage of Bird-like PRA.

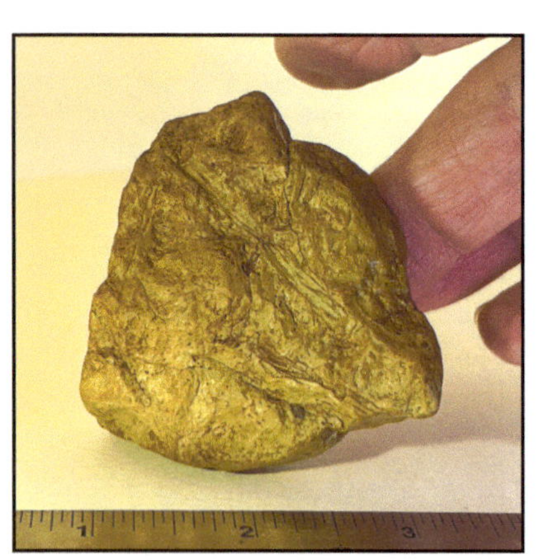

Over and beyond the utilitarian value of bird shaped PRA, birds held a special place in the cosmology of the Ancients. The Mayan vulture glyph cited in Figure 60 is indicative of the importance of bird motifs, specific shapes, and their multiple meanings within a specific cultural context. As it relates to Portable Rock Art, many researchers including Alan Day and Dr. Harrod, have noted the importance of birds in the mythology of Native Americas. Other collectors have examples of specific birds, based on the beak and head shape, attesting to the diversity of different types of birds represented in PRA.

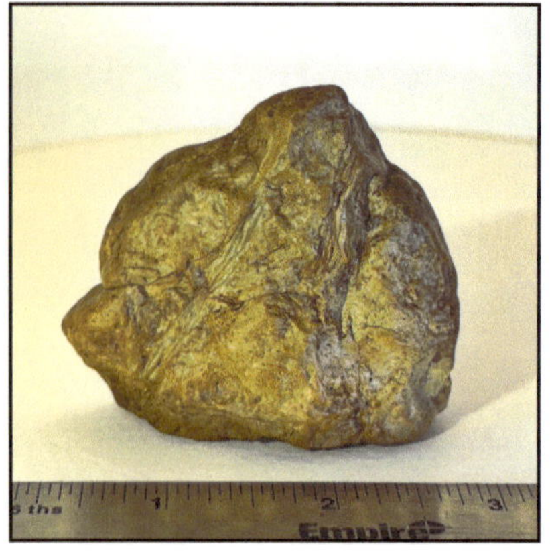

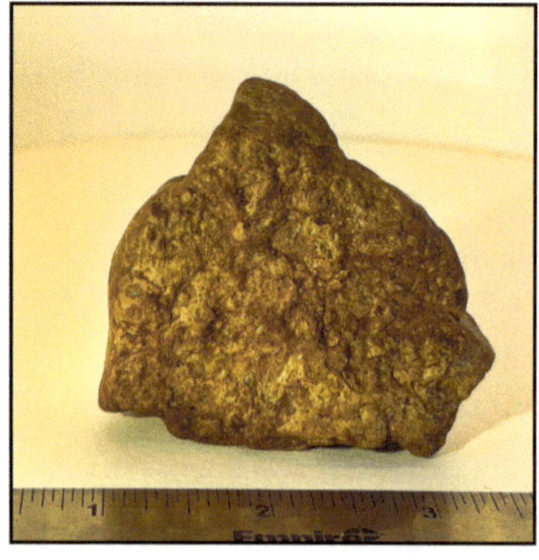

Figure 116: Artifact with Bird-Like Qualities, Kansas (Tim Banninger). This artifact from Kansas reveals well-shaped head variants. Photos above left and far left show the front side with right- and left-facing bird shapes. The near left photo, the backside, has a right-facing cat-like head with pointy top.

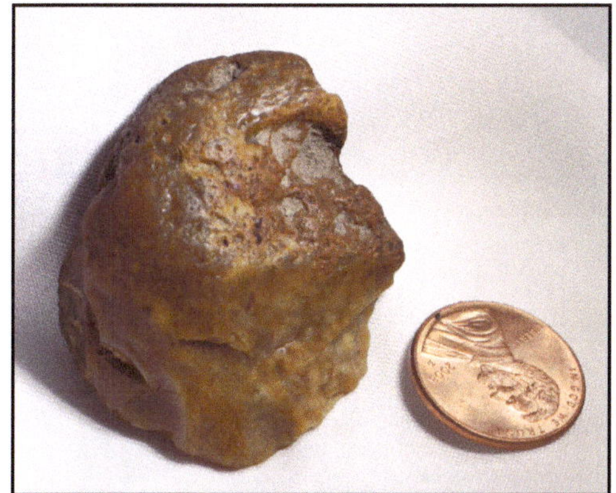

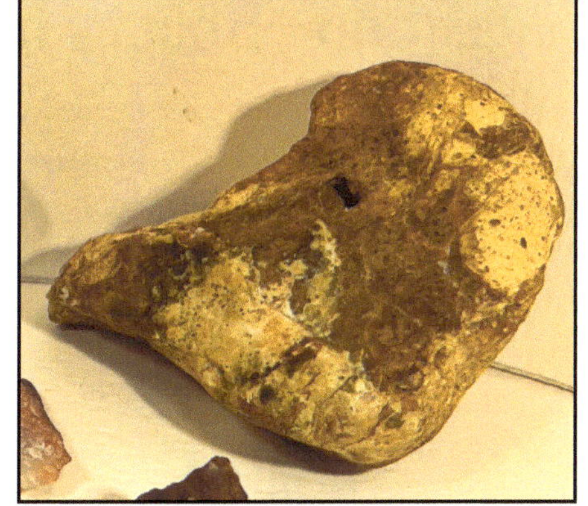

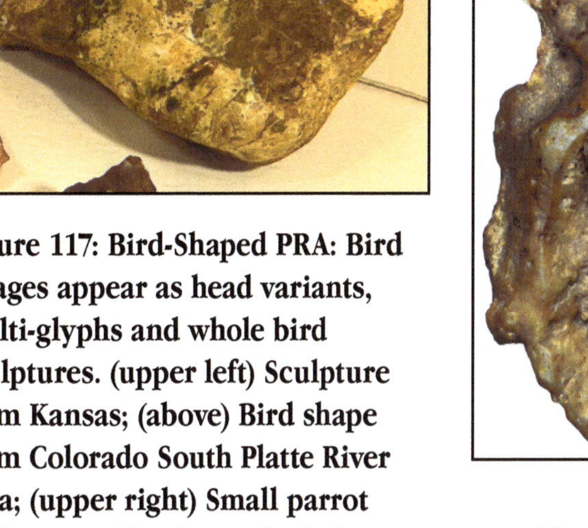

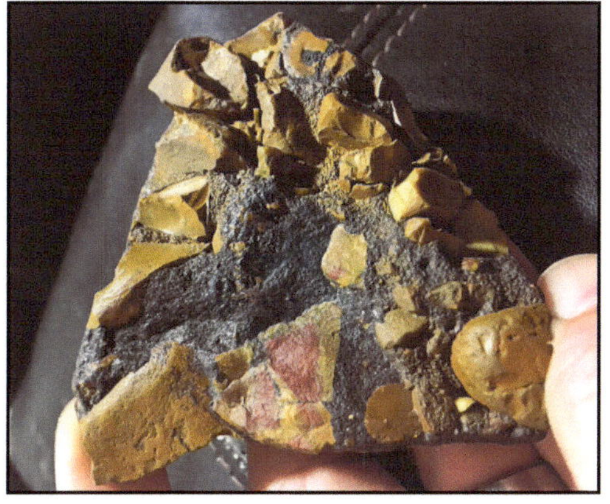

Figure 117: Bird-Shaped PRA: Bird images appear as head variants, multi-glyphs and whole bird sculptures. (upper left) Sculpture from Kansas; (above) Bird shape from Colorado South Platte River area; (upper right) Small parrot sculpture with a heart depicting a man on a blue-colored stone from Kansas; (left) Black vulture image in middle from Alabama (Jamie Collier).

PRA imagery includes an abundance of different types of animals, along with many variations of them. In addition to birds and specific types of birds, important PRA zoomorphs include mastadons, serpents, bears, cat-like animals, turtles and many more.

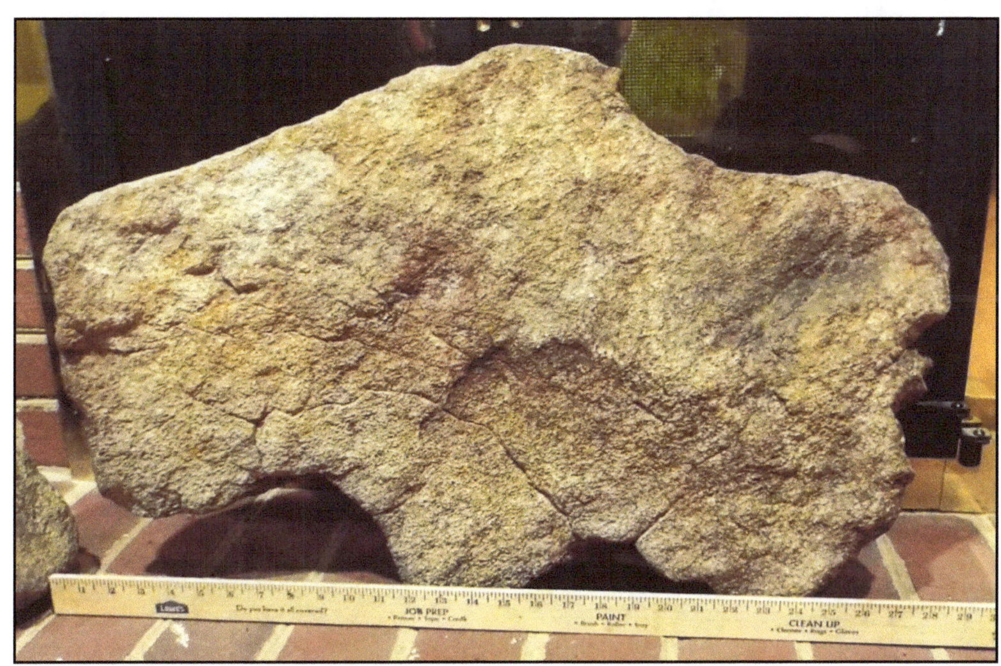

Figure 118: Bison PRA, Virginia (Alan O'Hara).

Mastodon Images in Stone

The American mastodon roamed the Americas beginning around 3.75 million years ago up until their extinction about 10,000 years ago. While mastodons resemble mammoths and elephants (all belonging to the order *Proboscidea*), mastodons are distinct and belong to the family *Mammutidae*, while the larger mammoths and elephants belong to the more recent *Elephantidae* family.

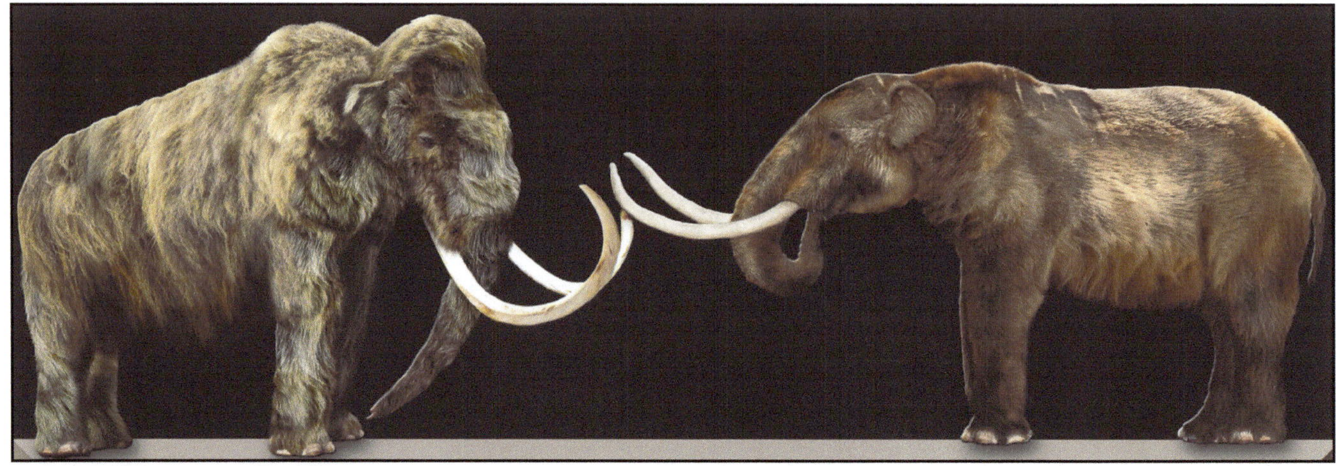

Figure 119A. A woolly mammoth (left) and an American mastodon (right) demonstrate their differences[63] (Wikipedia).

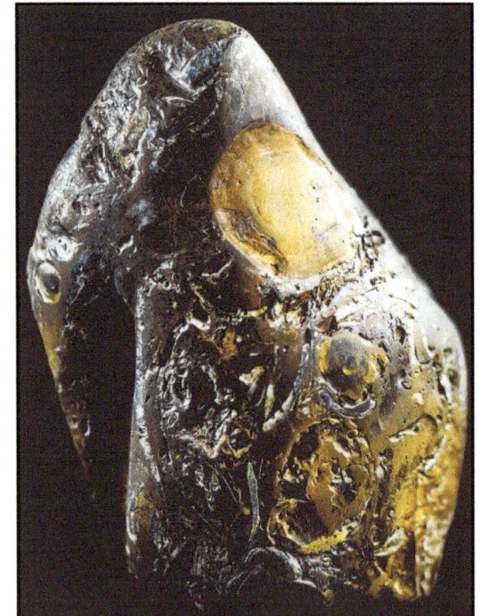

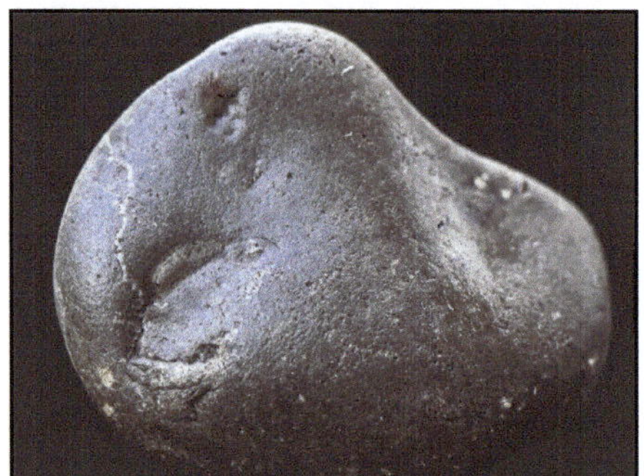

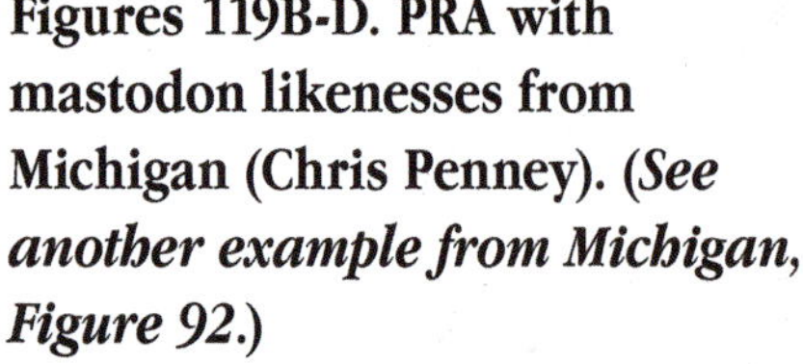

Figures 119B-D. PRA with mastodon likenesses from Michigan (Chris Penney). (*See another example from Michigan, Figure 92.*)

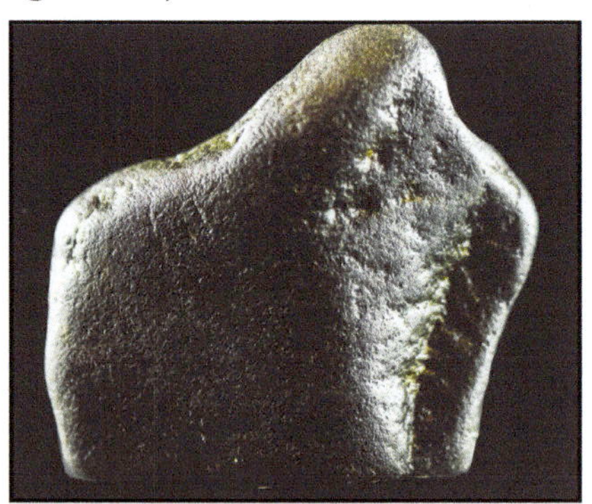

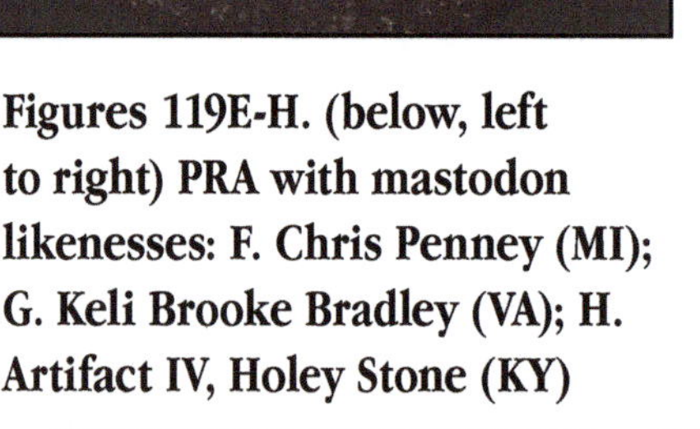

Figures 119E-H. (below, left to right) PRA with mastodon likenesses: F. Chris Penney (MI); G. Keli Brooke Bradley (VA); H. Artifact IV, Holey Stone (KY)

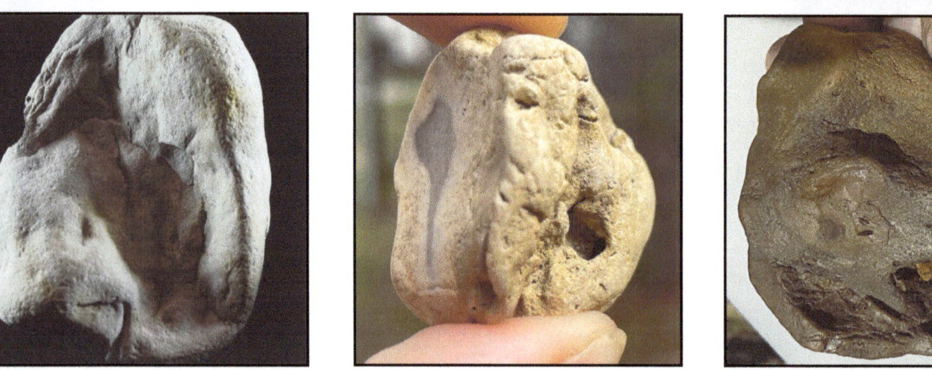

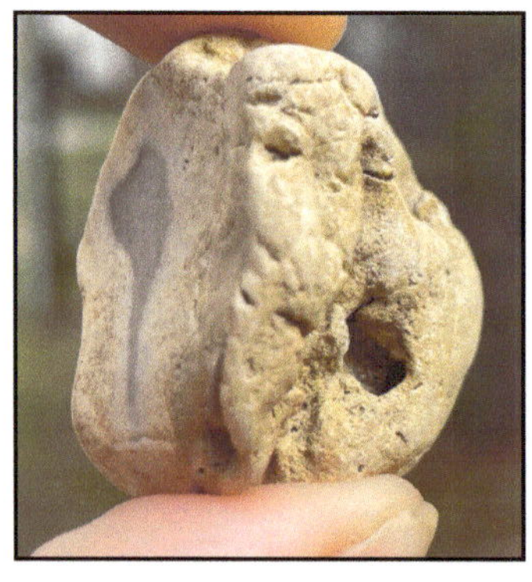

Crystals, Metal and Beads

While PRA is abundant, some types are rare, including paleo art created on crystals, metal and beads. Metal PRA objects can be found, especially along riverbanks. An avid collector from southern Colorado has amassed a significant PRA collection that includes pieces of metal. In one example, a natural pyrite cube extending from the stone, was integrated into a PRA head variant. Head variant sculptures created out of other types of metal have also been found in the Arkansas Valley. The author has also recovered a zinc serpent-shape object with eye holes, that is suitable for stringing.

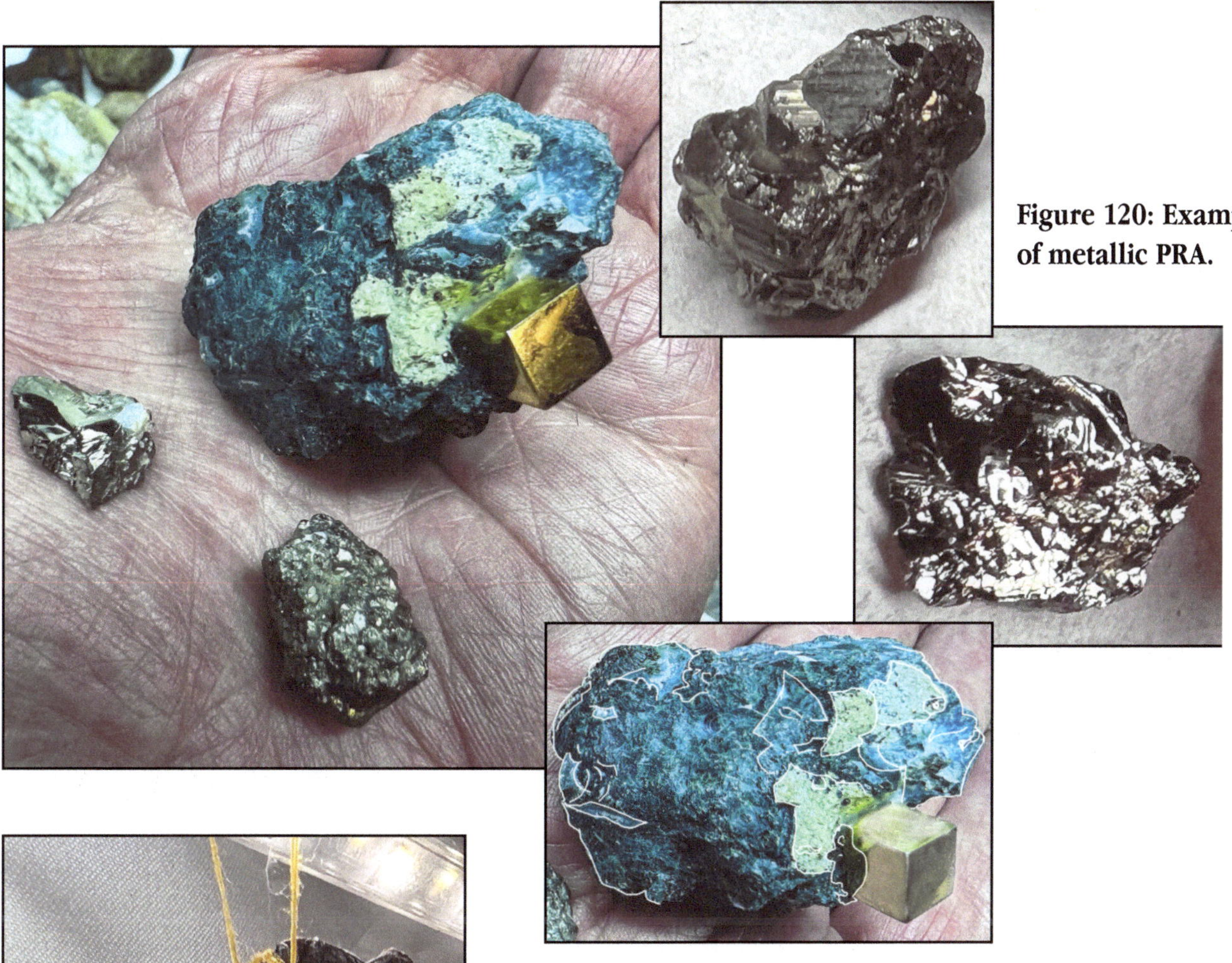

Figure 120: Examples of metallic PRA.

Figure 121: Metallic PRA recovered from rock fill bordering a residential street in Denver, Colorado, this object is probably made of zinc. Its serpentine shape is consistent on both sides. The tiny holes, discovered after cleaning and holding it to the light, are positioned above the divot that serves as an eye.

Volcanic glass and semi-precious stones were prized material to create PRA. The same Colorado collector has recovered examples of small, translucent, and transparent PRA from the Arkansas River Valley, Colorado with fine artistic details.

In addition to these examples of fine paleo creations, other rare and less obvious finds may include beads, worked crystal along with metal objects. These small creations can be easily overlooked when found in the field, caked in sediment.

Figure 122: Transparent, translucent PRA, Colorado.

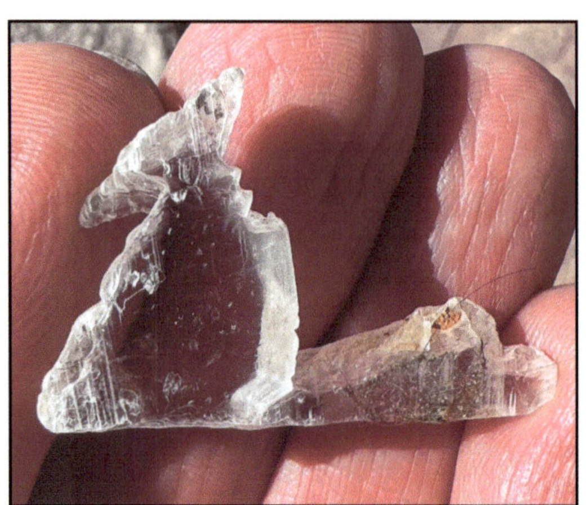

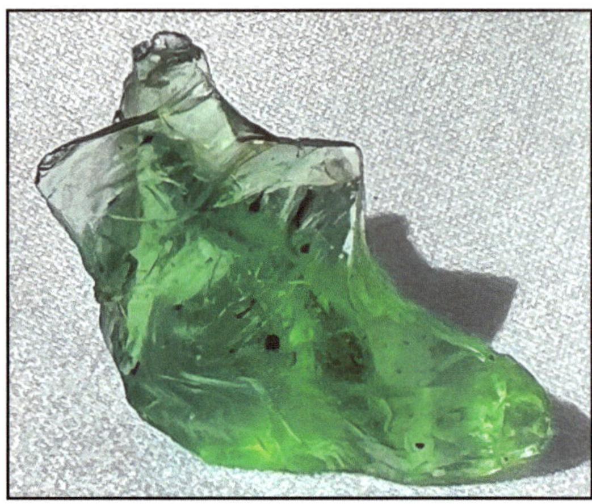

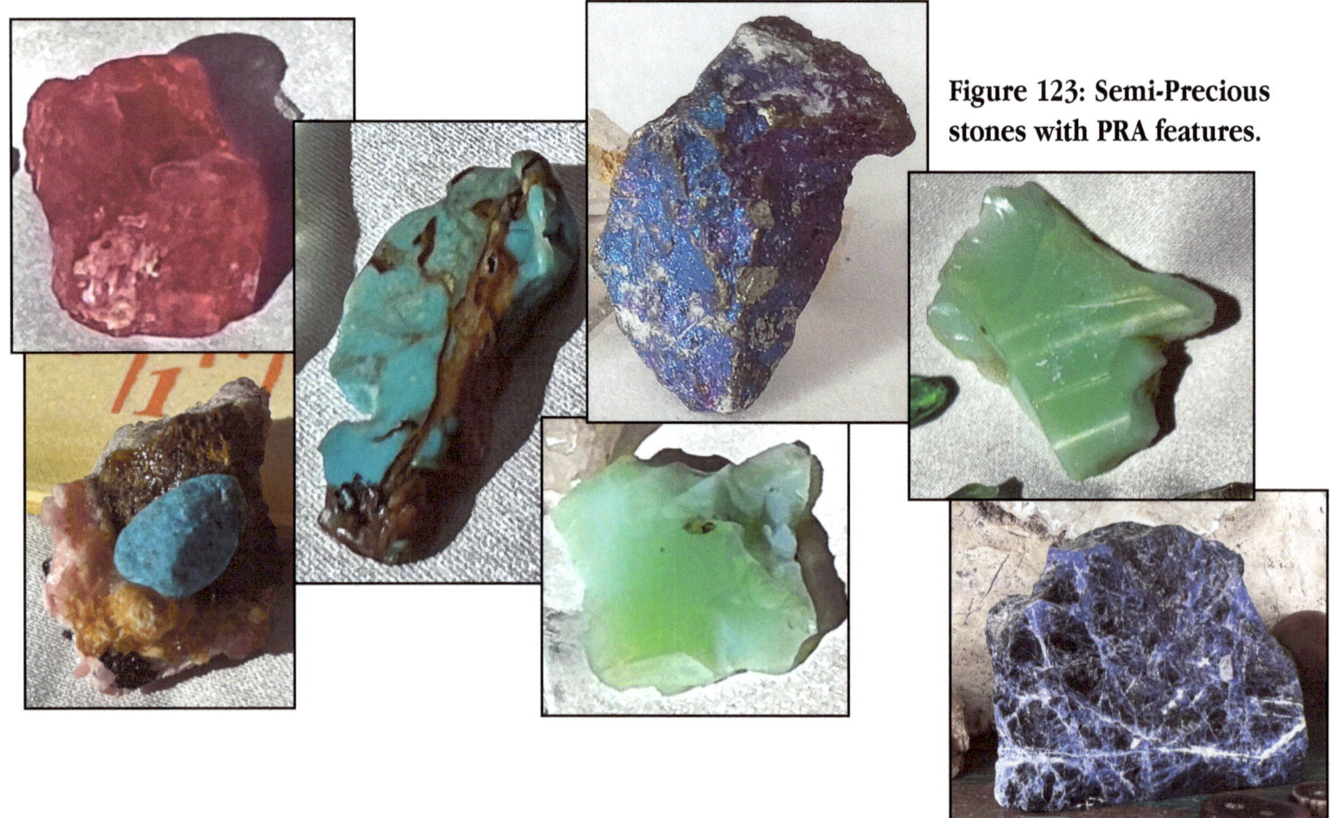

Figure 123: Semi-Precious stones with PRA features.

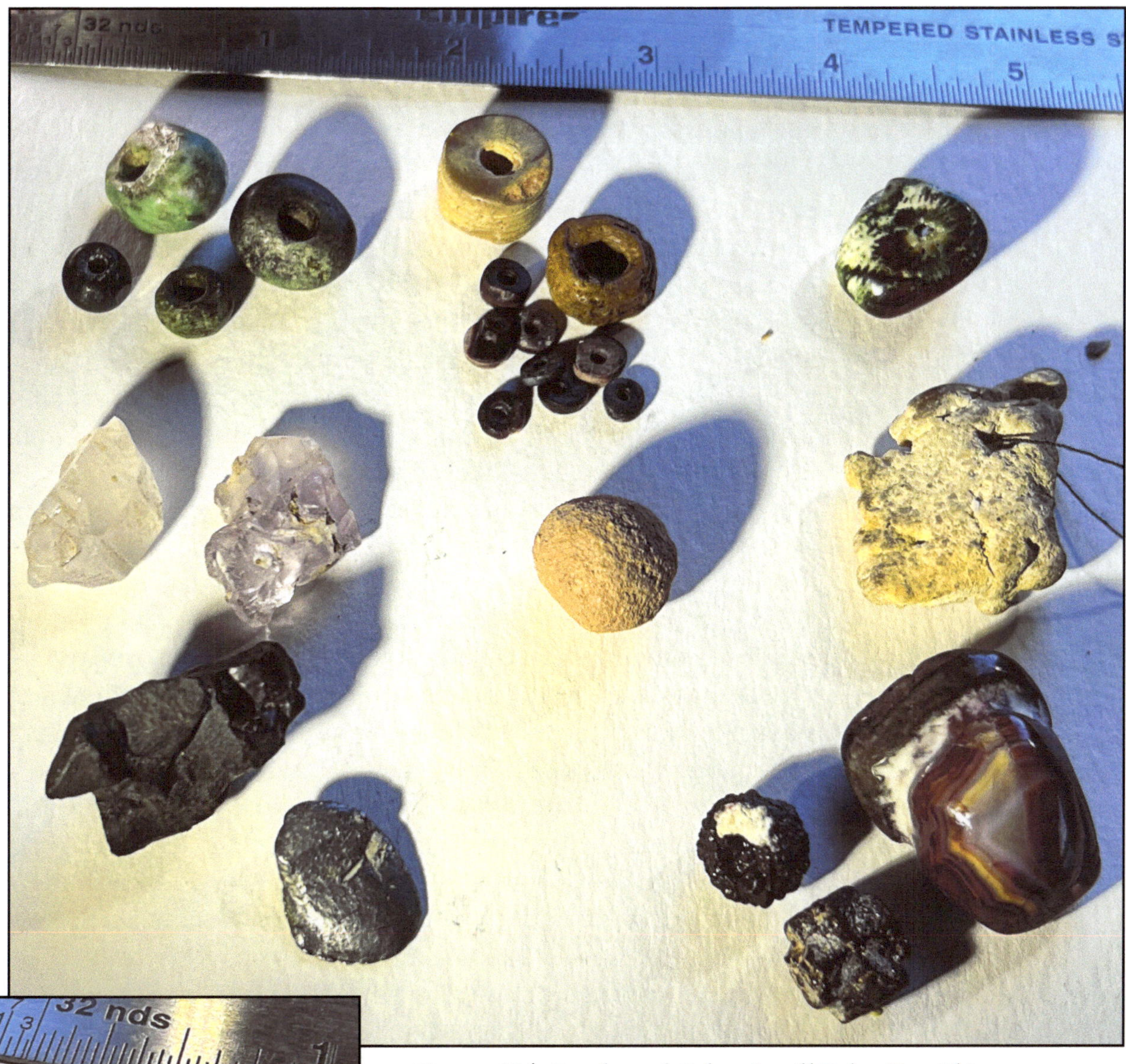

Figure 124: Beads and Other Small Paleo Era Objects. Top row contains three types of beads (left to right)—Mesoamerican jade; Beads from Kentucky; A bead from Colorado. Continuing clockwise from upper right—PRA with hole and string; Three decorative "pebbles" from Colorado; Two metal tools; Two carved crystals (one from Arkansas River Valley, Colorado, and the other from the Oklahoma Panhandle); Round stone in the center is a crafted marble from New Mexico.

Figure 125: Detail of Bead with Hole from upper right corner of above examples, Colorado.

Is There a Code?

Can we determine if PRA has a language or code? Do PRA artifacts head variants and sculptures have specific meanings as the previously described Mayan head variants?

Paleo rock art traditions have apparently all but disappeared, in part due to the conquest of indigenous peoples and destruction of native cultures. Yet, PRA artifacts remain along with the many mysteries they invoke. Once we begin to see what was intended, Moderns can begin to ask, "What do they mean?" A simple explanation is the images are just representational: a bird shape is a generic or specific representation of a bird and there is no code or language at all. Given the complexity of many PRA pieces, along with connected glyphs and sculptures, this seems unlikely in the author's view.

There are, of course, many other possibilities as to their meanings: remembrances of family and tribal members; a memento to accompany the dead; a guardian stone; an offering; a gift; a game tied to how many images could be identified; a commodity used in commerce; or simply a personal quest to create beautiful artwork.

Perhaps, as Frank Cushing suggests, like fetishes they are messengers and intermediaries between humans and Nature. As a result of the abundance of PRA, it is likely our Ancestors surrounded themselves with PRA, during life and after passing, to create sacred space.

For Moderns who think and see in established linear patterns, interpreting artifacts is fraught with challenges. These include multi-glyph imagery that defies a singular name or designation. Sometimes PRA imagery is so clear and pronounced that a consensus will clearly see the same image or series of images. For example, specific head variants that can be distinguished, like a distinguishable bird with pronounced beak. In other cases, there may be a lack of consensus of what an image could be or represent. With such an assortment of views, how are we to interpret what we see and what was intended, especially with faces-in-faces and moving 3-D imagery?

Grouping PRA by head variants and animal motifs found throughout a broad spectrum of locations can be useful in identifying generic and regionally shared characteristics. The author believes faces-in-faces and multi-glyph petroglyphs offer a beginning point to "reading" PRA. However, this assumes that we take PRA seriously and make the time and effort to find, properly clean and restore the best examples.

If there is a paleo code or language, it could involve how an individual head variant relates to: 1) the changing overall shape as the object moves; and 2) identifying specific head variants in a series, including faces-in-faces and totem-style images.

ARTIFACT XI: *A Pointy Head Guy*

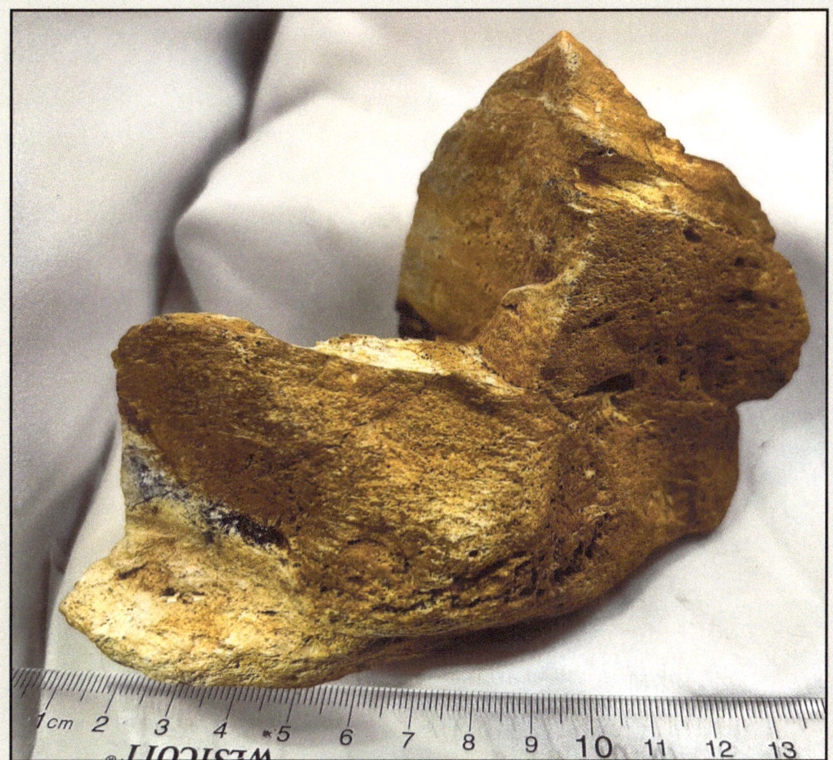

Figure 126: One of Many Views of Artfact XI. When viewed from another position, Artifact XI petroglyphic images become apparent. A series of different head variants could provide clues to an intended order or meaning.

Figure 127: Artifact XI PRA Features. The series of micro head variants within the upper left-side appendage offer the viewer a mosaic of discernible faces. The juxtaposition of offsetting dark and lighter layers adds yet another dimension to this 3-D creation. From this view (near right), a bird with beak profile sits on top; (far right) Details of upper section from a different view; (center) Author's drawing of petroglyphs. (*See Figures 99 and 100 on pages 78-79* for a different aspect of this incredible find retrieved from a gravel pit in Kentucky.)

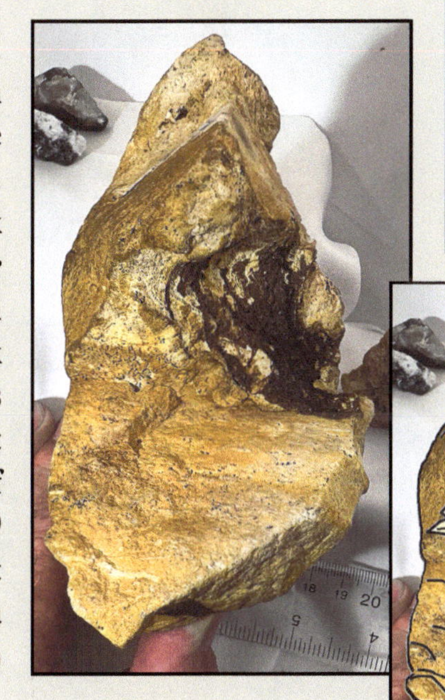

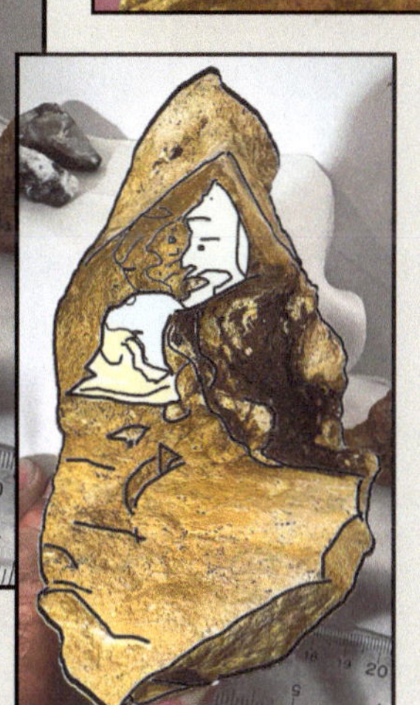

Rock art readers must be able to determine which side presents the main theme if there is such a thing? As previously noted, many artifacts have a base, some have many, but others have none. For those with an obvious base, this is perhaps the best starting point to finding a central artistic feature.

Artfact XI demonstrates the difficulty of finding any clear starting position to begin interpreting, storytelling or recognizing other-wordily symbology, as shown below. With so many perspective and different viewing positions, where do we begin?

Totem-style and horizontally connected images can provide clues on how to read the petroglyphic head variants and in what order, because like a totem pole, these glyphs may have a prearranged order to them. However, even though this may sound like a reasonable methodology, finding the starting position to determine any order of the images remains one of many challenges.

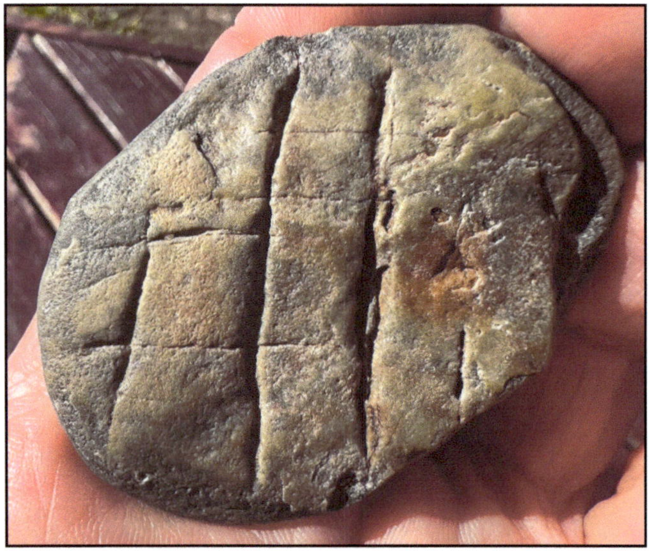

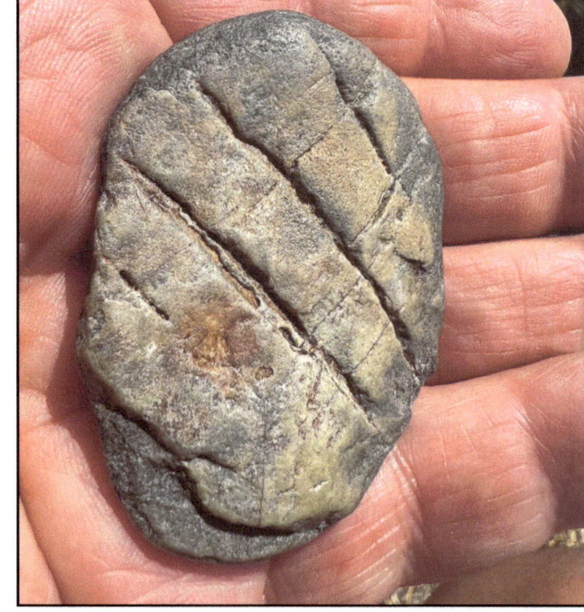

Figure 128: PRA Head Variant. (above) This flat two-inch diameter stone has natural-lookimg crosshatches, some containing apparent carved head variant details; (upper right) Left- facing head variant using the entire stone with cross hatches positioned in the upper head; (right) Detail of section with apparent head variants next to color overlays showing multiple faces and "faces-in-faces" images. While most of the highlighted head variants are left-facing, a right-facing image appears in green. The connected images and their order are potential clues to PRA interpretations.

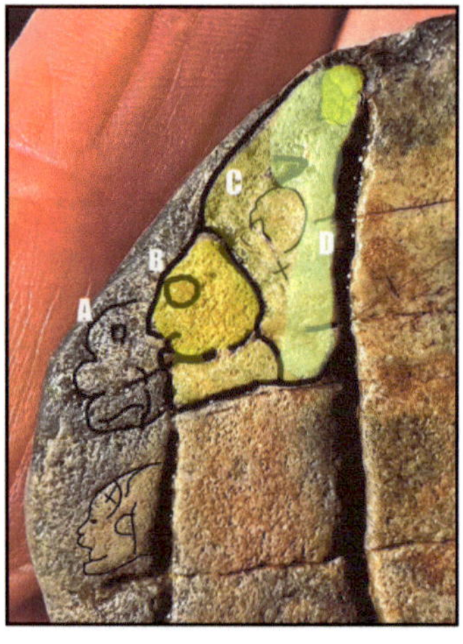

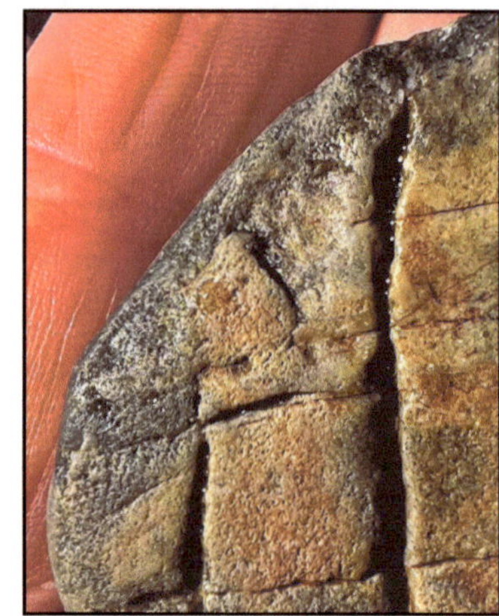

Paleo art examples like this and Artifact XI can offer opportunities to determine if there is a code or language. Even though much more restoration is required to actually to see all the workmanship, what can be seen offers insights on how one might approach "reading" an appendage or the images.

Ascribing a specific identity or meaning to specific paleo art configurations and motifs, except for an obvious image encompassing the whole stone, requires significantly more investigation before any such "language" or code is validated. Even so, Dr. James Harrod offers a

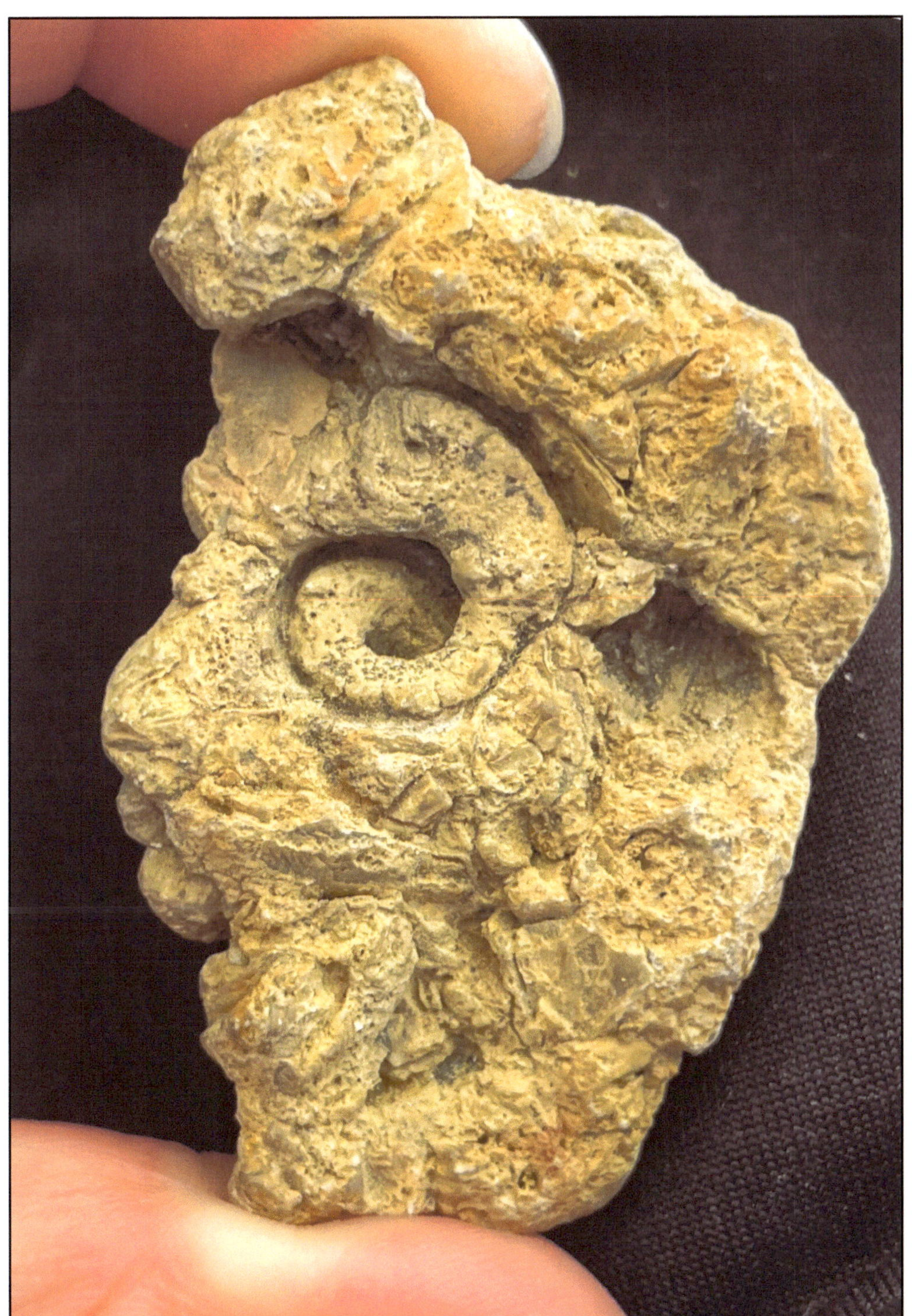

Figure 129: Beautifully carved head variant with detailed misculptures from Virginia (Kelly Brooke Bradley).

profound interpretation of some of the paleo art he has researched. In documenting paleo art from a clovis archaeological site in Montana, he identified portable art depictions that appear to represent "spiritual-ecological, mortuary and 'afterlife' beliefs." The research report, "Portable Art Sculptures from the Anzick Clovis Site, Wilsall, Montana," documents portable paleo art from a 13,000 year old clovis-era site, offering evidence of shamanistic practices of our Ancestors.[64]

Dr. Harrod has also proposed that the paleoart may have been integrated into shamanistic practices to help guide humans in our journeys between the upper and lower worlds. In this context, the animals represented in PRA are the spirit of the animal, here to assist humans navigate life's transitions.

Regarding interpretation of PRA imagery, we Moderns have a long ways to go to catch up to the Ancients. We can pick out the shapes and head variants if properly cleaned and positioned. But for most rock art enthusiasts, academics and collectors it would be wise to focus on restoring artifacts so the enhancements are recognizable and let them tell their own story.

PART VIII

A NEW WAY OF SEEING

A Universe Beyond Conventional Thinking

The implications of reviving this ancient paleo art platform known as Portable Rock Art can be profound, impacting human education and history, while providing new insights into art, anthropology and archaeology. The impediments to recognizing PRA artifacts can be overcome as we learn to use inherent mental pattern recognition capabilities and imagination to see paleo art and symbols. Once it becomes readily comprehensible, this dynamic viewing platform can begin to vanquish fixed patterns of perception as we awaken to the gifts of our Ancestor's creations.

While it may sound wild, the intimate physical and psychic connection with a rock is an opportunity to expand and arouse one's consciousness. In that moment while beholding PRA, Moderns can relate to the Ancestors and to Nature. This is not an abstract connection but something one can hold, touch and experience. An essential aspect of this alchemical process is being able to disengage from the present paradigm of "just a rock" to the greater awareness of being "part of our living world." In other words, understanding that we are part of Nature.

Learning to recognize artistic patterns disguised and hidden from view over a mellennia can advance slowly or instantaneously. Keeping an open mind to the possibilities of experiencing intentionally created art, among what appears to be common rocks, is the key to enhanced understanding.

Can this aha moment become a prelude to a new way of seeing, with PRA artifacts becoming a valuable tool for integrating the artistic and analytical minds as a means to advance human consciousness. Sounds farfetched, but. . . .

In his writings, Buckminster Fuller presented new ways of thinking that resulted in new ways of viewing the world. As this could relate to recognizing PRA, Fuller wrote:

> *Everything you've learned in school as "obvious" becomes less and less obvious as you begin to study the universe. For example, there are no solids in the universe. There's not even a suggestion of a solid. There are no absolute continuums. There are no surfaces. There are no straight lines.*[65]

PRA presents subject matter that requires the comprehensive thinking Fuller advocated. To see it, we need to rid ourselves of the "obvious" we've been taught, and instead become open to a new universe whose boundaries extend beyond conventional thinking.

A dynamic aspect of expanding one's consciousness is a newly realized relationship between Moderns and the Ancestors. Thus, the alchemy of transformation entails the dance of awakening the modern mind to the deeply rooted connections to our Ancestors imbued in paleo art.

Learning to See Again

In my archaeological travels I always wondered how the Ancients were able to navigate and return to the same location in the vast wildernesses of North America. I came to realize the familiar looking mountains and rock formations along the river valleys were markers that could be referred to as "Bear" mountain, "Eagle" mountain, "Elephant" hill, etc.

This realization came about after a fellow rock art reader bragged about seeing an "elephant petroglyph." As we were driving in southern New Mexico through a large valley created by surrounding mountains, I implored him to show me the elephant petroglyph. He laughed as he pointed toward a series of mountains in front of us and said, "It's right there, brother, can't you see it?" At first I didn't get it, because I imagined the petroglyph to be a carving on a rock. But I soon realized the mountains on the horizon resembled an elephant with a discernable trunk and ears. It wasn't that the Ancients carved the mountains, but resemblances were discernable and shared, like the Makapansgat Pebble previously mentioned in Part IV (*Fig. 49*).

Recognizing paleo art, including multi-glyphs and faces-in-faces imagery, will impact our understanding of fixed petroglyphs as well. An influence of PRA on archaeology may be anticipated in recognizing the 3-D platform at petroglyph locations.

I have often observed at petroglyphic rock art sites that large rock boulders and outcroppings that appear natural seem to be integrated into the petroglyphs themselves. With a fixation on the petroglyphs, the archeologists often miss the larger picture before them, which can encompass the surrounding rocks on which the images were made (*Fig. 129*).

Another example of the same phenomena can be observed at a Mojave Desert petroglyph site (*Fig. 130*). While great efforts have been made to interpret the inscription on the vertical rock panel, little observations have been made of the head variant sculptures that surround the inscription.

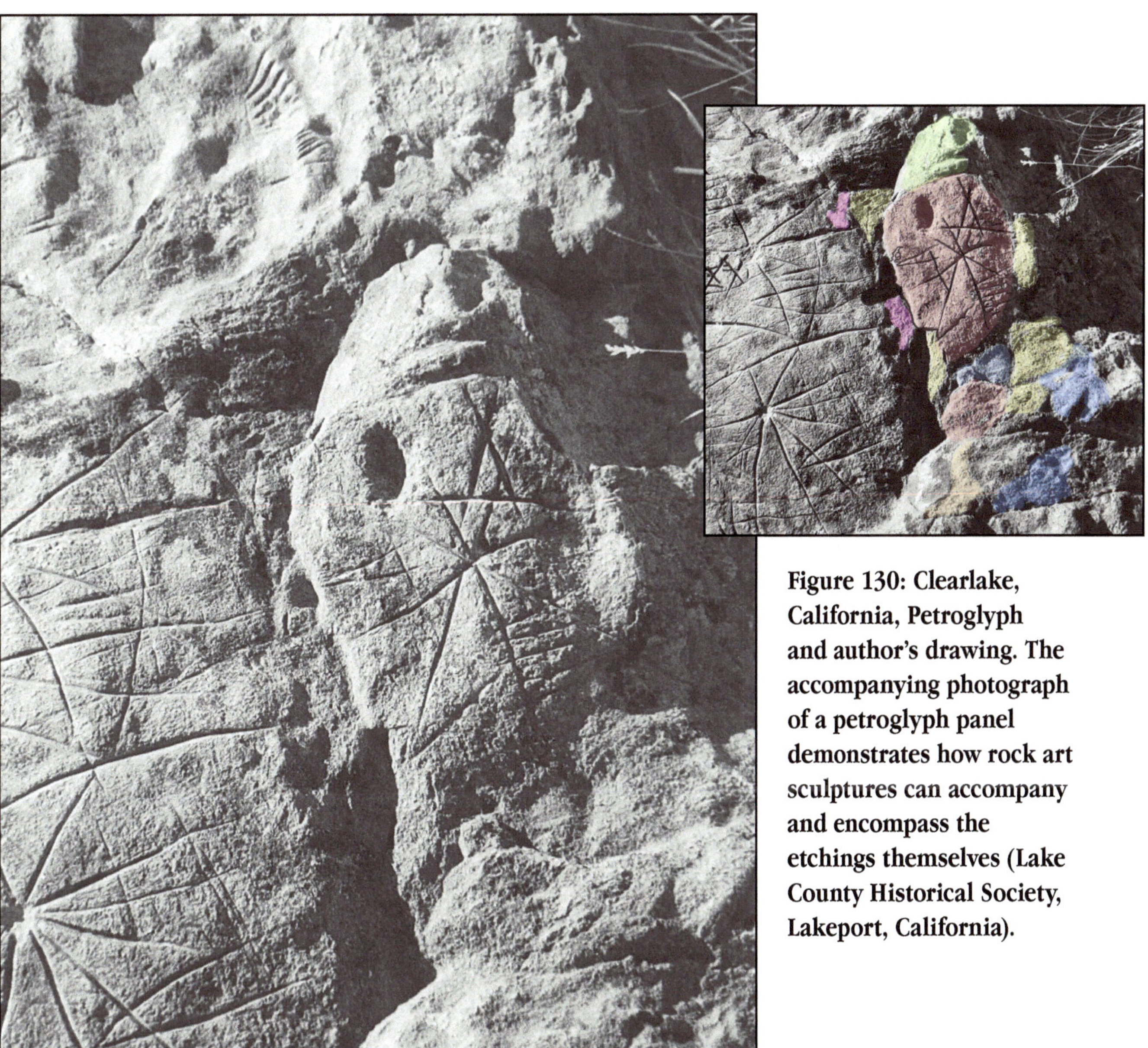

Figure 130: Clearlake, California, Petroglyph and author's drawing. The accompanying photograph of a petroglyph panel demonstrates how rock art sculptures can accompany and encompass the etchings themselves (Lake County Historical Society, Lakeport, California).

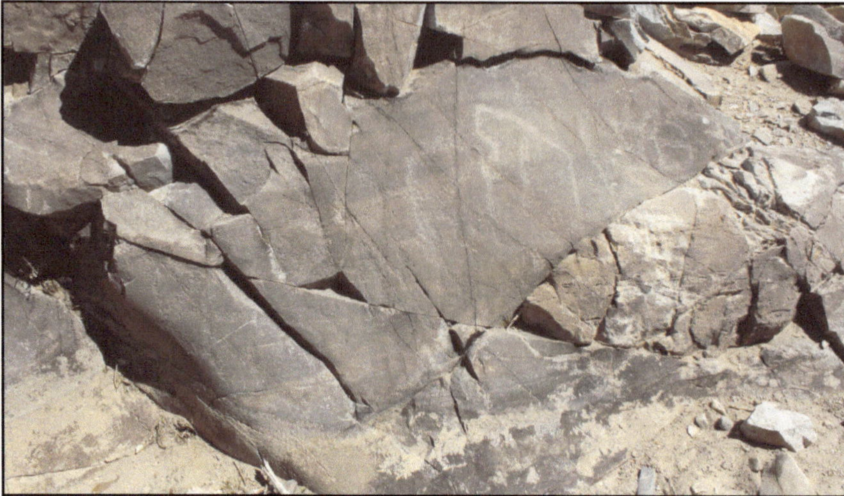

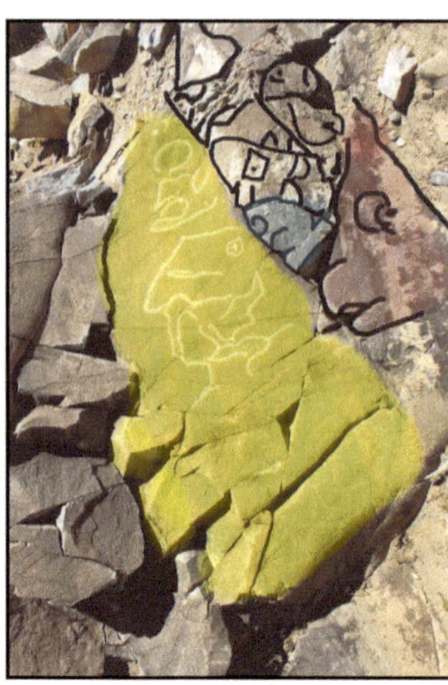

Figure 131: Rock Sculptures Among Petroglyphs, Mojave North. Above left is a vertical rock outcropping with petroglyphs. Looking straight on, some of the surrounding rock appendages resemble PRA caricatures. When rotated 90 degrees counterclockwise, the imagery begins to make sense, including a rendition (right) showing left-facing head variants.

In addition to the archaeological ramifications, the impact of discovering these paleo traditions can influence our idea of what "art" is. Moderns often revel at modern art, including contemporary art, cubism, and surrealism. Imagine Modern artists incorporating ancient paleo art techniques into their paintings and sculptures. As the PRA platform becomes more accepted, it can also impact architecture, urban design and landscaping.

Another significant implication of appreciating PRA will be our understanding of the ancient mindset. We may come to learn the reoccurring images over time and location represent more than "birds" or "humans" have specific characters, stories and meanings.

But before any of these innovations can transpire, we first must learn to see PRA and its dynamic viewing platform. Moderns need to look beyond the apparent, to the depth of human imagination outside the veils protecting a limited worldview. Perhaps with a new way of seeing, we can relearn our relationship to Nature, and understand that instead of being at war, we are one.

A Transformational Opportunity

There is always something new to see from a well-constructed and cleaned PRA artifact. Reconstructing what appears to be a simple rock into an artifact that expresses its creator's intent and abilities can be a time consuming, slow task, as anyone who spends time "brushing stones" knows. In the process, an alchemical transformation happens as the artifact reveals and the mind begins to comprehend a new view—not "just a rock."

Finding, cleaning, identifying and honoring PRA is a transformation process in which both the stone and the collector are changed.

This transformation begins with the recognition in the eye of the beholder, seeing the dynamic 3-D artistic platform and appreciating newly discovered and now comprehensible artistic achievements. This can involve an actual transformation of the brain itself, as it grows to integrate new artistic dimensions with newfound neural pathways, as one begins to see what was previously invisible.

Sometimes to see PRA, one has to conjure up that "marvelous state of ignorance," as Alan Watts encouraged.[66] Watts (1915-1973) was a brilliant British writer and lecturer best known for interpreting and popularizing eastern philosophy in the West. In his many lectures and writings, Watts admonished that our sometimes abstract and incomplete concepts of reality actually can disguise it, thus deluding the mind by confusing the world with our embedded concepts of the world. Rigid concepts of art and beauty need to evolve beyond the senses, he taught. Watts quotes Taoist master Lao Tzu suggesting, "Five colors make a man blind, five tones make a man deaf."

Beyond Human Suicide

While this book addresses PRA, the world today seems to care less as rocks and minerals are mostly viewed through the eyes of the extraction industries as resources for the taking. The devastating environmental effects of prioritizing money-making extraction businesses above protecting Nature are all around us. Meanwhile, solutions to the growing environmental destruction, loss of species, habitats and increasing human population remain elusive.

Can the rediscovery of PRA lead to a new state of being, inspiring individuals and transforming the human race?

Alan Watts and many others have suggested our modern-day conditioning measures nearly everything in terms of profit and material gain, blinding us to the devastating impacts of short-term material aspirations.

The human relationship with the mineral kingdom has built a destructive environmental legacy. The global extractive industries continue to pollute with reliance on old technologies with destructive impacts locally and globally. The rush to destroy the natural environment in pursuit of profit and wasteful consumption is unconscionable. We must challenge social conditioning and the modern paradigm that portrays human beings outside of and alienated from Nature, with a single-minded mission to exploit it.

There is a connection between the PRA legacy of our Ancestors and the ongoing destruction of the environment for short-term, commercial gain. In America, and throughout the world, indigenous, community and environmental organizations continue the battle to protect Mother Earth and rescue local economies from the extraction industries. In a short piece entitled "With Her: Women, Mother Earth, and Our Collective Humanity," Anrianna Quintero, an environmental and indigenous rights activist, chronicled this familiar story.

> *Driven by greed, polluting industries have exploited our planet with reckless abandon as if they were entitled and justified to carry out this destruction as business as usual. From the exploitation of native and even sacred lands (Bears Ears, Dakota Access Pipeline, Keystone Pipeline, to name a few), to the ongoing reckless extraction in the name of corporate profits, the list of offenders is long and the crimes span centuries. Drilling, mining, pillaging, raping, our misogynistic society has reduced our living,breathing Mother Earth to a faceless sea of resources ripe for the taking—robbing her of her dignity and sovereignty and harming us all.*[67]

To be fully aware in this perilous time, we must wake up to the violence our cultural behavior imposes on Spaceship Earth and learn respect for our mothers, daughters and Mother Earth. Both the individual and global awakening must continue to grow to overcome the many veils that blind us to a destructive and suicidal course.

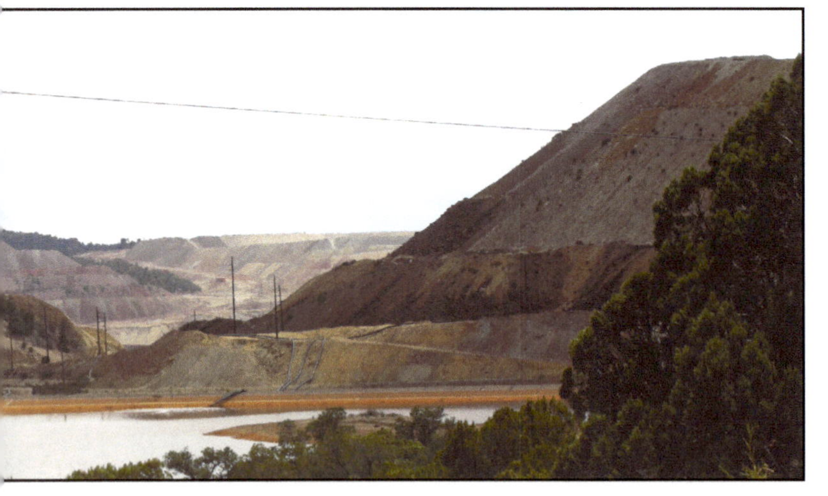

Figure 132: Open pit mining operations (above) continues to destroy the environment, as evidenced from this New Mexico copper mine.

There may be no simple way to awaken Moderns to comprehensive thinking and overcome limited dimensionality. Yet, if seen as a metaphor, the PRA phenomenon connects all of us to our past, and in the process of discovery offers an opportunity to heal the corrupted relationship between humans and the natural world.

PRA can accelerate expanding consciousness, guide us to explore other dimensions of perceptions and create new ways of relating to the Earth, our Ancestors and the future. This new way of seeing, stimulated by learning to see and appreciate our Ancestor's artistic creations, offers an opportunity to grow as individuals and as Humans.

Reconstructing the past and restoring ancient PRA will not solve human-created problems; but perhaps becoming aware of our legacy will contribute to greater reverence in a newly found heritage that is powerful enough to challenge the modern-day suicidal war on Nature.

APPENDIX

A BRIEF GUIDE TO PRA

Respect for Nature and the Ancestors

Respect embraces the awe and the acknowledgement that Portable Rock Art (PRA) connects us with the Ancients and the Earth. The transformation of a rock into an artifact reveals the mysteries imbued by the Ancients. As we begin to understand the significance of these newly appreciated millennia-old artifacts, the important work of rock art collectors and rock art readers is to restore the grandeur of this lost ancient art. Finding, cleaning and honoring PRA is an act of restoration and transformation that reinforces the connection to our Ancestors while expanding our understanding of a shared but elusive history.

Once identified, it is strongly encouraged to approach PRA with a deep sense of reverence, along with the passion and feelings of connection to the Ancestors. Some PRA artifacts are unique, mind-bending creations, while most appear crudely fashioned, yet with something profound to convey. Become open to a new way of being and seeing, based on receptivity to extraordinary experiences.

By restoring the past, there is a connection to the future. As humanity learns to appreciate paleo artistic creations, even as common as PRA artifacts may be, they are destined to be inherited by future generations as part of a common heritage.

Complex and Not So Simple

With most observers, PRA is anything but simple to visualize much less easy to understand. Once identified as an artifact distinguishable from a natural stone, the 3-D artistic platform requires imagination to

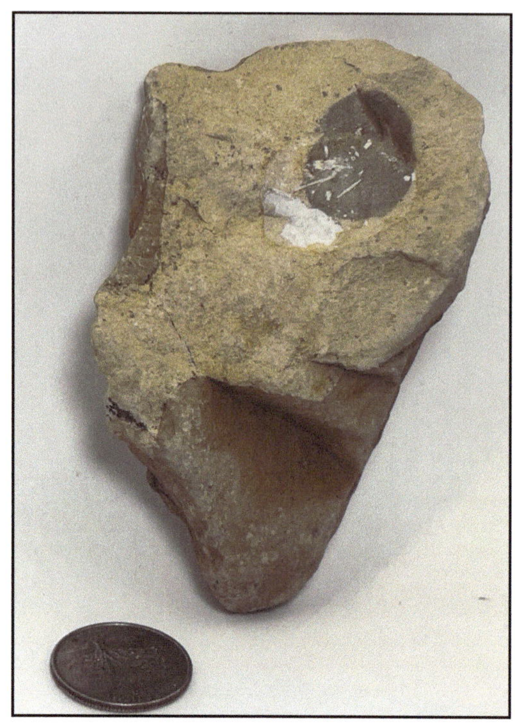

Figure 133: Single Eye Serves Two Head Variants. The dark circle serves as an eye for right- and left-facing head variants in this Platte River Valley, Colorado, artifact.

recognize a specific appearance or feature. Some of these enhancements were created out of simulacra features, integrating natural rock appearances with human crafted elements— a fine line of distinction. Imagination, as a subjective mental construct, will not necessarily validate human workmanship, an intentionally made image or conclusively determine that it is not pareidolia. Thus, it will take more than imagination to validate PRA.

Artistic characteristics include whole stone likenesses, which change when rotated in the hand under varying lighting conditions. Part of demystifying artifacts is to hold and move them with proper side lighting. It is a process of discovery. The challenge is being able to identify a singular and/or interconnected multiple images. In some cases, a single eye will serve as the eye for different but connected head variants (*Fig. 133*).

As one studies paleo art, the intricate details become more evident. These details can be just as profound on larger artifacts as on smaller stones measuring an inch in diameter or less. The ability of Ancient craftsmen to sculpt imagery relied on four dimensions: width, length, height and turning the object to view different positions. In this regard PRA is akin to holding a rotating hologram with multiple sides visible to the viewer.

Seeking, Finding and Recognizing PRA

When prospective PRA objects are found disguised by millennia of dirt, mud, and patina among thousands of similar looking rocks, how does one find and identify artifacts? The answer: become familiar with common PRA shapes and head variants.

Most PRA collectors have a moment of discovery that begins a journey. Part of the drive to collect is to learn more, while traversing the edge of a rediscovered archaeological paradigm. Collectors are surprised by the lack of attention paid to PRA by the archaeological and scientific institutions yet continue their quest to bring to light this barely recognized phenomenon.

Identifying imagery using the whole stone is a first step. To orient oneself, identify any head variant shapes using the whole stone and then look for eye/mouth/nose/chin/beak configurations. Rotating the object to determine if there are other head variants and animal shapes made out of the entire stone often yields unexpected results.

When observed in the field, holes and indentations usually are covered with residue, making the artifact appear to have flat surfaces. These depressions, holes and uneven surfaces may only be visible after a thorough cleaning. The same is true of what appear to be sharp edges, which can become more rounded and sculpted when cleaned.

PRA integrates abnormalities and special attributes, including shapes, natural patterns, layers, and colors, which may distinguish it from surrounding rocks. Watch for tool functions, including sharp points and somewhat beveled edges for scrapping or cutting. Tools will fit naturally in one's hand or fingers, often rotated in several positions. In addition to the overall shape, the most common identifier of a PRA artifact is the eye placement. These may be natural or worked areas central to any head variant.

When looking at hundreds, sometimes thousands of rocks, it's important to watch for special and attractive features in addition to the overall shape. These include reflective surfaces (like mica) that "wink" with the changing light position. Other special features are placements of grooves and holes; beaks/noses/pointed extensions that predominately extend outward; and at least one flat surface functioning as a base allowing the stone to rest naturally.

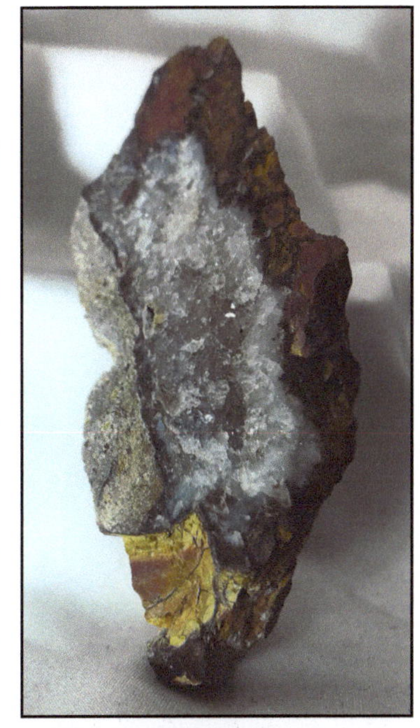

Handheld paleo creations were made from practically any type of rock, including granite, quartz, sandstone, dolomite, petrified wood, basalt, jasper and in rare cases soft metals like copper. Prized pieces include those with surfaces/facets with detailed sculptures and etchings; translucent qualities, especially quartz; clearly identifiable micro-sculptures; and "X"s usually found in or below the eye. Where mica-laced stones were in abundance, artistic enhancement emphasized natural layers of glitter.

Sometimes the quality of a stone is so extraordinary with dynamic and contrasting colors, shapes and contortions they reach out to you, as they did to the Ancients. Artistic features, including head variant designs, are often identifiable in crystalline structures, most notably quartz embedded in multi-mineral PRA.

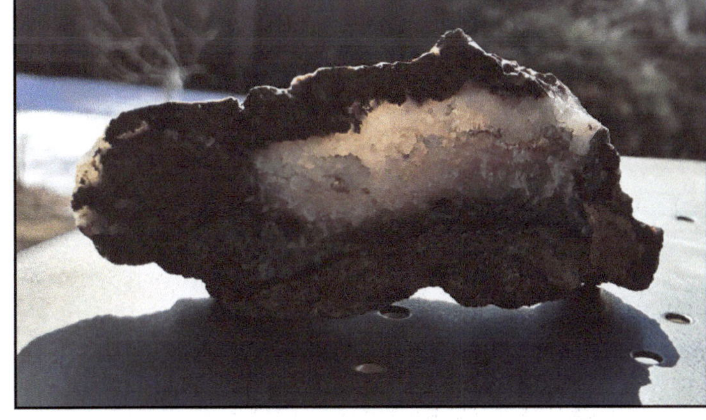

Figure 134: Quartz Embedded in a Multi-Mineral Artifact. The stone knife from Arizona is a multi-mineral artifact with sharpened edges and fits well in one's hand. It has functionality as a scraper or potentially a cutting implement. This specimen hosts a quartz center that has translucent qualities, something to look for with crystalline artifacts (Carrie Bell).

As noted throughout this book, positioning is key when looking into the PRA realm. When possible, hold the stone in one's hand and look for profiles and/or sculptures resembling a human, bird or animal utilizing the entire rock. Rotate to view the different angles where the overall shape and any facets, layers, grooves, holes, extrusions, or edges resemble part or all of an image. Experiment with identifying base(s) where the stone rests naturally—many do not have a base, while others have multiple bases. Be especially mindful of how edges, holes and indented/depressed surfaces may have their own enhancements including micro-sculptures and petroglyphs.

Where to Look

Artifacts, large and small, are widely distributed and can be found both in Nature and urban environments. An abundance of PRA remain on the surface, indistinguishable from common rocks to the untrained eye.

As a general rule, wherever the Ancients dwelled PRA is to be discovered. This includes on the surface in dry, wind-swept, arid climates; along river and creek banks; in open fields; and on dirt roads and trails. A significant reservoir of undiscovered PRA objects lay below the surface, often in concentrated caches. Researchers have collected significant quantities of PRA twelve to fifteen feet below the surface at a gravel extraction operation in Kentucky and at other locations.

A cache of artifacts was found within a perimeter of several square yards at the intersection of two dirt roads in rural Kansas. Other collectors have reported similar finds both above and below the ground. PRA artifacts are also readily seen in regularly plowed agricultural fields, especially after a rain. It is not uncommon to spot an artifact in the rows of gravel and small rocks along the sides that make up the edges of rural highways. Stone fill in gardens and commercial properties in urban environments may contain PRA when the stones originate from layers of sand, dirt and gravel extracted from river beds and banks, as is common throughout much of the country.

Stone and gravel fill come in two main types: (1) natural, screened and washed stones transported to wholesale gravel bunkers/piles and (2) crushed stone.

Crushed stones are reduced to a common size and look, which destroys any art and sculpted shapes of the original stones. Accordingly, do not expect to find PRA in crushed gravel, although you are sure to find many resemblances. If authentic they will have a dirty appearance, contrasted with more newly crushed stone exhibiting a

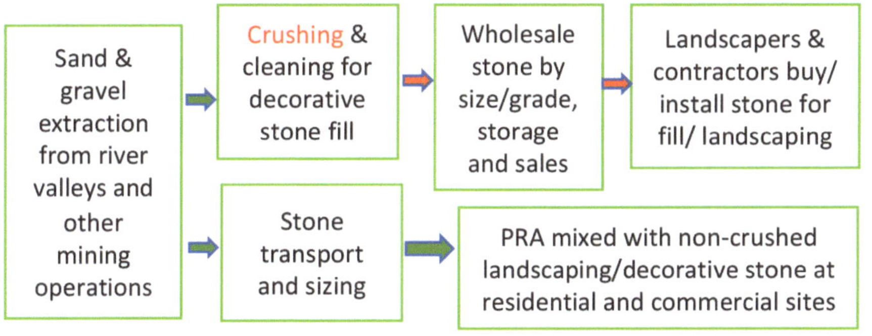

Figure 135: PRA Pathway Diagram: Mining to residential and commercial properties. (PRA pathways indicated by green arrow.)

cleaner, shinier appearance with sharp edges. Another tip off of a pareidolia look-alike is found among similar stones in concentrations. However, a PRA prospect made of quartz dispersed among different rocks exhibiting a dull patina is a likely candidate.

When homes, municipal and commercial properties are decorated with small stone fill, PRA may be present. When present, worked pieces of stones are most often encrusted with age-old residue and blend into the surrounding rocks. Therefore, to find them, look for the basic shapes and anomalies including color or type of stone, presence of glitter and out of place features.

A walk down a dirt road in a small New Mexico township, yielded remarkable finds. The regular monsoon rains clean the top surfaces of rock allowing worked artifacts to become readily visible. Similarly, unpaved rural roads and driveways in rural America, may have PRA embedded in the exposed dirt.

The author has found PRA artifacts in gardens, driveways and in

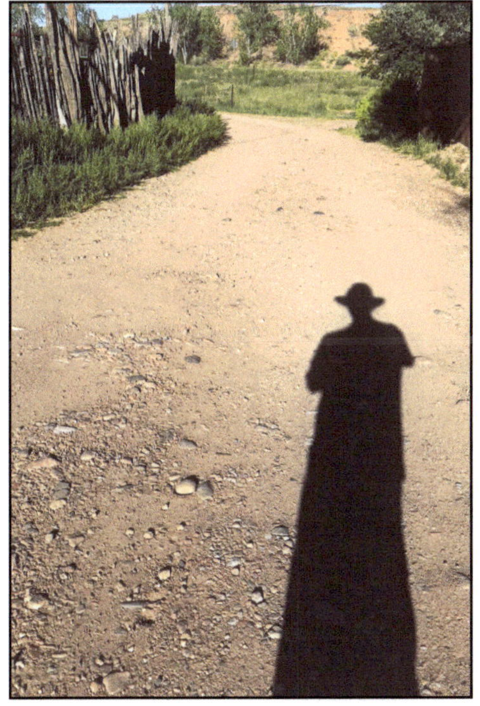

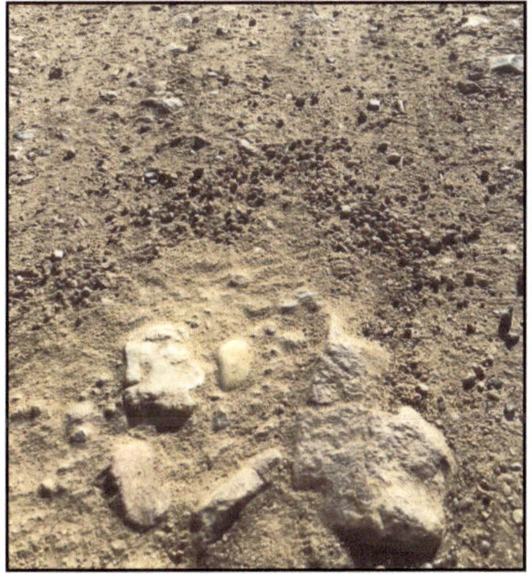

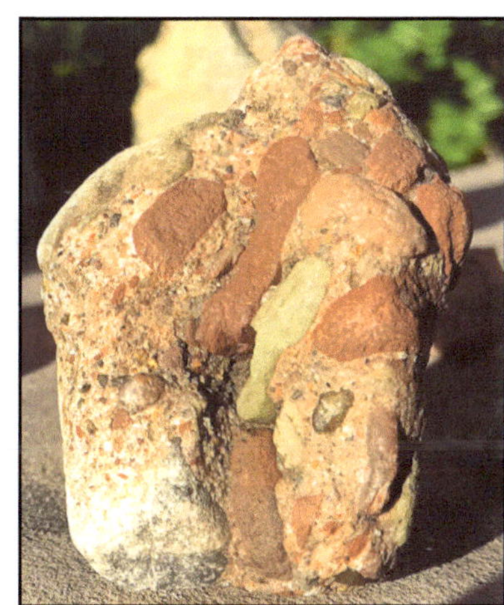

Figure 136: Village Dirt Road with Buried Artifacts: (left) A New Mexico dirt road in a small village without paved roads with exposed cobbles and stones. Center photo shows "possible-maybe" artifact. The best find of the day on the right.

neighborhood alleys. It is almost irresistible not to pick up ancient relics that people drive their cars over daily or situated in decorative gardens, unrecognized after decades and centuries. As further described below, collectors need to be mindful of private property restrictions in taking stones, as well as federal, state and local laws governing removing them from designated locations.

Cleaning

Proper cleaning is a critical element to revealing PRA. Layers of built-up, hardened residue and patina must be removed without damaging embellishments to see carvings and petroglyphs hiding underneath. A serious challenge to thorough cleaning is the irregularity of surfaces, populated with grooves, indentations, facets, corners, edges and holes. Accordingly, one needs to brush in many different directions to remove dirt, patina and residues from the surface. Circular brushing works well, as does the "shoe shine" approach in two directions.

Although there may be more efficient ways of cleaning artifacts, washing and brushing is highly recommended to remove the black, brown and/or red layer(s) of patina that cover the surface.

Some collectors use ultrasonic (US) baths to clean their stones. US baths are cleaning devices that clean most metal, stones, and other material and are especially helpful for removing dirt and the smallest particles on rocks. The US method allows cleaning of the difficult crevices in PRA. US baths use ultrasound and a liquid to create cavitation bubbles induced by high-frequency pressure waves to mix the liquid. The ultrasound frequencies (usually 25-42 kHz) are adjustable and create millions of imploding bubbles that make the ultrasonic cleaning process effective. For cleaning rocks, it is advised to begin with a low frequency setting before using higher frequencies. Prices range for US baths from several hundreds to several thousands of dollars.

Chemical cleaning solutions along with wire brushes should not employed, depending on the type of stone, degree of residue buildup, tightness of holes, ridges and corners, and the artifact size. Ultrasonic cleaning, combined with the brushing techniques described below, is an excellent PRA cleaning regiment.

Fine horsehair brushes are among the best. Synthetic brushes seem less effective but can get the job done. Electric Dremel drill brushes are useful but wear out quickly and are expensive to replace. Larger electric drills outfitted with synthetic brushes can be effective on larger stones.

After a preliminary washing and brushing, an electric toothbrush is beneficial for a final brushing of small depressions, grooves, corners and flat surfaces with prospective etchings. Expect to spend more than the few minutes it takes to brush your teeth in the morning. This process often takes hours to achieve successful results.

It may sound surprising, but just rubbing one's fingers on the stone, like a brush, can clean flat surfaces better than brushing.

For larger pieces try an electric drill outfitted with brush attachments, once again avoiding metal brushes. The larger the artifact, the longer it takes to properly clean, so tackling large pieces could take years. Also, extensive brushing can make for sore wrists, arms and shoulders.

Regrettably, a better approach to removing the patina has yet to be identified by the author. Perhaps a reader can provide a quicker and more thorough solution. Until then, I continue to clean them the old fashion way.

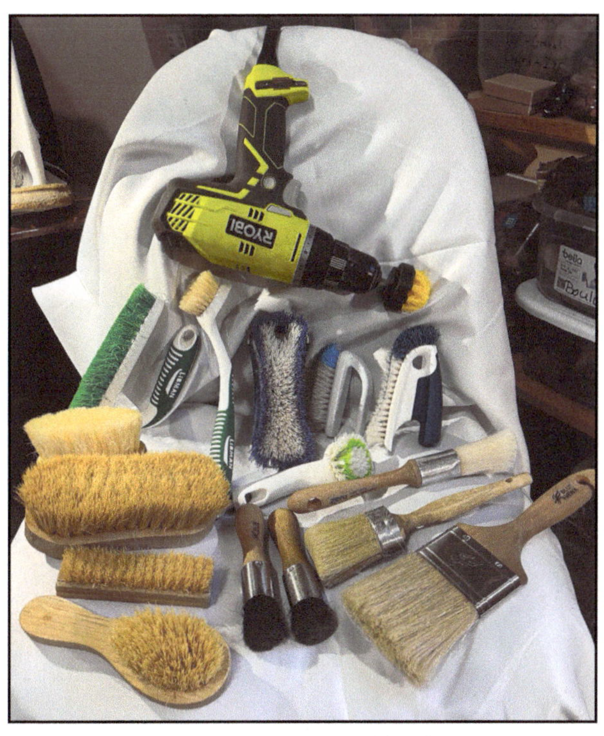

Figure 137: A variety of brushes, including horsehair, synthetic, and mechanical.

My Cleaning Regiment

Before cleaning, it is suggested to take a "before" photo to contrast with the "after" cleaning look.

1. Wash stones in water to remove outside mud and caked dirt. Sturdy brushes can be used, detergent not necessary.
2. While wet, vigorously brush the entire object using a coarse brush. Identify key elements and focus initial efforts on the sides, edges, depressions and imagery that jump out. Brushing takes time, so get used to it. It involves both circular and back-and-forth movements. If the stone is big enough, a shoeshine brush and stroke work well.
3. Next, a more thorough washing using water pressure. I apply water under pressure from a water spicket, bathtub, sink, or hose with spray attachment, focusing again on the key artistic elements. Move the object under the spicket or hose to expose different angles of surface to the pressurized water. This can be accompanied by wet brushing using a synthetic brush. The imagery should slowly become more visible if it exists.
4. Soaking in water for hours often softens the now exposed deeper surfaces. Some collectors recommend soaking in Dove brand liquid soap overnight; others use vinegar.

5. Repeat step 2 with a finer brush. Focus on emerging artistic elements that should now include head variant eyes, mouths, and identifiable head variant outlines. Make sure edges are well brushed to reveal any chipping or rounding surfaces that may appear as sharp edges.
6. Repeat step 3. This time use an electric toothbrush to reach into small corners, cracks, and depressions. Abrasive toothpaste seems to help but leaves a white residue that must be washed off.
7. Depending on the quality of the artifact, this regimen may need to be repeated several times to prepare it for photography.
8. Many collectors brush a little olive oil on the artifact to highlight surface features prior to showing and photography.

Lighting, Positioning and Viewing

In addition to cleaning, optimum lighting of surface etching and abnormalities is required. Direct light can disguise, while sidelighting can accentuate PRA layers, etchings, and sculpting. Surprisingly, PRA is sometimes best seen with less, not more light, but sufficient light to see micro shadows as the light grazes the surface. We assume our Ancestors created and viewed PRA at night by firelight. The dancing flames would have added a strobe lightshow effect, revealing subtle artistic features on appendages and layers.

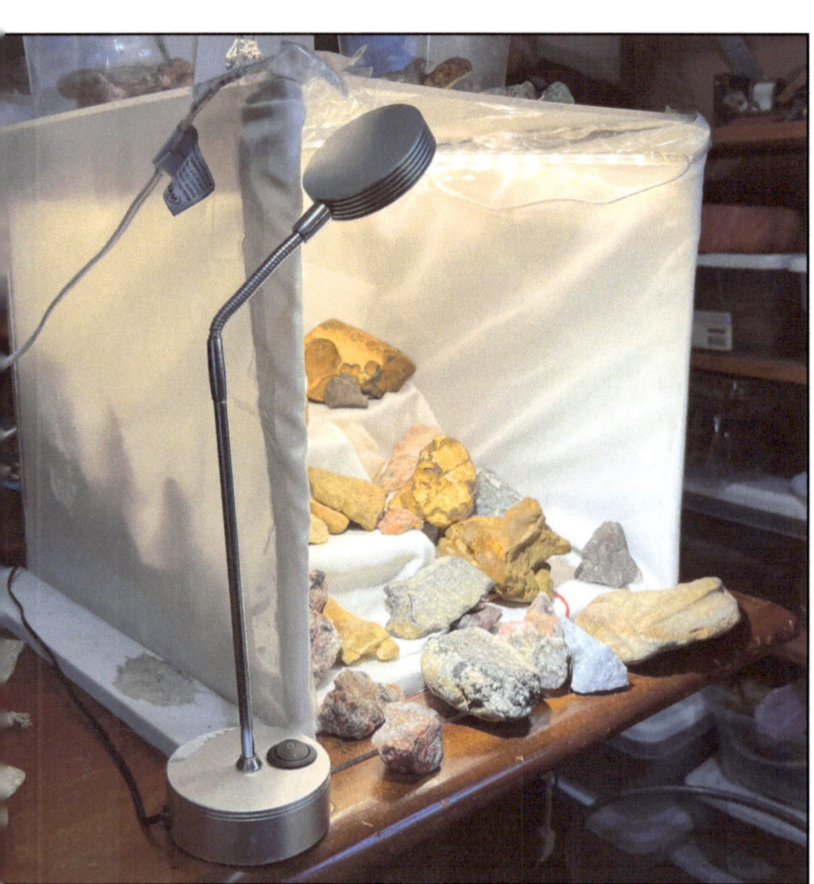

Figure 138: Light box.

Small handheld florescent lights can be easily moved to achieve sidelighting. Finding the "sweet spot" takes coordinating the light source(s) with the position of the artifact. As the object and/or lights move, imagery can be seen on adjoining surfaces, planes and appendages.

Sidelighting brings out subdued PRA imagery and surface embellishments become clearer, both of which can be seen under natural and artificial lighting. Slowly moving the artifact into the optimum position can create shadows on the surface from small indentations and surface irregularities. These shadows help accentuate shapes and profiles. (*See page 38, Artifact VI, for more details.*)

Viewing three-dimensional art requires optimum viewing positions of the object while rotating the piece and/or the light source(s). Placing larger pieces on a table or revolving turntable is practical for viewing all sides.

For some, distinguishing PRA is akin to viewing Magic Eyes™ 3-D art. If one stares intently, the eyes learn to refocus on the disguised Magic Eyes images. At first Magic Eye graphics appear confusing and fuzzy as the mind fails to recognize images among the repeating patterns. With practice, a focused eye will penetrate the flat looking surface and the "hidden" three-dimensional world opens up. The same is true of viewing PRA.

Photography and Photo Editing

Much can be written on this topic and the many challenges faced trying to capture handheld paleo sculptures. Of course, there are multiple variables to consider: *Photography or video? Inside or outside? Type of camera? Handheld or stationary placement? Use of tripods? Type of lighting? Degree and type of photo editing?*

Each variable must be considered within the context of the photographer's goals, equipment, expertise and the artifact(s) themselves. For most of us, the quality of cameras now available on cellular phones is sufficient to capture PRA details with the right lighting.

In addressing photography, four main considerations apply to PRA:

1. **The artifact:** Handheld or stationary? I like handheld to show relative size to a hand and how it might have been held and employed. If photographed in a stationary position, include a tape measure or a coin in the image to show relative size.
2. **Light sources:** Stationary or mobile? A light box provides stationary light, while small florescent lights are mobile and well suited for positioning in one hand while using the camera in the other. Taking photos in direct sunlight can be a superior method of capturing details, especially with shiny objects.
3. **Viewing position:** Is the camera handheld or fixed on a tripod? Especially when trying to capture micro-details, a tripod is recommended. If handheld, try to stabilize the camera, for example by leaning on a stationary object.
4. **For video, what is moving?** Are the lights, the camera or the artifact in motion? I advise the artifact should be moving in one's hand.

Among the best photographic results, using a handheld camera in one hand while holding the object in direct sunlight can produce high quality photos. Alternatively, a camera tripod can achieve different angles as the object moves.

Other photo techniques to consider:

- Light box in conjunction with a handheld florescent light source(s) with either a handheld camera or a camera on a tripod
- Rotating table with a fixed camera
- Time lapse photography
- Dampen the artifact to bring out the art or use a little dab of olive oil.
- Reflectance Transformation Imaging (RTI) which uses multi-lighting conditions to capture a set of images. These many images are combined into single images, with computational variations created by finding the optimum composite light angles to achieve the clearest surface images.

Photo editing is another effective tool to bring out the art. With a good photo-editing program, one can readily adjust light levels, colors, contrast, saturation, and shadows to reveal subtle artistic enhancements. Photo editing allows one to add drawing layers to highlight images by adding colors and accentuating lines and borders.

When editing photos, beware of distortions created by the effects of pixilation when enlarging graphics, which tends to misrepresent small micro images. In this regard, using the highest resolution photographs is key to mitigating distortions and pixilation.

What Are They Worth?

I am regularly asked about the "value" of Figure Stones and am often approached by collectors seeking to sell PRA pieces. Among the obstacles to valuing artifacts is the sheer number of them and the difficulty in verification. Nevertheless, some PRA artifacts are so exquisite they clearly are artistically superior and of such qualities to qualify them as masterpieces—recognizable sculpted and/or etched images that are unmistakably sophisticated artistic embellishments.

At this writing PRA as paleo art remains generally unaccepted by the establishment, inclusive of art galleries and mineral and gem stores. Therefore, the Internet provides the best opportunity for collectors to sell their pieces.

Since many PRA artifacts appear "crude" and can be confused with pareidolia phenomena, those seeking to sell or buy PRA should look for obvious workmanship and well-constructed artistry and head variant and animal shapes, along with documentation and confirmation of the PRA validation criteria previously noted.

The author views PRA as sacred. These *artfacts* are imbued with days, perhaps years of workmanship, and untold ceremonial excursions into dimensions beyond the imagination of most Moderns. These gifts from the Ancestors deserve respect and gratitude. Gifting and trading are the most appropriate pathways for collectors. But for those who do engage in PRA commerce, please offer thanks to the creators and show respect when pursuing, acquiring and collecting PRA.

Honoring, Displaying and Sharing

Most collectors I know experience an intimate, deep connection with the stones, which transcend conventional assumptions of the nature of these ancient relics. Capturing the dynamic qualities of PRA can be illusive and conveying artistic embellishments challenging in a skeptical world. Yet, within the context of lost history and newly discovered art, restored PRA can be shared. As more videographers and authors find success, there will be opportunities to integrate PRA into conventional academic presentations for teaching including textbooks, videos and field trips.

For individual collectors, opportunities to locate, identify and share PRA are vast. Especially when finding PRA in an urban setting—removed from any cultural context—these ancient creations are literally there for the collecting. Treat each with respect and select quality, not quantity for personal collections. Honor the Ancestors by properly cleaning, documenting and displaying so they can be admired, held and respected.

Museums, universities, mainstream archaeologists, and geologists are likely to be the last to accept PRA as anything other than pareidolia. Within each of these institutions, there will be early adapters willing to challenge the establishment along with ridicule and other potential repercussions. While we don't know how long the skeptics can maintain their stronghold of dismissing it, PRA can be shared in books, photographs and video presentations.

For those that do collect, there are many ways to display PRA as shown on the following page.

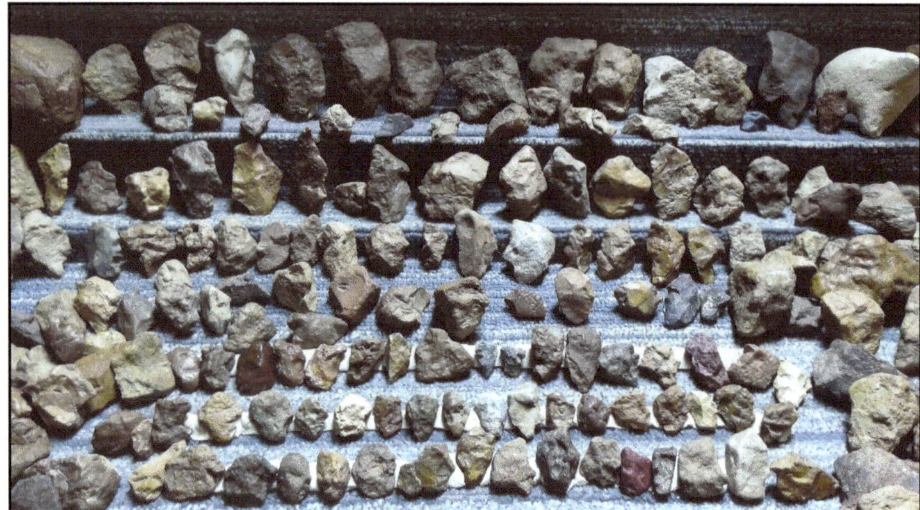

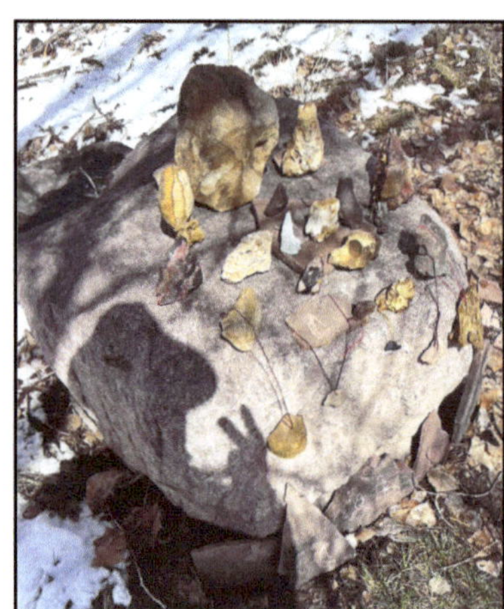

Figure 139: Displaying PRA. (clockwise from top) PRA from Kansas collected by Tim Banninger; An outdoor display of some of the author's larger PRA examples arranged into mandalas, hung and perhaps most notably, arranged outside in Nature to create sacred space; A conventional arrowhead display in a small town museum; A display case from Ursel Benekendorff's paleo art collection, Germany; A beautiful blue lapis PRA sculpture from Colorado sits among other found treasurers.

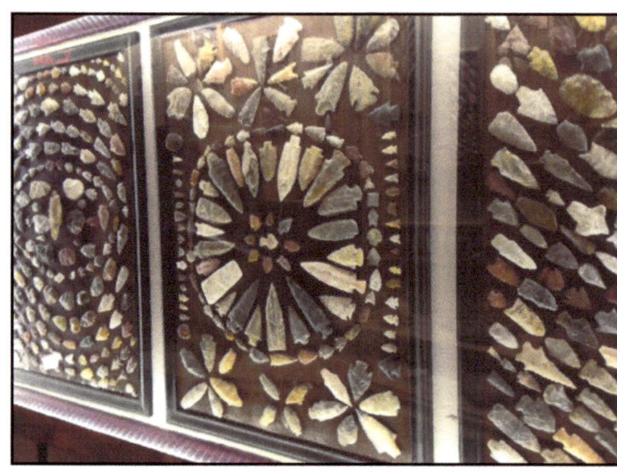

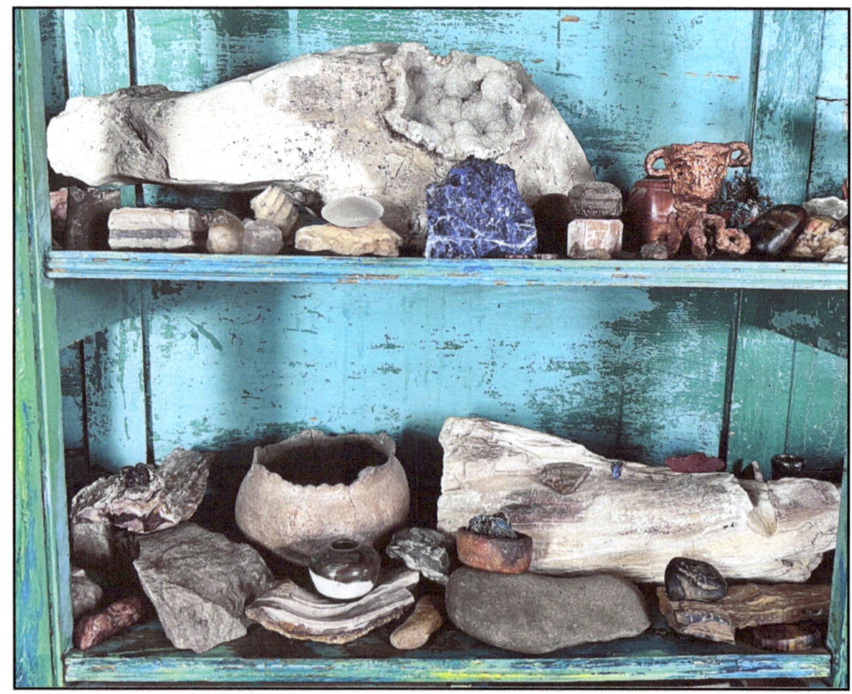

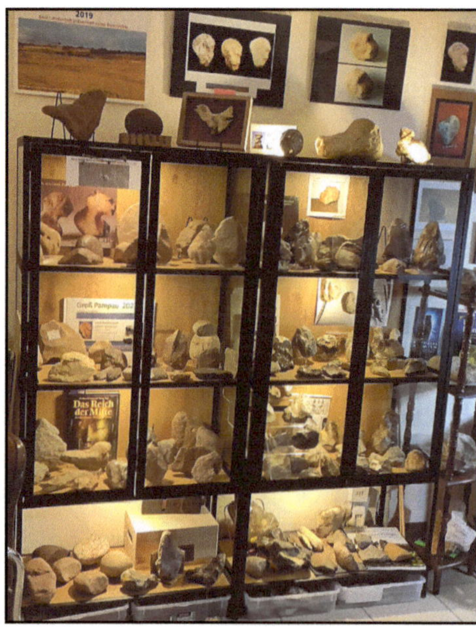

Cautionary Notes for Collectors

I offer several cautionary notes regarding collecting PRA.

Burial Sites and Public Land: When caches of PRA are found, one must consider they may be indicative of a burial site. In such a case, state and federal historical preservation laws and jurisdiction could apply, and it is best not to disturb the site. Also, when on public lands, it is illegal to take any artifact, and in most cases this includes "just rocks."

Private Property: Collectors should be mindful of taking stones from people's private property. Looking for artifacts should be accompanied by respectful behavior, including not trespassing and taking the property of others. Having said that, especially in residential environments and around commercial buildings, retrieving and honoring ancient artifacts from indifferent and unaware Moderns can preserve lost history.

Document Locations: It is also suggested to note locations where artifacts are found for future reference. One approach is to use small colored labels affixed to each cleaned specimen, with each color denoting the city/town, neighborhood, etc., alternatively, scotch tape with ID. Take photos of prospective pieces in their original landscape to help record the location and to document the original condition before cleaning.

A New Obsession: Once one discovers PRA, seeking, finding, and collecting can become an obsession. Many PRA collectors seem to emphasize the quantity, with some collections in the thousands. Hoarding PRA is something to be mindful of and I urge collectors to focus on each artifact when discovered. This means thorough cleaning and documentation as one begins to look for, and hopefully find, artistic enhancements.

Be Judicious: Be kind and return the ones that you may not be interested in. Instead of hiding them away in a box, display and honor them.

Be Open to a New Way of Seeing: Moderns so often believe we are the smartest and most intelligent humans that ever existed. But in our evolution, something important was left behind—honor and respect of Nature. Humanity couldn't be that smart if we wage a destructive war on Nature and continue down a suicidal course.

We humans must expand our awareness to include our important role in maintaining the delicate balance of life on Planet Earth. Perhaps a growing awareness of the wisdom of the Ancients will invite a new way of seeing and a new way of being human for the benefit of Spaceship Earth, all earthly creatures and for future generation.

NOTES

INTRODUCTION

1. Greg Darby, Pareidolia stone example, https://www.boredpanda.com/funny-pareidolia-examples/, posted on Reddit. Photograph by Greg Darby, 2018.
2. Carl Lehrburger, "Ancient Colorado Rock Art Site Employs Light Animation to Mark Equinoxes: Astronomical Alignments Predate Anasazi Civilization, Part One," *Ancient American Magazine* 10, no. 65, [December] 2005, 12-17; and Carl Lehrburger, "Pathfinder Petroglyphs and Possible Associations with Native American Mythology" Part Two, *Ancient American Magazine* 10, no. 66, February 2006, 15-19.
3. William R. McGlone, Phillip M. Leonard, and Ted Barker, *Archaeoastronomy of Southeast Colorado and the Oklahoma Panhandle*. (Kamas, Utah: Mithras, Inc, 1999). Out of print.
4. Lehrburger, "Ancient Colorado Rock Art," 12-17.
5. A video of the Sunset Equinox Animation (SEA) by Carl Lehrburger can be found at https://www.newhistoryofamerica.com/video/
6. Carl Lehrburger, "Ancient Micro Art Discovery, California Heliolithic Petroglyph Animation Revealed on Equinox—Old World Origin Proposed," *Ancient American Magazine* 14, no. 87, April 2010, 20-23.
7. Carl Lehrburger, "Lost Rock Art Found—Portable Rock Art—Changing Archaeology Forever?" *Ancient American Magazine* 23, no. 123, June 2019, 26-29, https://newhistoryofamerica.com/lost-rock-art-found/.
8. Carl Lehrburger, "Petroglyphic Features of Portable Rock Art," *Ancient Origins® Magazine,* 16 December 2020, https://www.newhistoryofamerica.com/wp-content/uploads/2021/11/Rock-Art_2021.pdf.
9. Carl Lehrburger and Scott Monahan, "Evidence of Old World Travelers in Colorado: The Sun Temple and Crack Cave," *Ancient American*

11, no. 70, [October] 2006, 2-17; "The Anubis Caves: Mithraic Religion in the Oklahoma Panhandle, Part Two," *Ancient American* 11, no. 69, [August] 2006, 26-30, "The Anubis Caves: Evidence of Mithraism and Celtic Religion in the Oklahoma Panhandle, Part One," *Ancient American* 11, no. 68, June 2006, 8-12.

10. William R. McGlone, Phillip M. Leonard, et. al, Ancient American Inscriptions: Plow Marks or History? (n.p.: Early Sites Research Society, 1993). Out of print.

II. PRA TRAILBLAZERS

11. Pietro Gaietto, "The Intuition by Boucher de Perthes," *Paleolithic Art Magazine,* December 2000, http://www.paleolithicartmagazine.org/pagina20.html; James Sackett, "Boucher de Perthes and the Discovery of Human Antiquity," *Bulletin of the History of Archaeology* 24, (n.d. 2014): Art, 2, 1–11, DOI: http://dx.doi.org/10.5334/bha.242. James Sackett, Professor Emeritus, Department of Anthropology, Director, European Laboratory, Cotsen Institute of Archaeology, University of California, Los Angeles, USA. jsackett@ucla.edu.
12. Gaietto, "Intuition by Boucher de Perthes," http://www.paleolithicartmagazine.org.
13. Gaietto, "Intuition by Boucher de Perthes," http://www.paleolithicartmagazine.org.
14. Mary D. Leakey, *Olduvai Gorge: Excavations in Beds I & II, 1960–1963,* Vol. 3, (Cambridge, UK: Cambridge University Press, 1971).
15. Mary Leakey, "Grooved and pecked cobble" photo, FLK North-1, Olduvai Gorge, 1.8 million years ago, (1971): 84 & 269, plate 18; reprinted in James B. Harrod, "Palaeoart at Two Million Years Ago? A Review of the Evidence," *Arts* 3, no. 1, (2014): 135-155, Fig. 1; https://doi.org/10.3390/arts3010135.
16. Ursel Benekendorff, "Lower Paleolithic 'Figure Stones' from the Ohle Gravel Pit, Gross-Pampau, Germany," *Pleistocene Coalition News* 4, no. 1, (January-February 2012): 17, http://pleistocenecoalition.com/newsletter/january-february2012.pdf#page=17.
17. Ursel Benekendorff's website http://www.schafftwissen.de/.
18. "Archaeology of Portable Rock Art," *Portable Rock Art Blog,* 16 November 2014, http://portablerockart.blogspot.com/2014/06/archaeology-of-jan-van-es-roermond.html.
19. A full report on the Boukoulian is given in J. van Es and C. J. H. Franssen. Een vroege microkern-traditie van de Peelhorst het Boukoulien. *Archaeologische Berichten* 19 [An early microcore

tradition of the Peelhorst het Boukouline. *Archaeological Messages* 19] (1989): 6-25, 93-133.

20. Additional information is available at "Archaeology of Portable Rock Art," *Portable Rock Art Blog.* Archaeology of Jan van Es, Roermond, The Netherlands, http://portablerockart.blogspot.com/2014/06/archaeology-of-jan-van-es-roermond.html, Jan Van Es' Facebook page is https://www.facebook.com/jan.vanes.98.
21. "Archaeology of Portable Rock Art," *Portable Rock Art Blog,* 16 November 2014, http://portablerockart.blogspot.com/2014/.
22. Brett Martin, Eoliths @ Revelation in Stone, https://eoliths.blogspot.com/2021/02/portable-rock-art.html.
23. Martin, Eoliths @ Revelation in Stone.
24. Alan Day, "Figure Stones (Pierres Figures), Portable Rock Art, America's (Almost) Invisible Prehistory, Day's Knob in Guernesy County Ohio," http://www.daysknob.com/index.html#Top_of_Page
25. Day, "Figure Stones (Pierres Figures)," http://www.daysknob.com/index.html#Top_of_Page
26. Day, "Figure Stones (Pierres Figures)," http://www.daysknob.com/index.
27. James B. Harrod, "North, Central, South America Paleo and Early Archaic Archaeological Sites with Zoomorphic or Anthropomorphic Sculptures (including Ornaments with Sculptures)." 2 December 2021, https://www.researchgate.net/publication/356748143_North_Central_South_America_Paleo_and_Early_Archaic_Archaeological_Sites_with_Zoomorphic_or_Anthropomorphic_Sculptures_62_sites_126_depictions
28. James B. Harrod, "Paleoart at Two Million Years Ago? A Review of the Evidence," *Arts* 3, no. 1, 2 March 2014, 139, Table 1, https://doi.org/10.3390/arts3010135
29. Harrod, "Paleoart at Two Million Years Ago?" 139.
30. James B. Harrod, 2020) Discovery of Portable Art Zoomorphic Sculptures from the Clovis Zone, Hiscock Site, New York quoted in Richard Michael Gramly (ed.), *Human and Proboscidean Interactions in Northern North America: New Evidence, Fresh Interpretations and Revisited Data*, (North Andover, MA: ASAA/Persimmon Press, 2020), Chapter 4, https://www.researchgate.net/publication/350409697_Discovery_of_Portable_Art_Zoomorphic_Sculptures_from_the_Clovis_Zone_Hiscock_Site_NY_Pre-Publication_Print_Version.
31. Rock Art Museum, Jul Jones, Curator, www.Rockartmuseum.com.
32. Rock Art Museum, www.Rockartmuseum.com
33. Robert G. Bednarik, "Characterization of Petroglyphs," *The Encyclo-*

pedia of Archaeological Sciences, (Hoboken, NJ: Wiley-Blackwell, November 2018), DOI: 10.1002/9781119188230.saseas0079.

34. Professor Bednarik's website is https://www.ifrao.com/robert-g-bednark/. A list of his publications can be found at Auranet, R. G. Bednarik Library, http://www.ifrao.com/robert-g-bednarik/r-g-bednarik-library/.
35. Chris Penney, "Ancient Artifact Hunters," 2023, https://www.imdb.com/title/tt23860458/?fbclid=IwAR22eZqHdv0dwcK0R6SN6iKH1A-j5KqyWki1hpLQ-v9NDU5zcAbf4fi_WxV0.

III. HANDHELD, MULTIFACETED PALEO ART

36. Carl Lehrburger, "Petroglyphic Features of Portable Rock Art," *Ancient Origins*, 16 December 2020, https://www.ancient-origins.net/artifacts-other-artifacts/portable-rock-art-0014678.
37. Jan Van Es photo from http://portablerockart.blogspot.com/2014/06/archaeology-of-jan-van-es-roermond.html.
38. Hobart M. King, "Types of Rock Art: Petroglyphs and Pictographs," *Geology.com Science News and Information,* https://geology.com/articles/petroglyphs.shtml.
39. Reflectance Transformation Imaging, https://culturalheritageimaging.or/Technologies/RTI/.

IV. GRAND ARTISTRY OR PAREIDOILA

40. Robert G. Bednarik, *Rock Art Science: The Scientific Study of Palaeoart*, IFRAO-Brepols Series 1, (Turnhout, Belguim: Brepols Publishing, 2001), ISBN 2-503-99124-6.
41. Robert G. Bednarik, "Rock Art and Pareidolia," *Rock Art Research* 33, no. 2 (April 2016): 167-181.
42. Bednarik, "Rock Art and Pareidolia," 168.
43. Bednarik, "Rock Art and Pareidolia," 179.
44. James Harrod, Personal Communications, in addition to many referenced research papers.
45. Happy Pareidolia Potato, photo by Andy Mabbett, Wikipedia, Creative Commons Share Alike 4.0 International License, *https://en.wikipedia.org/wiki/Pareidolia,*
46. Frank Hamilton Cushing, "Zuni Fetishes," *Second Annual Report of the Bureau of Ethnology, 1880-81,* 8th printing, (Las Vegas, NV: KC Publications, 1988): 31.

47. Photo by Robert G. Bednarik, Wikipedia, https://commons.wikimedia.org/wiki/File:Makapansgat_pebble.webp. Reprinted under the Creative Commons license.
48. Bednarik, "Rock Art and Pareidolia," 151.
49. Harrod, "Paleo Art at Two Million Years Ago," n.p.
50. James B. Harrod, *Categories and Principles of Proto-Art: Hypotheses on Early and Middle Paleo Art, Symbols and Religion,* (November 20, 2001), https://www.academia.edu/61945841/Categories_and_Principles_of_Proto_Art_Hypotheses_on_Early_and_Middle_Palaeolithic_Art_Symbol_and_Religion
51. Harrod, "Paleo Art at Two Million Years Ago," Table 1 Symbolic Behavior—Taxonomy.
52. Cushing, "Zuni Fetishes," 31.
53. Tom Bahti, "Introduction—Zuni Fetishes," *Second Annual Report of the Bureau of Ethnology, 1880-81,* 8th printing, (Las Vegas, NV: KC Publications, 1988): 2.
54. Photo by El Comandante, Wikipedia, Creative Commons Share Alike 3.0 Unported, 2.5 Generic, 2.0 Generic, and 1.0 Generic license.

V. PRA TECHNIQUES AND TOOLS

55. John J. Shea, *Stone Tools in the Paleolithic and Neolithic Near East: A Guide* (Cambridge University Press, 2013): 17-46, https://www.cambridge.org/core/books/stone-tools-in-the-paleolithic-and-neolithic-near-east/lithics-basics/487AB7381E1E3B42C4980448AF364C40
56. Peter A. Bostrom, photo from Gravers, Single and double spurred gravers from early archaic Dalton habitation site (III), http://lithiccastinglab.com/gallery-pages/2008augustgraverspage1.htm
57. Jean M. Pitzer, "A Guide to the Identification of Burins in Prehistoric Chipped Stone Assemblages," Center for Archaeological Research, *The University of Texas at San Antonio Guidebooks in Archaeology,* no. 1, (1977:) 1, [2nd printing, 1979]; H. L. Movius Jr. "Notes on the History of the Discovery and Recognition of the Function of Burins as Tools," *Societe Prehistoriquie Francaise* 63 (1968): 50-65; H. Noone, "Notes on Flint Burins of the Ve-zere (Dordogne) Sites," *Proceedings of the Prehistoric Society* 16, (1950): 186-191. doi:10.1017/S0079497X00019022.

VI. HOW OLD ARE THEY?

58. Harrod, "Paleoart at Two Million Years Ago?" https://doi.org/10.3390/arts3010135.
59. L. Benson, E. Hattori, J. Southon, B. Aleck, "Dating North America's Oldest Petroglyphs, Winnemucca Lake Subbasin, Nevada," *Journal of Archaeological Science* 40, no. 12 (December 2013): 4466-4476; doi: 10.1016/j.jas.2013.06.022. https://www.donsmaps.com/winnemucca.html.
60. "Spanish Cave Art Was Made by Neanderthals, Study Confirms," *The Guardian,* 2 August 2021, https://www.theguardian.com/science/2021/aug/02/tinted-cave-stalagmites-are-neanderthal-art-say-archaeologists.
61. Andrew Curry, "Were Neanderthals Making 'Art' in Europe's Fabled Unicorn Cave?" *National Geographic* 240, no. 1 (July 5, 2021): n.p.
62. Curry, "Were Neanderthals Making 'Art'," n.p.

VII. RECOGNIZING PETROGLYPHIC FEATURES

63. Dantheman9758 at en.wikipedia, (Wikipedia, "Mastodon"), (April 6, 2007): https://en.wikipedia.org/wiki/Mastodon. Licensed under GFDL by the author; released uner the GNU Free Documentation License.
64. Harrod, "Portable Art Sculptures," 26.

VIII. A NEW WAY OF SEEING

65. R. Buckminster Fuller, *Operating Manual for Spaceship Earth,* (Baden, Switzerland: Lars Müller Publishing, reprint 2008): 107, [1969]. Fuller writes regarding the difference between mind and the brain, "The brain deals only with memorized, subjective, special-case experiences and objective experiments, while mind extracts and employs the generalized principles and integrates and interrelates their effective employment. Brain deals exclusively with the physical, and mind exclusively with the metaphysical."
66. Alan Watts, *Philosophy of the Tao Part 3* (2.4.6), Audio Lectures.
67. Adrianna Quintero, "#WithHer: Women, Mother Earth, and Our Collective Humanity" with Mary Annaise Heglar, *Huffington Post,* (Jan 17, 2018): https://www.huffpost.com/entry/withher-women-mother-earth-and-our-collective-humanity_b_5a5fc81de4b048d1c498787a.

GLOSSARY

Anubis Caves. A series of caves in the Oklahoma Panhandle, documented by William R. McGlone, Philip M. Leonard, et al., of Celtic origin with multiple solar alignments, Celtic and Mithraic iconography and Ogam (Celtic) inscriptions estimated to be around 1,700 years old. The name references a central petroglyph of a canine with a crown depicting the Egyptian god Anubis, the guide to the underworld. Referring to the Equinox sunset archaeoastronomical alignment at the site, Anubis rules over the night, contrasted to the Sun God (Mithras) who rules over the day.

Apophenia. The tendency to perceive meaningful connections between unrelated things. *Also see **Pareidolia.***

Archaeoastronomy. An integrated field of study relying on astronomy, archaeology, anthropology, philosophy, and epigraphy (the study of writing) to identify and interpret the meaning of astronomical alignments at large structures and petroglyphs.

Arrowheads. A broad term to describe different size and shaped hunting points, ranging from small bird points to larger spear points. Arrowheads represent a small fraction of stone age tools.

Artfact. The author has created and uses the term artfacts to distinguish Portable Rock Art with artistic features that often include stone tools, from traditionally understood artifacts. See Portable Rock Art and figure stones.

Artifact. Typically, an item of cultural or historical interest, showing human workmanship or modification as distinguished from a natural object.

Boukoulian. From Boukoul, Netherlands, where artifacts identified by Jan Van Es were dated to be 400,000-450,000 years old.

Burins, Prehistoric stone or metal tools with sharp points, sometimes beveled, used to engrave surfaces and to create fine petroglyphs. *Also see **Gravers**.*

Celtic. Early Indo-European people who came from the second millennium bce to the first century bce and spread over much of Europe. The word is connected with the people and the culture of Scotland, Wales, Ireland, and other areas such as Brittany. Celtic languages include Irish, Scottish Gaelic, Welsh, Breton, Manx, and Gaulish.

Celt. A prehistoric stone or metal implement with beveled edges, used as a cutting tool, weapon and for ceremonial purposes.

Chert. A type of stone similar in quality to flint, often used for making stone tools. Flint is a type of chert.

Conglomeration Stones. A sedimentary rock made of rounded pebbles and sand usually held together by silica, calcite or iron oxide. Conglomeration stone elements are rounded or angular gravel rather than of sand found in sandstone.

Crack Cave. A cave located in Picture Canyon in southeastern Colorado, where Celtic inscriptions and petroglyphs memorialize the Equinox (Day of Bel) in a sunrise morning alignment.

Cross-Quarter Days. The cross-quarter days occur midway between the Equinoxes and Solstices. Today, the four cross-quarter days have become Groundhog Day (February 2), May Day (May 1), Lammas (August 1) and Halloween (October 31).

Effigy Stones. A broad category of objects representing human or animal forms made from multiple material, including stone, clay, shell, wood and bone. Broadly, effigy stones are distinguished from Portable Rock Art by having a single aspect/image compared to multiple imagery found in PRA.

Eoliths. In the nineteenth century these items were considered to be the original tools created by early humans, but later came to be seen as natural, or geofacts (nature-fact). Today, the term eolith is often used to dismiss as "natural" the unknown or unrecognized features that exist in artifacts or rocks. *Also see **Geofact**.*

Equinox. The two times each year, about March 21 and September 21, when the sun crosses the celestial equator and day and night are the same length.

Face-in-Face. A PRA artistic feature where a single petroglyph or sculpture incorporate many connected images, specifically several faces within a single head variant. For example, a face-in-face image could share a single hole representing the eye for two different head variants.

Fetish (or **Fetich**). Small stone carvings of animals believed to be imbued with magical power. Fetishes are generally a singular image compared to multiple images found in PRA.

Figure Stones (French: Pierre's figures). A stone depicting familiar representations of animals and head variants in stone. Considered synonymous with the term Portable Rock Art, some consider figure stones a type of Portable Rock Art. *Also see* ***Portable Rock Art.***

Geofact. Taken from "geology" and "artifact" (geo-fact), a natural stone formation or rock difficult to distinguish from a man-made artifact. Geofacts can be misinterpreted as artifacts, especially when compared to paleolithic artifacts.

Glitter. A term used by the author to reference minerals with reflective qualities often integrated into Portable Rock Art, primarily mica, but also quartz, gold and other minerals with shiny qualities.

Glyph. Any kind of purposeful mark, such as a single letter in script or a carved symbol intended to denote unique characters that collectively convey a written meaning or message.

Gravers. From the word to engrave, metal or stone tools with sharp points or "spurs" used to make impressions on stone including etching fine petroglyphs. Authors from Europe often refer to burins as gravers, while American authors consider gravers to be stone tools created by pressure flaking and created to have functional points. *Also see* ***Burins.***

Great Basin. An area in the western U.S. spanning nearly all of Nevada, much of Utah, and portions of California, Idaho, Oregon, Wyoming, and Baja California. Both the North American lowest point (Death Valley) and the highest point less than 100 miles (160 km) away (Mount Whitney) are within the Great Basin. The region encompasses Death Valley, Mojave, and Great Salt Lake Deserts.

Head Variant. Adaptation or depiction of a human or animal head shape. The overall shape of a stone may resemble PRA head variants, which can include human and animal likeness carved or etched details. Also, variations of head shapes employed in writing, such as Mayan glyphs.

Heliolithic Animation. Heliolithic combines "sun" and "stone," and most often refers to observing changing solar phenomena on petroglyphs and megalithic structures. Also referred to as moving picture shows, solar animations involve the appearance of sunlight and shadow on structures, rock art panels and petroglyphs designed for a particular day (e.g. Equinox). The Temple of Kukulkan at Chichén Itza, Mexico, is known for its equinox alignment depicting a heliolithic animation of an undulating serpent with light and shadow interplay on its back, mimicking its movement down the pyramid. Other heliolithic animations cited include Anubis Cave, Crack Cave and the Pathfinder site.

Lithic. Pertaining to or consisting of stone.

Makapansgat Pebble. The jasperite 7 cm wide pebble with a resemblance to a human face, found in 1925 in South Africa among bones of a forerunner to humans who lived three million years ago. Considered natural, not carved, the resemblance to a human face and it having been transported 20 miles by the Australopithecus human predecessors suggests the connection between pareidolia and paleo art.

Maya. An ethnolinguistic group of indigenous peoples of Mesoamerica whose chief members are Maya, Quiché and Tzeltal. "Maya" is used to describe the Maya civilization, people, places and other non-linguistic aspects of their culture, while the "Mayan" is used to describe the languages that are spoken by them.

Mesoamerican, Mesoamerica. The diverse civilizations that shared similar cultural characteristics in the geographic areas comprising Mexico, Guatemala, Honduras, Belize, El Salvador, Nicaragua, and Costa Rica.

Microlithic Sculptures. Term coined by Jan Van Es, synonymous with paleolithic sculptures and aspects of Portable Rock Art.

Mimeotoliths. Rocks that mimic recognizable forms through random processes of formation, weathering and erosion.

Mojave Desert. An arid region of southeastern California and portions of Nevada, Arizona, and Utah, in the Southwestern United States, named for the Mojave people.

Multi-glyphs. Multiple glyphs and images incorporated into a single petroglyph or sculpture. Multi-glyphs include "faces-in-faces" imagery.

Multi-Tool. Stone tools with utilitarian functions on different sides or planes (for example scraper, awl and cutting functions on multiple edges of a single tool), akin to a modern Swiss Army Knife.

Olduvai Gorge (or **Oldupai Gorge).** Located in Tanzania, Northeast Africa, where anthropologists found some of the earliest human remains going back two million years.

Neanderthal. An extinct species or subspecies of archaic humans who lived in Eurasia until about 40,000 years ago. Neanderthals made stone tools and had the ability to make fire, weave, create art and build seafaring boats.

Paleo. Relating to or typical of the ancient period when people used tools and weapons made of stone. Also means old and ancient.

Paleolithic Sculptures. *See Portable Rock Art.*

Pareidolia. The perception of apparently significant patterns or recognizable images, especially faces, in random or accidental arrangements of shapes and lines. The word is associated with faulty perception of seeing patterns in random details on rocks and in natural features, often referred to as *apophenia* and *simulacra.*

Patina. A thin surface layer that develops on an object or surface because of use, age, or chemical action. Regarding stones, PRA and petroglyphs, a layer of residue covering rock surfaces, changing the natural rock color and appearance.

Pathfinder Site. Native American petroglyph rock art panel located in southeastern Colorado with morning and noon Equinox alignments.

Petroglyph. From the Greek words petros meaning *stone* and glyphein *to carve,* it also means to shape, fashion and sculpt. Petroglyphic images are inscribed in stone and are common worldwide, found predominately on fixed boulders, large rocks, rock outcroppings, and cave walls, in addition to on PRA.

Pictographs. Images painted on rock surfaces, as opposed to being carved or etched.

Portable Rock Art (PRA). Also referred to as paleo art, familiar stones, figure stones, microlithic sculptures as well as anthropomorphic paleolithic sculptures. The author has created and uses the term artfacts to distinguish these human worked stones with artistic features that often include stone tools, from traditionally understood artifacts.

Purgatory River / Purgatory River Valley. Located in Southeastern Colorado and named by early Spanish explorers. Various styles of rock art have been found along this tributary of the Arkansas River.

Rock Art. Broadly speaking, rock art is human-made markings on natural stone surfaces. It includes petroglyphs and pictoglyphs created on rock surfaces and cave walls, cave paintings, sculpted stoneworks, and Portable Rock Art. Prehistoric rock art survives today throughout Europe, Australia, Asia, Africa and the Americas.

Sunset Equinox Animation (SEA). Petroglyph at a Mojave Desert location known as Mojave North with a sundown Equinox alignment displaying a multi-glyph with a face within a face image.

Sidelighting. Commonly referred to as **Raking Light.** A sharp angle of light striking rock surfaces brings out details created by pecking, abrading and etchings on rock surfaces, both on fixed petroglyphs and Portable Rock Art. In PRA the sidelighting effect is achieved by moving the properly positioned artifact under the right lighting conditions and angles to create shadows that bring out surface details.

Simulacrum (plural **Simulacra**)**.** Used in referring to natural landscapes, geological features and objects such as rocks appearing to have organized attributes that are unreal, usually resembling faces.

Solstice. The time or date (twice each year) at which the sun reaches its maximum or minimum declination, marked by the longest and shortest days (about June 21 and December 22).

Taxonomy. Classifying groupings of paleo art inclusive of symbolic behavior applicable to distinguishing human-made art from pareidolia.

The Unicorn Cave Bone. Found in the Unicorn Cave in West Harz, Germany, it is estimated to be 50,000 years old, made from the toe bone or phalanx of a deer and was reported to have been created by Neanderthals.

Widapokwi. Also called *Changing Woman,* considered to be the *First Mother* and the *Mother of Mankind* in some Native American mythologies, including a Yavapai-Apache tradition.

INDEX

Q

R

S

T

www.ingramcontent.com/pod-product-compliance
Lightning Source LLC
LaVergne TN
LVHW070123110826
845147LV00002B/178